CCCC

Bibliography of Composition and Rhetoric

1990

Erika Lindemann
Editor

Sandra Monroe Fleming
Associate Editor

Conference on College Composition and Communication, A Conference
of the National Council of Teachers of English

Southern Illinois University Press
Carbondale and Edwardsville

ISSN 1046–0675
ISBN 0-8093-1811-3
ISBN 0-8093-1812-1 (pbk.)

The paper used in this publication meets the minimum requirements of
American National Standard for Information Sciences—Permanence
of Paper for Printed Library Materials, ANSI Z39.48-1984. ∞

Contents

Preface

Erika Lindemann

The *CCCC Bibliography of Composition and Rhetoric,* published by the Conference on College Composition and Communication, offers teachers and researchers an annual classified listing of scholarship on written English and its teaching. This volume cites 1849 titles that, with few exceptions, were published during the 1990 calendar year. The bibliography lists each work only once, but it descriptively annotates all citations, cross-references them when appropriate, and indexes all authors and editors. A group of 136 contributing bibliographers, listed on pages xi to xii, prepared the citations and annotations for all entries appearing in this volume.

SCOPE OF THE BIBLIOGRAPHY

The *CCCC Bibliography* includes works that treat written communication (whether the writing people do is in English or some other language), the processes whereby human beings compose and understand written messages, and methods of teaching people to communicate ef-

fectively in writing. The bibliography lists entries in five major categories (see the Contents for a fuller description of these categories):

Section 1. Bibliographies and Checklists

Section 2. Theory and Research

Section 3. Teacher Education, Administration, and Social Roles

Section 4. Curriculum

Section 5. Testing, Measurement, and Evaluation

The bibliography makes few restrictions on the format, medium, or purpose of the works it includes, so long as the subject of the work falls into one of the five categories described in the preceding list. It lists only published works: books, articles, monographs, published collections (of essays, conference presentations, or working papers), bibliographies and other reference works, films, microforms, videotapes, and sound recordings. It includes citations for unpublished doctoral dissertations appearing in *Dissertation Abstracts International.* It also includes review articles that discuss several works, define movements or trends, or survey an individual's contribution to the discipline. It excludes master's theses, textbooks, computer software, book reviews, and works written in a language other than English.

SOURCES

The *CCCC Bibliography* cites works from four major sources.

Periodicals. Journals publishing articles on composition and its teaching are the source for approximately 1000 entries. Each journal is identified by an abbreviation; an alphabetical list of Journal Abbreviations begins on page xiii. With few exceptions, the contributing bibliographers preparing entries for journal articles examined the material firsthand.

Publishers. A second source of materials are commercial publishers and university presses. These publishers, whose participation in the bibliography project is voluntary, provided contributing bibliographers with written information for approximately 170 books listed in this volume. By and large, contributing bibliographers were unable to examine these materials firsthand.

This volume also includes scholarly essay collections, books that bring together essays, articles, or papers by several authors. The bibliography annotates these collections, but does not annotate each essay. Unless the annotation for a collection says otherwise, all authors contributing to the collection are listed in the Name Index.

Dissertation Abstracts International (DAI). *DAI* represents a third source for over 500 citations. Not all degree-granting institutions list their unpublished doctoral dissertations in *DAI*, and as a rule, the contributing bibliographers have not examined these dissertations firsthand. The citations in this volume serve only to direct readers to abstracts in *DAI*. Users will want to consult the *DAI* abstracts for additional information, including who supervised the degree candidate's work and which institution granted the degree.

Resources in Education (RIE). A fourth source of materials in the *CCCC Bibliography* is the Educational Resources Information Center (ERIC), a federally funded document retrieval system coordinated by sixteen clearinghouses.

ERIC indexes its materials in two reference works. Journal articles appear in *Cumulative Index to Journals in Education (CIJE)*. *Resources in Education (RIE)*, on the other hand, indexes documents in the ERIC microfiche collection, which is available in 2600 regional libraries or directly from ERIC. These documents, frequently published elsewhere, include government documents, research and project reports, bibliographies, and conference papers. Documents indexed in *RIE* receive a six-digit "ED" number (e.g., ERIC ED 305 701) and are cross-referenced under various subject headings or "descriptors."

Some documents may be listed in *RIE* and may become available through ERIC several years after they were written. For convenience and to ensure comprehensiveness, the *CCCC Bibliography* reports ERIC documents cited in *RIE* during the years covered in the current volume; that is, this volume cites over 150 ERIC documents listed in *RIE* in 1990, even though the works themselves may have an earlier "date of publication." Also as a convenience, each ERIC entry includes the six-digit "ED" number.

Contributing bibliographers working with ERIC materials have developed the following criteria for determining what documents to include in this volume:

Substantiveness. Substantive documents of general value to college composition teachers and researchers are included. Representative publications are curriculum guides, federal government final reports, and technical reports from various publication series, such as those published, for example, by the Center for the Study of Writing and the Center for the Study of Reading.

Relevance. Documents that seem to represent concerns of high interest to researchers are included. The topics of functional literacy, computer-assisted instruction, and revision, for example, represent concerns of greater relevance than the teaching of handwriting.

Inclusiveness. All papers on composition and rhetoric available in ERIC and delivered at the annual meetings of the Conference on College Composition and Communication (CCCC) and the National Council of Teachers of English (NCTE—Fall and Spring conventions) are included. Papers delivered at other regional and national meetings—for example, meetings of the American Educational Research Association (AERA), the International Reading Association (IRA), and the Modern Language Association (MLA)—are selected for inclusion on the basis of their substantiveness and relevance.

Reference value. Items for which the ERIC microfiche system might provide unique access are included. Representative of entries meeting this criterion would be books or collections of articles no longer available from their original publishers.

Alternate access. Many professional organizations regularly make copies of book and monograph publications available as ERIC microfiche. And many papers presented as reports or conference talks and available in ERIC are later published as monographs or as articles in journals. When such information is available, the entry in this volume will include ERIC ED numbers to indicate an alternate source of access to the document. However, users of this volume should keep in mind that, although a book in ERIC reflects the exact contents of the published work, an article in ERIC is a manuscript that may see substantial revision before it is published.

The following criteria determine which items cited in *RIE* are excluded from this volume:

Communication theory. ERIC documents broadly concerned with human communication or with language study in general, rather than with college composition and rhetoric, are routinely excluded.

Local interest. ERIC documents concerned with composition and rhetoric but judged to be primarily of local interest are excluded. For example, this volume omits annual evaluation reports of writing programs in local schools.

Availability. Publications of commercial publishers and other organizations that are listed in *RIE* and assigned an ERIC ED number but are not available through the ERIC microfiche system are omitted.

Users of the *CCCC Bibliography* may wish to supplement this resource by consulting *RIE* or various computer-assisted retrieval systems that access ERIC documents. Copies of most documents indexed in *RIE* can be purchased in paper or microform from the ERIC system. ERIC clearinghouses also make available free or inexpensive guides to special topics of interest to rhetoric and composition teachers and researchers. Order forms and current addresses for these clearinghouses appear at the back of each monthly issue of *RIE*.

A few entries in this volume show publication dates earlier than 1990. By and large, these materials have two sources. They represent articles published in 1990 but appearing in journals showing earlier volume numbers, or they represent materials accessioned by ERIC clearinghouses in 1990 but originally published earlier.

Authors, publishers, and editors may send offprints of articles, copies of books and journals, or microforms to me for possible inclusion in the *CCCC Bibliography;* however, I will be unable to return them.

The items listed in the annual bibliography are not housed in any single location or owned by any single individual. The *CCCC Bibliography* lists and describes these materials but does not provide users of the bibliography any additional means of retrieving them. However, users of this volume will find librarians extremely helpful in finding copies of particular works to examine firsthand. Some materials may be available through interlibrary loan, OCLC and on-line catalogues, ERIC and other information retrieval systems, or in state and university libraries. To locate materials cited in this volume, ask your librarian to help you.

CONTRIBUTING BIBLIOGRAPHERS

The reliability and usefulness of these annual volumes depend primarily on a large group of contributing bibliographers. Contributing bibliographers accept responsibility for compiling accurate entries in their areas of expertise, for preparing brief, descriptive annotations for each entry, for determining where each entry will appear within one of the five sections of the bibliography, for cross-referencing entries when appropriate, and for submitting completed entries by a specified deadline.

To ensure consistency, contributing bibliographers receive a *Handbook for Contributing Bibliographers* to guide them in their work and fill out a printed form for each entry. Contributing bibliographers agree to serve a three-year term and, thereafter, may request reappointment for another two-year term. In return for their valuable service to the profession, they receive a copy of each annual volume they have helped to prepare. Graduate students, teachers, researchers, or other individuals who wish to become contributing bibliographers may write to me.

ANNOTATIONS

Annotations accompany all entries in this volume. They describe the document's contents and are intended to help users determine the document's usefulness. Annotations are brief and, insofar as the English language allows, are meant to be descriptive, not evaluative. They explain what the work is about but leave readers free to judge for themselves the work's merits. Most annotations fall into one of three categories: they present the document's thesis, main argument, or major research finding; they describe the work's major organizational divisions; or they indicate the purpose or scope of the work.

CROSS-REFERENCES AND INDEXES

This volume cites and annotates each document only once, in one of the five major sections of the bibliography. Every entry, however, receives an "entry number" so that cross-references to other sections are possible. Cross-references are necessary because much scholarship in composition and rhetoric is interdisciplinary. Cross-references appear as a listing of entry numbers preceded by "See also," found at the end of each subsection of the bibliography.

The Subject Index lists most of the topics discussed in the works cited in this volume. Consulting the Subject Index may help users locate sections and subsections of the bibliography that contain large numbers of entries addressing the same topic.

The Name Index lists all authors, editors, and contributors to publications cited in this volume.

ACKNOWLEDGMENTS

My editorship ends with this volume. A decade has passed since I first contemplated how I might organize the project, how scholars in the field of composition studies conduct their teaching and research, and how computer technology might make the undertaking feasible. Throughout this period, colleagues within and outside the profession challenged and encouraged me, sustaining the project with their own good work.

I owe special thanks to the contributing bibliographers, whose conscientious efforts represent a significant contribution to the profession. I am also grateful to the CCCC officers, CCCC Executive Committee members, and CCCC Chairs—especially David Bartholomae, Andrea Lunsford, Jane Peterson, and Don McQuade— whose advocacy have made this project possible. The University Research Council and the Department of English at the University of North Carolina-Chapel Hill offered generous financial support. Joseph M. Flora and Robert A. Bain encouraged the work month after month, year after year. Larry Mason and Mike Padrick contributed important technical expertise in computer programming. I have also appreciated the exceptional help of talented associate editors— J. Randal Woodland, Elizabeth Denton Burrows, Mary Beth Harding, Terri O'Quin, and Sandra Monroe Fleming—who devoted their summers to coding data, verifying sources, and proofreading entries. Kenney Withers, Susan H. Wilson, and Robyn Laur Clark of Southern Illinois University Press offered sound editorial advice and production assistance, always with good cheer and extraordinary professionalism.

Our profession is fortunate to number among its ranks two scholars who have agreed to serve as coeditors for the project, Gail Hawisher of the University of Illinois at Urbana-Champaign and Cynthia Selfe of Michigan Technological University. Their commitment to sustaining and improving this bibliography deserves our thanks. We wish them every success in their important work.

Contributing Bibliographers

Elizabeth Addison
Jim Addison
Clara Alexander
J. D. Applen
Ken Autrey
Linda Bannister
Richard Behm
Kelly Bellanger
Pam Besser
Laurel Black
Virginia A. Book
Robert Broad
Jody Brown
Lady Falls Brown
Collin G. Brooke
Mary Louise Buley-Meissner
Dan Callahan
Barbara Cambridge
Gary Caret
Gregory Clark
Irene Lurkis Clark
John Clifford
Laurie A. Coene
Joseph Colavito
Rick Cypert

Donald A. Daiker
Thomas E. Dasher
Kenneth W. Davis
Bonnie Devet
William M. Dodd
Robert Donahoo
Suellynn Duffey
Ann Hill Duin
Elizabeth Ervin
Chuck Etheridge
Timothy J. Evans
Marisa Farnum
Lauryl Fife
Janis Forman
Richard Fulkerson
T. Clifford Gardiner
Beate Gilliar
Gregory R. Glau
Joan I. Glazer
Judith Goleman
Gwendolyn Gong
Alice Goodwin
Patricia Goubil-Gambrell
Barbara Griffin
C. W. Griffin

Stephen Hahn
Liz Hamp-Lyons
Kathy Haney
Kristine Hansen
Sarah E. Harrold
Patrick Hartwell
Gary Hatch
Malcolm Hayward
Nancy Hayward
Cozette Heller
Marguerite H. Helmers
Alexandra R. Henry
John F. Heyda
Dixie Elise Hickman
Betsy Hilbert
Elizabeth Hoger
Deborah H. Holdstein
Sylvia A. Holladay
Elizabeth Huettman
Zita Ingham
Rebecca Innocent
Deborah James
Jack Jobst
Patricia Kedzerski
Joyce Kinkead

Elizabeth Larsen
Janice M. Lauer
Cynthia Lewiecki-Wilson
Maggy Lindgren
Marilyn Serraino Luecke
James McFadden
Geraldine McNenny
Dana Gulling Mead
Stephen Merrill
Vincent P. Mikkelsen
Max Morenberg
Neil Nakadate
Terence Odlin
Rory J. Ong
Suzanne C. Padgett
Peggy Parris
Christine Pellar-Kosbar
Michael A. Pemberton
Elizabeth F. Penfield
Virginia Perdue
Virginia G. Polanski

Deborah L. Pope
James Postema
John W. Presley
Paul W. Ranieri
D. R. Ransdell
Tom Reigstad
Valerie Reimers
Duane Roen
Audrey J. Roth
Sara Sanders
John Scenters-Zapico
Judith Scheffler
Marian Sciachitano
Erica L. Scott
Stuart Selber
Cynthia L. Selfe
Cynthia Miecnikowski
   Sheard
Barbara M. Sitko
Betsy Smith
Penelope Smith

Susan R. Smith
Wayne Sneath
James Strickland
Suzanne Swiderski
Dan J. Tannacito
Josephine K. Tarvers
Nathaniel Teich
Patricia Terry
Laura Thomas
Myron Tuman
Lisa Tyler
Elizabeth Vander Lei
Rex Veeder
Billie J. Wahlstrom
Keith Walters
Robert H. Weiss
Jacqueline Wheeler
David E. Wilson
J. Randal Woodland
George Xu

Journal Abbreviations

Contributing bibliographers reviewed the journals listed below in preparing entries for this volume. Entries for journal articles cited in this volume will include an abbreviation identifying the journal or serial in which it was published.

A&E	Anthropology and Education Quarterly	BL	Brain and Language
AdEd	Adult Education	Boundary	Boundary 2
AdLBEd	Adult Literacy and Basic Education	BRMMLA	Rocky Mountain Review of Language and Literature
AERJ	American Educational Research Journal	CACJ	Computer-Assisted Composition Journal
AJS	American Journal of Semiotics	CalE	California English
AM	Academic Medicine	CC	Computers and Composition
AmA	American Anthropologist	CCC	College Composition and Communication
AmE	American Ethnologist		
AmP	American Psychologist	CCR	Community College Review
Annals	Annals of the American Academy of Political and Social Science	CCrit	Cultural Critique
		CE	College English
		CEAC	CEA Critic
ArEB	Arizona English Bulletin	CEAF	CEA Forum
Arg	Argumentation	CHE	Chronicle of Higher Education
AS	American Speech	CHum	Computers and the Humanities
ASch	The American Scholar	CI	Cognition and Instruction
		CJL	Canadian Journal of Linguistics
BABC	Bulletin of the Association for Business Communication	CLAJ	College Language Association Journal
BADE	Bulletin of the Association of Departments of English	Cognition	Cognition
		CollL	College Literature

CollM	Collegiate Microcomputer		HT	History Teacher
CollT	College Teaching		IE	Indiana English
ComEd	Communication Education		IL	Informal Logic
ComM	Communication Monographs		IlEB	Illinois English Bulletin
CompC	Composition Chronicle		Intell	Intelligence
CompEd	Computers and Education		IPM	Information Processing and Management
ComQ	Communication Quarterly			
ComR	Communication Research		IRAL	International Review of Applied Linguistics in Language Teaching
ComS	Communication Studies			
CPsy	Cognitive Psychology			
CritI	Critical Inquiry		Issues	Issues in Writing
CSc	Cognitive Science			
CSWQ	Center for the Study of Writing Quarterly		JAC	Journal of Advanced Composition
			JAF	Journal of American Folklore
D&S	Discourse and Society		JBC	Journal of Business Communication
Daedalus	Daedalus: Journal of the American Academy of Arts and Sciences		JBS	Journal of Black Studies
			JBTC	Iowa State Journal of Business and Technical Communication
DAI	Dissertation Abstracts International		JBW	Journal of Basic Writing
DP	Developmental Psychology		JC	Journal of Communication
DPr	Discourse Processes		JCBI	Journal of Computer-Based Instruction
EdM	Educational Measurement: Issues and Practice		JCE	Journal of Chemical Education
			JCS	Journal of Curriculum Studies
EdPsy	Educational Psychologist		JCST	Journal of College Science Teaching
EEd	English Education			
ELT	English Language Teaching Journal		JDEd	Journal of Developmental Education
EnEd	Engineering Education		JEd	Journalism Educator
EngR	English Record		JEdM	Journal of Educational Measurement
EngT	English Today			
EQ	English Quarterly		JEdP	Journal of Educational Psychology
ESP	English for Specific Purposes			
ET	English in Texas		JEdR	Journal of Educational Research
ETC	ETC: A Review of General Semantics		JEngL	Journal of English Linguistics
			JEPG	Journal of Experimental Psychology: General
ExES	Explorations in Ethnic Studies			
ExEx	Exercise Exchange		JEPH	Journal of Experimental Psychology: Human Perception and Performance
FEN	Freshman English News			
FLA	Foreign Language Annals		JEPL	Journal of Experimental Psychology: Learning, Memory, Cognition
Focuses	Focuses			
FS	Feminist Studies			
GR	Georgia Review		JFR	Journal of Folklore Research
HCR	Human Communication Research		JGE	JGE: The Journal of General Education
HD	Human Development			
HER	Harvard Educational Review		JL	Journal of Linguistics

JLD	Journal of Learning Disabilities		PMS	Perceptual and Motor Skills
JML	Journal of Memory and Language		PPR	Philosophy and Phenomenological Research
JNT	Journal of Narrative Technique		PR	Partisan Review
JPsy	Journal of Psychology		Pre/Text	Pre/Text
JPsyR	Journal of Psycholinguistic Research		PsyR	Psychological Review
			PsyT	Psychology Today
JR	Journal of Reading		PT	Poetics Today
JRB	Journal of Reading Behavior: A Journal of Literacy		QJS	Quarterly Journal of Speech
			QRD	Quarterly Review of Doublespeak
JT	Journal of Thought			
JTEd	Journal of Teacher Education		R&W	Reading and Writing: An Interdisciplinary Journal
JTW	Journal of Teaching Writing			
JTWC	Journal of Technical Writing and Communication		Raritan	Raritan
			Reader	Reader
			RER	Review of Educational Research
L&M	Literature and Medicine			
L&S	Language and Speech		Rhetorica	Rhetorica
Lang	Language		RIE	Resources in Education
Lang&S	Language and Style		RR	Rhetoric Review
LangS	Language Sciences		RRQ	Reading Research Quarterly
Leaflet	The Leaflet		RSQ	Rhetoric Society Quarterly
Learning	Learning		RTE	Research in the Teaching of English
Ling	Linguistics			
LSoc	Language in Society			
LT	Language Testing		SAF	Studies in American Fiction
M&C	Memory and Cognition		SAm	Scientific American
MCQ	Management Communication Quarterly		SCJ	Southern Communication Journal
MEd	Medical Education		SCL	Studies in Canadian Literature
MissQ	Mississippi Quarterly		SFS	Science Fiction Studies
MLJ	The Modern Language Journal		SHum	Studies in the Humanities
MLQ	Modern Language Quarterly		SLang	Studies in Language
MLS	Modern Language Studies		SNNTS	Studies in the Novel
MM	Media and Methods		ST	Science Teacher
MSE	Massachusetts Studies in English		Style	Style
			SubStance	SubStance
MT	Mathematics Teacher			
			TC	Technical Communication
NYRB	The New York Review of Books		TESOLQ	Teachers of English to Speakers of Other Languages Quarterly
OralH	Oral History Review		TETYC	Teaching English in the Two-Year College
P&L	Philosophy and Literature			
P&R	Philosophy and Rhetoric		TWM	Teachers and Writers of Magazines
PC	The Professional Communicator		TWT	Technical Writing Teacher
PhiDK	Phi Delta Kappan		UEJ	Utah English Journal
PhS	Philosophical Studies			
PMLA	Publication of the Modern Language Association		V&R	Visions and Revisions
			VLang	Visible Language

WC	Written Communication	WLN	Writing Lab Newsletter
WCJ	Writing Center Journal	WLWE	World Literature Written in English
WE	Writing on the Edge	WPA	Journal of the Council of Writing
WI	Writing Instructor		Program Administrators
WJSC	Western Journal of Speech	Writer	The Writer
	Communication	WS	Women's Studies

Abbreviations in Entries

ABC	Association for Business Communication	ERIC/FLL	ERIC Clearinghouse on Language and Linguistics
ABE	Adult Basic Education	ERIC/RCS	ERIC Clearinghouse on Reading and Communication Skills
ACT	American College Test		
ACTFL	American Council on the Teaching of Foreign Languages	ESL	English as a Second Language
		ESP	English for Specific Purposes
ADE	Association of Departments of English	EST	English for Science and Technology
AERA	American Educational Research Association	ETS	Educational Testing Service
		FIPSE	Fund for the Improvement of Postsecondary Education
AP	Advanced Placement		
CAI	Computer-Assisted Instruction	GED	General Education Development
CBI	Computer-Based Instruction	GPA	Grade Point Average
CCCC	Conference on College Composition and Communication	GRE	Graduate Record Examination
		IRA	International Reading Association
CEE	Conference on English Education	LEP	Limited English Proficiency
CSR	Center for the Study of Reading	LES	Limited English Speaking
CSW	Center for the Study of Writing	L1	First Language
EAP	English for Academic Purposes	L2	Second Language
EDRS	ERIC Document Reproduction Service	MCAT	Medical College Admission Test
EFL	English as a Foreign Language	MLA	Modern Language Association
ERIC	Educational Resources Information Center	NAEP	National Assessment of Educational Progress

NCTE	National Council of Teachers of English	SLATE	Support for the Learning and Teaching of English
NEA	National Education Association	TESOL	Teachers of English to Speakers of Other Languages
NEH	National Endowment for the Humanities	TOEFL	Test of English as a Foreign Language
NIE	National Institute of Education		
NIH	National Institute of Health	TSWE	Test of Standard Written English
OCLC	Online Computer Library Center	WPA	Council of Writing Program Administrators
SAT	Scholastic Aptitude Test		
SCA	Speech Communication Association		

CCCC

Bibliography of Composition and Rhetoric

1990

1
Bibliographies and Checklists

1   BIBLIOGRAPHIES AND CHECKLISTS

1. Adult Literacy and Technology Project. *Adult Literacy and Technology: Guide to Literacy Software, 1989 Edition.* San Ramon, Calif.: Adult Literacy and Technology Project, 1989. ERIC ED 314 607. 126 pages

   Offers an annotated listing of software.

2. Benoit, William L., and Michael D. Moeder. *Bibliography of Several Approaches to Rhetorical Criticism.* Bloomington, Ind.: ERIC/RCS, 1989. ERIC ED 312 685. 9 pages

   Contains over 150 items treating criticism that were published between 1952 and 1989.

3. Benoit, William L., and Michael D. Moeder. *The Theory of Rhetorical Criticism: A Bibliography.* Bloomington, Ind.: ERIC/RCS, 1989. ERIC ED 312 686. 9 pages

   Contains 132 items published from 1933 to 1980 listed in three sections: books, articles, and book chapters.

4. *Bibliographic Guide to Education.* Boston: G. K. Hall, 1990.

   Lists material recorded on the OCLC tapes of Columbia University Teachers College during the year, supplemented by listings from New York Public Library for selected publications. Covers all aspects of education, including composition pedagogy.

5. Bosley, Deborah S., Meg Morgan, and Nancy Allen. "An Essential Bibliography on Collaborative Writing." *BABC* 53 (June 1990): 27–33.

   An annotated bibliography on interdisciplinary aspects of collaborative writing, particularly in business communication. Treats research, theoretical foundations, cooperative learning, small-group dynamics, pedagogy, and textbooks.

6. Chapman, David W. "Checklist of Recent Writing Center Scholarship: April 1989–March 1990." *WCJ* 11 (Fall-Winter 1990): 95–99.

   A 78-item checklist of articles appearing primarily in *The Writing Center Journal* and *Writing Lab Newsletter*. Includes articles from other journals as well as a few books.

7. Collins, Norma Decker. "Reducing Writing Apprehension through the Writing Process." *CompC* 3 (October 1990): 8–9.

Offers eight annotated ERIC citations.

8. Durst, Russel K., and James D. Marshall. "Annotated Bibliography of Research in the Teaching of English." *RTE* 24 (December 1990): 441–457.

Selections are grouped into four major categories: writing, language, literature, and teacher education.

9. Greene, Beth G. "International Business Communication: An Annotated Bibliography." *BABC* 53 (December 1990): 76–79.

Selects and annotates sources appearing in the ERIC data base from 1983 to 1990.

10. Hayward, Nancy M. *Recent Trends in Error Treatment: An Annotated Bibliography*. Washington, D.C.: ERIC/FLL, 1989. ERIC ED 314 962. 87 pages

Offers an annotated bibliography of 80 items published from 1975 to 1985.

11. Hayward, Nancy M. *A Selected Annotated Bibliography of Vocabulary in Teaching ESL and EFL, 1976–1985*. Washington, D.C.: ERIC/FLL, 1989. ERIC ED 314 963. 40 pages

Offers an annotated bibliography of 38 items published from 1976 to 1985.

12. Horner, Winifred Bryan. "Nineteenth-Century Rhetoric at the Universities of Aberdeen and St. Andrews with an Annotated Bibliography of Archival Materials." *RSQ* 20 (Summer 1990): 287–299.

Gives historical sketches of the universities of Aberdeen and St. Andrews and their professors of moral philosophy and logic. Annotates archival materials, primarily lecture notes written by students and professors.

13. Horner, Winifred Bryan. "Nineteenth-Century Rhetoric at the University of Glasgow with an Annotated Bibliography of Archival Materials." *RSQ* 20 (Spring 1990): 173–185.

Offers a brief history of the University of Glasgow and biographical sketches of nineteenth-century professors of logic and rhetoric. Annotates archival materials about these teachers, including students' notes, course descriptions, and commission reports.

14. Horner, Winifred Bryan, ed. *The Present State of Scholarship in Historical and Contemporary Rhetoric*. Rev. ed. Columbia, Mo.: University of Missouri Press, 1990. 288 pages

Arranged chronologically by period, each section contains an introductory essay providing an overview of existing scholarship and suggesting new avenues of research. Each essay is followed by a bibliography of selected primary and secondary sources.

15. Johns, Jerry, and Roberta L. Berglund. *Reading-Writing Relationships*. Focused Access to Selected Topics Bibliography, no. 42. Bloomington, Ind.: ERIC/RCS, 1990. ERIC ED 313 691. 5 pages

Provides an annotated bibliography of 31 items published between 1955 and 1989.

16. Keeler, Heather. "Portrait of a Technical Communicator: A Bibliographic Review of Current Research." *TC* 37 (February 1990): 41–48.

Reviews surveys published since 1980 of professional technical communicators. Data on skills required, communication tasks, and other concerns are useful for planning technical communication curricula.

17. Lutz, William. "Keeping Up with Your Reading." *QRD* 16 (April 1990): 10–11.

Provides an annotated bibliography of six recent books treating doublespeak.

18. Lutz, William. "Keeping Up with Your Reading." *QRD* 16 (July 1990): 4–6.

Provides an annotated bibliography of seven recent books treating doublespeak.

19. Lutz, William. "Keeping Up with Your Reading." *QRD* 17 (October 1990): 10–11.

Provides an annotated bibliography of seven recent books treating doublespeak.

20. Mabrito, Mark. "Annotated Bibliography of Resources in Computer Networking." *CC*7 (August 1990): 23–39.

Cites resources on computer-mediated communication in writing instruction, distance education, social and psychological influences, and the language of computer-mediated communication.

21. Maine State Department of Education. *Language and Cultural Minorities Resource Catalog*. Bangor, Maine: Maine State Department of Education, 1988. ERIC ED 313 906. 197 pages

Lists 1000 resources for ESL literacy instruction at all levels.

22. Marshall, James D., and Russel K. Durst. "Annotated Bibliography of Research in the Teaching of English." *RTE* 24 (May 1990): 205–221.

Annotates 134 articles, papers, and dissertations from 1987 through 1989. Covers writing, language, literature, and teacher education.

23. Miller, Thomas. "The Formation of College English: A Survey of the Archives of Eighteenth-Century Rhetorical Theory and Practice." *RSQ* 20 (Summer 1990): 261–286.

Outlines sources that document the origins of college English and cites collections of primary materials that can relate the origins of college English to social developments beyond the classroom.

24. Moran, Michael G., and Martin J. Jacobi, eds. *Research in Basic Writing: A Bibliographic Sourcebook*. New York: Greenwood Press, 1990. 268 pages

A survey of research on the teaching of unprepared writers. The 11 bibliographic essays are grouped into social science perspectives, linguistic perspectives, and pedagogical perspectives. Name and subject indexes are included.

25. Morgan, Bradford A. "Computers and Writing on the Verge of the 1990s: A Bibliographic Foreword to Scholarship and Pedagogy in a Time of Technological Change." *Research in Word Processing Newsletter* 7 (May 1989): 2–38.

Lists over 700 articles, books, and papers dealing with the processing of words by computers. Entries are unannotated.

26. Nakamura, Mitsuo. "An Annotated Bibliography of *The Journal of Technical Writing and Communication,* 1971–1989." *JTWC* 20 (1990): 45–107.

Describes all items published in *JTWC* between 1971 and 1989, grouping them under the profession; pedagogy; preparation and presentation of information; research and theory; and application of technology.

27. NCTE Commission on Media. *Visual Media for English Teachers: An Annotated Bibliography*. Urbana, Ill.: NCTE, 1990. ERIC ED 312 692. 23 pages

Contains nearly 100 items divided into seven sections: film studies, television studies, response and intertextuality, video production, computers and English, imaging, and textbooks.

28. Ramsey, Richard David, and Bobbye J. Davis. "Jay Reid Gould: A Checklist." *JTWC* 20 (1990): 25–44.

A "comprehensive listing" of Professor Gould's publications, including books, plays, short stories, articles, and essays, as well as unpublished materials and items about him.

29. "Resources." *QRD* 16 (April 1990): 9.

Lists 36 sources for research on doublespeak, including books, articles, and software.

30. "Resources." *QRD* 17 (October 1990): 9–10.

    Lists nine books helpful for research on doublespeak.

31. Rothschild, Joyce, and others. "1989 ATTW Bibliography." *TWT* 17 (Fall 1990): 272–296.

    Lists books and articles on theory and philosophy, research, pedagogy, and writing practice for technical writing teachers and researchers.

32. Scott, James Calvert. "An Annotated Reference List of Publications Relating to International Business Communication." *BABC* 53 (December 1990): 72–76.

    Includes sources beyond textbooks and publications of the Association for Business Communication.

33. Shermis, Michael. "Research, Activities, and Writing Assignments in Persuasion." *CompC* 3 (December 1990): 8–9.

    Lists 10 annotated ERIC citations.

34. Shermis, Michael. "Using Word Processing for Writing Instructors." *CompC* 2 (January 1990): 9–10.

    An annotated bibliography of eight ERIC citations.

35. Shermis, Michael. *Writing and Literature.* Focused Access to Selected Topics Bibliography, no. 29. Bloomington, Ind.: ERIC/RCS, 1989. ERIC ED 311 425. 4 pages

    Contains 28 references on using writing to study literature and using literature to foster invention in student writing.

36. Shields, John C., and William E. Hull. "Stylistics Annotated Bibliography for 1989." *Style* 24 (Winter 1990): 503–563.

    Covers bibliographical resources, general theory, culture and history, the author, the text, and the reader.

37. Speck, Bruce W., and Lynnette R. Porter. "Annotated Bibliography for Teaching Ethics in Professional Writing." *BABC* 53 (September 1990): 36–52.

    Cites works that focus on theory, teaching, the teacher, and related subjects.

38. Tannacito, Dan J., ed. *ESL/EFL Methodology: Topical, Annotated Bibliographies, vol. 2.* Washington, D.C.: ERIC/FLL, 1989. ERIC ED 314 961. 128 pages

    Offers two annotated bibliographies of materials published between 1975 and 1985. The first lists 80 items on treating error; the second, 38 items on vocabulary instruction.

39. Wolff, William C. "Annotated Bibliography of Scholarship on Writing Centers and Related Topics, 1988–1989." *Focuses* 3 (Spring 1990): 37–73.

    An annual listing of 191 entries, including books, collected essays, and journal articles.

40. Xu, George Q. *ESL/EFL Composition: A Selected Annotated Bibliography.* Bloomington, Ind.: ERIC/RCS, 1989. ERIC ED 309 645. 27 pages

    Offers 84 briefly annotated citations of ESL/EFL pedagogical literature written since 1983.

See also 615, 1789, 1826

2
Theory and Research

2.1 RHETORICAL THEORY, DISCOURSE THEORY, AND COMPOSING

41. Ackerman, John M. *Reading, Writing, and Knowing: The Role of Disciplinary Knowledge in Comprehension and Composing.* CSW Technical Report, no. 40. Berkeley, Calif.: CSW, 1990. ERIC ED 318 008. 48 pages

Compares two groups of 20 graduate students from two disciplines. Think-aloud protocols show the interrelatedness of composing and comprehension.

42. Allen, Mike, and Nancy A. Burrell. "Resolving Arguments Accurately." *Arg* 4 (May 1990): 213–221.

Examines how 46 subjects resolved disagreements over solutions to categorical syllogisms. Subjects most frequently argued the merits of the positions and appealed to precedents.

43. Anderson, Lawrence Edmund. "Incubation and Interruption: An Experimental Study of Idea Elaboration in the Impromptu Writing of College Students." *DAI* 50 (April 1990): 3170A.

A study of 140 students shows that impromptu writing benefits from interruptions of 15 minutes, 24 hours, and 48 hours, with fewer benefits for longer interruptions.

44. Anson, Chris M., and L. Lee Forsberg. "Moving beyond the Academic Community: Transitional Stages in Professional Writing." *WC* 7 (April 1990): 200–231.

A qualitative study of six writers, senior English majors participating in an off-campus intern program. Proposes a three-stage model of expectation, disorientation, and transition and resolution.

45. Armstrong, Nancy, and Leonard Tennenhouse. "Gender and the Work of Words." *CCrit* 13 (Fall 1989): 229–278.

Argues that rhetoric "genders" occupations, making some labor men's work and some labor women's. Examines texts from the seventeenth through the nineteenth centuries.

46. Atkins, G. Douglas. "The Return of/to the Essay." *BADE* 96 (Fall 1990): 11–18.

Distinguishes the contemporary essay from the belletristic form of the article. Argues for reestablishing ties between the critical and the personal essay.

47. Balwanz-Emmel, Barbara A. "Model Essays in the Classroom: An Organic Approach to Understanding the Epistemological Basis of Form and Argument in the Essay." *DAI* 50 (May 1990): 3567A.

Enthymematic analyses of essays reveal logical constructions of knowledge that inform the development of those essays.

48. Bannister, Linda. "Examining Contemporary Women Rhetoricians: Is There a Feminine Rhetoric?" Paper presented at the CCCC Convention, Chicago, March 1990. ERIC ED 317 996. 15 pages

Sees the work of Mina Shaughnessy, Linda Flower, and Janet Emig as comprising a feminine rhetoric.

49. Barton, Ben F., and Marthalee S. Barton. "Postmodernism and the Relation of the Word and Image in Professional Discourse." *TWT* 17 (Fall 1990): 256–270.

Explores the relation between words and graphics at both the theoretical and practical levels.

50. Barton, Fred. "A Description of the Effects of Certain Spatial Visualization Techniques on the Composing Processes of Selected Two-Year College Students." *DAI* 51 (August 1990): 436A.

Examines nonlinear organizing strategies such as clusters and hierarchical maps. Finds that maps help control the process, especially for invention.

51. Baum Brunner, Shelley. "Talk about Writing and the Revision of Rough Drafts." *DAI* 51 (November 1990): 1535A.

Explores the nature of oral responses, qualities of effective response, the development of respondents and response, and the impact of individual personalities on response and revision.

52. Baumlin, James S., and Jim W. Corder. "Jackleg Carpentry and the Fall from Freedom to Authority in Writing." *FEN* 18 (Spring 1990): 18–20.

Values seeing writing as the search for authority rather than as definitive. Regards authorship as a continuous search.

53. Bavelas, Janet Beavin, Alex Black, Nicole Chovil, and Jennifer Mullett. *Equivocal Communication.* Sage Series in Interpersonal Communication, vol. 11. Newbury Park, Calif.: Sage, 1990. 344 pages

Uses psychological research methods to examine ambiguity or equivocation in communicative contexts.

54. Bayer, Gertrude J. "The Silenced Voice of Feminist Rhetoric: A Critique of Social Movement Theory and a Framework for Reconceptualizing the Feminist Movement." *DAI* 51 (August 1990): 659A.

Concludes that five existing rhetorical theories inadequately describe the rhetorical transactions of the women's movement. Suggests a historical analysis centered on biological-social contradictions.

55. Bender, John, and David E. Wellbery, eds. *The Ends of Rhetoric: History, Theory, Practice.* Stanford, Calif.: Stanford University Press, 1990. 238 pages

Twelve essays discuss concepts of rhetorical theory, the work of major proponents, and breaks and continuities in the history of rhetoric. Most of the essays were originally presented at a 1987 conference at Stanford University.

56. Beniger, James R. "Who Are the Most Important Theorists of Communication?" *ComR* 17 (October 1990): 698–715.

A review essay of the 1800-page *International Encyclopedia of Communication*

(Oxford University Press) describing how such a volume defines the field.

57. Berthoff, Ann E. *The Sense of Learning.* Portsmouth, N.H.: Boynton/Cook, 1990. 160 pages

Argues that teaching, learning, and reading are all still possible so long as the act of interpretation stands at the center of education.

58. Birth, Kevin K. "Reading and the Righting of Writing Ethnographies." *AmE* 17 (August 1990): 549–557.

A review article discussing ethics and the writing of ethnographies.

59. Bizzell, Patricia. "Beyond Antifoundationalism to Rhetorical Authority: Problems Defining 'Cultural Literacy.' " *CE* 52 (October 1990): 661–675.

Demonstrates that English studies, by shifting from a philosophical to a rhetorical orientation, could assert antifoundationalist authority in the name of democratic social change.

60. Bonk, Curtis. "A Synthesis of Social Cognition and Writing Research." *WC* 7 (January 1990): 136–163.

A critical review of literature from the last two decades on the relationship between social cognition and writing. Proposes an agenda for future theorizing and research.

61. Booth-Butterfield, Melanie, and Steve Booth-Butterfield. "Conceptualizing Affect as Information in Communication Production." *HCR* 16 (Summer 1990): 451–476.

Four studies investigate how affect relates to other communication constructs and behaviors such as recall and communicating emotional events.

62. Bouldin, Thomas Tyler. "Composing as Symbolization: A Systemic Perspective on Composing and Composition Research." *DAI* 51 (November 1990): 1535A.

Describes a composing and research methodology based on the principles of general systems theory.

63. Bowman, Joel P. "Response to Johan van Hoorde [*JBC* 27 (Winter 1990)]." *JBC* 27 (Winter 1990): 71–74.

A sympathetic critique of van Hoorde's modification of the Targowski/Bowman communication model.

64. Boyanowski, Ronald Thomas. "Attitudes of High School Seniors towards Writing: A Phenomenological Investigation." *DAI* 50 (March 1990): 2685A.

Explores the effects of apprehension and anxiety on the attitudes towards writing of 11 high school students. Finds them most influenced by the kinds of compositions required.

65. Brand, Alice G. "Social Cognition, Emotions, and the Psychology of Writing." Paper presented at the CCCC Convention, Chicago, March 1990. ERIC ED 318 001. 28 pages

Argues that social-cognitive approaches have neglected the emotional components of writing.

66. Brand, Alice G. "Writing and Feelings: Checking Our Vital Signs." *RR* 8 (Spring 1990): 290–307.

Reports on a study evaluating the effect of emotions on writing and of writing on emotions in various contexts.

67. Brooke, Robert. "Robert Brooke Responds [to Steinberg, *CE* 52 (January 1990)]." *CE* 52 (January 1990): 100–102.

Defends his exploration of the metaphors that describe control in writing. Suggests deconstruction as a way of gaining access to complex writing such as Flower's.

68. Brown, Stuart C. "Reconsidering I. A. Richards' Role in the New Rhetoric: Predecessor, Prestidigitator, Proponent." Paper presented at the CCCC Convention, Seattle, March 1989. ERIC ED 311 471. 18 pages

Argues that Richards' work has more to offer than is presently recognized.

69. Bruffee, Kenneth A. "Response to the *JAC* Interview with Richard Rorty [*JAC* 9 (1989)]." *JAC* 10 (1990): 145–146.

Criticizes Richard Rorty's interviewers for improperly situating their questions in a foundational mode and for making a theory/practice dichotomy.

70. Burke, Kenneth. *On Symbols and Society.* Edited by Joseph R. Gusfield. Chicago: University of Chicago Press, 1989. 332 pages

Brings together Burke's writing on symbols and social relations.

71. Campbell, John Angus. "Between the Fragment and the Icon: Prospect for a Rhetorical House of the Middle Way." *WJSC* 54 (Summer 1990): 346–376.

Explores possibilities for synthesizing the two perspectives.

72. Campbell, John Angus. "Introduction: Special Issue on Rhetorical Criticism." *WJSC* 54 (Summer 1990): 249–251.

Establishes a focus on specific issues in two diverse programmatic orientations.

73. Campbell, Jonathan L. "The Relevant Communication of Rhetorical Arguments." *DAI* 51 (December 1990): 2001A.

Argues that rhetorical arguments are made and understood in three contexts: spatial/temporal, sequential, and cultural/historical.

74. Campbell, Kim Sydow, Kathryn Riley, and Frank Parker. "You-Perspective Insights from Speech-Act Theory." *JTWC* 20 (1990): 189–199.

Describes principles that help determine precisely when and where first- and second-person pronouns are most effectively used in two types of professional communication.

75. Capps, Douglas, and Kenneth Mendoza. "Writing as Cognitive Mapping." *WI* 9 (Fall 1989-Winter 1990): 19–25.

Argues that an emphasis on writing as an "activity of mapping" rather than as a "process" can empower students, fostering in them confidence and independence.

76. Carey, Linda, Linda Flower, John R. Hayes, Karen A. Schriver, and Christina Haas. *Differences in Writers' Initial Task Representations.* CSW Technical Report, no. 35. Berkeley, Calif.: CSW, 1989. ERIC ED 310 403. 33 pages

Verbal protocols of 12 writers reveal that different initial representations of writing goals affect the quality of the final texts.

77. Carter, Michael. "The Idea of Expertise: An Exploration of Cognitive and Social Dimensions of Writing." *CCC* 41 (October 1990): 265–286.

Proposes a theory of expertise to account for local (social) and general (cognitive) knowledge. Expert writers use general and specific strategies but within domains.

78. Catano, James V. "Response to Coles [*CE* 52 (December 1990)]." *CE* 52 (December 1990): 931–932.

Reasserts the importance of his contribution to discussing the rhetoric of masculinity and its effect on writing pedagogy.

79. Catano, James V. "The Rhetoric of Masculinity: Origins, Institutions, and the Myth of the Self-Made Man." *CE* 52 (April 1990): 421–436.

Sees the work of Elbow, Coles, and Macrorie as masculine rhetoric, especially as it emphasizes individual self-making and institutional authority.

80. Cherwitz, Richard A., ed. *Rhetoric and Philosophy.* Hillsdale, N.J.: Erlbaum, 1990. 336 pages

Ten essays explore how speech communication specialists have attempted to find a philosophical grounding for rhetoric. Examines eight philosophies of rhetoric: realism, relativism, rationalism, idealism, materialism, existentialism, deconstructionism, and pragmatism.

81. Chiseri-Strater, Elizabeth. *Academic Literacies: The Public and Private Discourse of University Students.* Portsmouth, N.H.: Boynton/Cook, 1990. 256 pages

Draws upon a case study of two college students to argue that such factors as gender, human development, and private talents are routinely ignored in the reading, writing, and thinking called for in a college curriculum.

82. Chiste, Katherine Beaty, and Judith O'Shea. "The Prewriting of Unsuccessful Writers on Timed Writing Competence Tests." *EQ* 22 (1990): 45–54.

Finds that unsuccessful writers used limited and ineffective prewriting strategies, resulting in weak content, structure, and paragraphing.

83. Clark, Gregory, and Stephen Doheny-Farina. "Public Discourse and Personal Expression: A Case Study in Theory Building." *WC* 7 (October 1990): 465–481.

Examines from the conflicting perspectives of collectivist and individualist rhetorics the experience of a female college senior writing at school and at a volunteer organization.

84. Clifton, Linda. "Notes toward a Paper." *JTW* 9 (Spring-Summer 1990): 59–64.

Analyzes Style B as a heuristic for exploring the personal writing process. Includes prompts and examples of the author's own Style B writing.

85. Cline, Rebecca J. Welch. "Detecting Groupthink: Methods for Observing the Illusion of Unanimity." *ComQ* 38 (Spring 1990): 112–126.

Tests Janis' (1972) groupthink theory. Results show that groupthink discussions expressed greater agreement than nongroupthink discussions.

86. Coe, Richard M. "Defining Rhetoric—and Us." *JAC* 10 (1990): 39–52.

Explicates six elements of Burke's definition of man to provide a basis for reading Burke.

87. Coe, Richard M. "Richard Coe Responds [to McKendy, *CE* 52 (January 1990)]." *CE* 52 (January 1990): 104–106.

Defends the selection criteria for articles in *CE* 50 (December 1988) and defines his own position as an Anglo-Canadian.

88. Coles, William E., Jr. "A Comment on 'The Rhetoric of Masculinity: Origins, Institutions, and the Myth of the Self-Made Man' [*CE* 52 (April 1990)]." *CE* 52 (December 1990): 930–931.

Protests Catano's reducing Coles' work "to an unevolving perpetuation of the myth of the self-made man."

89. Colomb, Gregory C., and Joseph M. Williams. "A Comment on 'Textual Research and Coherence: Findings, Intuition, Application' [*CE* 51 (March 1989)]." *CE* 52 (February 1990): 208–212.

Argues that quantitative results measure only statistical significance, providing no insight into affective significance. Affective response is an integral part of effective writing.

90. Condit, Celeste. "Rhetorical Criticism and Audiences: The Extremes of McGee and Leff." *WJSC* 54 (Summer 1990): 330–345.

Argues that a move to extremes threatens to reintroduce the form/content dichotomy.

91. Cox, J. Robert. "On 'Interpreting' Public Discourse in Postmodernity." *WJSC* 54 (Summer 1990): 317–329.

Argues that interpretation is essential to understanding the construction of rhetorical texts and is a source for inventing social critique in postmodern culture.

92. Cragan, John F., and David W. Wright. "Small Group Communication Research of the 1980s: A Synthesis and Critique." *ComS* 41 (Fall 1990): 212–236.

Classifies and critiques studies representing seven lines of research. Suggests new methodologies and contextual settings for further study.

93. Crismore, Avon, and William J. Vande Kopple. "Rhetorical Contexts and Hedges." *RSQ* 20 (Winter 1990): 49–59.

Examines how students respond to texts that contain hedges, linguistic judgments of modality such as *perhaps, might,* and *it is possible that.*

94. Cross, Geoffrey A. "A Bakhtinian Exploration of Factors Affecting the Collaborative Writing of an Executive Letter of an Annual Report." *RTE* 24 (May 1990): 173–203.

Uses Bakhtin's language theory in exploring the drawbacks of peer and hierarchical editing in a largely unsuccessful collaborative writing effort.

95. Crowley, Sharon. *The Methodical Memory: Invention in Current-Traditional Rhetoric.* Carbondale, Ill.: Southern Illinois University Press, 1990. 229 pages

A sustained critique of current-traditional rhetoric that traces how formalized methods have influenced our perception of the act of invention.

96. Crusius, Timothy W. "Reflections on *A Pragmatic Theory of Rhetoric*." *JAC* 10 (1990): 53–72.

Attempts to situate the discourse theory proposed by Walter Beale in relation to theories such as Kinneavy's and Burke's. An extended positive review.

97. Cumming, Alister. "Metalinguistic and Ideational Thinking in Second Language Composing." *WC* 7 (October 1990): 482–511.

Offers quantitative analyses of concurrent ideational and metalinguistic thinking in protocols of L2 writers. Offers suggestions for reformulating Swain's notion of "comprehensible output."

98. D'Angelo, Frank. "Tropics of Arrangement: A Theory of *Dispositio*." *JAC* 10 (1990): 101–109.

Four master tropes identified by Burke and White are asserted to be the deep structure of all discourse. Applies the theory to Annie Dillard.

99. Davis, James S., and James D. Marshall, eds. *Ways of Knowing: Research and Practice in the Teaching of Writing.* Iowa City: Iowa Council of Teachers of English (distributed by NCTE), 1988. 177 pages

Sixteen essays examine the gaps and bridges among different kinds of training, experiences, obligations, methods, and goals of researchers and teachers. Suggests ways of integrating these ways of knowing about composition.

100. "Describing the Structure of Discourse: A Conversation with Joseph Williams." *Issues* 2 (Spring-Summer 1990): 98–116.

Touches on many subjects, among them his current research interests, consulting in business and professional settings, elements of discourse common to all genres, nominal versus verbal style, and the University of Chicago's writing program.

101. Dilworth, Collett B. "The Relationship of Reading and Writing: A Review of Research." *Leaflet* 89 (Winter 1990): 32–38.

Summarizes and discusses the findings of 13 studies showing that reading and writing are mutually reinforcing.

102. DiPardo, Anne. "Narrative Knowers, Expository Knowledge: Discourse as Dialectic." *WC* 7 (January 1990): 59–95.

Examines the contrast between objective exposition and personal narrative promulgated by rhetorical theory and pedagogical practice, arguing for a dialectic view of the two.

103. Downing, Robert H. "The Relationship between Writing Revision, Thinking about Revision, and Quality of Writing." *DAI* 50 (June 1990): 3894A.

Investigates the writing behavior and processes of university students. As writers change audience, goals, or strategies, they revise larger units of text and meaning.

104. Durst, Russel, Chester Laine, Lucille M. Schultz, and William Vilter. "Appealing Texts: The Persuasive Writing of High School Students." *WC* 7 (April 1990): 232–255.

A quantitative analysis of 198 holistically scored persuasive essays reveals a relationship between their quality and the use of logical appeals, five-paragraph structure, coherence, and the number of words.

105. Durst, Russel K. "The Mongoose and the Rat in Composition Research: Insights from the *RTE* Annotated Bibliography." *CCC* 41 (December 1990): 393–408.

Surveys the state of composition research as revealed in five years of annotated bibliographies published in *RTE*.

106. Dutton, Sandra Jeanne. "Writing as Sculpting: An Affective, Structural Model." *DAI* 51 (August 1990): 438A.

Based on six case studies. Extends and modifies Hayes and Flower's cognitive process model of composing by positing a "triangle" that unites structure, process, and emotion.

107. Eckert, Penelope. "Cooperative Competition in Adolescent 'Girl Talk.' " *DPr* 13 (January–March 1990): 91–122.

Six high school girls used language to influence the way others in thc group saw them.

108. Ede, Lisa, and Andrea Lunsford. *Singular Texts/Plural Authors: Perspectives on Collaborative Writing*. Carbondale, Ill.: Southern Illinois University Press, 1990. 295 pages

Combining theoretical and historical explorations with research on group writing, these authors explore the rationale for engaging in collaborative work.

109. Ewald, Helen Rothschild. "Mikhail Bakhtin and 'Expressive Discourse.' " Paper presented at the CCCC Convention, Chicago, March 1990. ERIC ED 318 031. 10 pages

Discusses how Bakhtin's dialogics lead to an emphasis on openness and change in the composing process.

110. Ewald, Helen Rothschild. "Schematic and Text-Based Arrangement Options, the Reading Process, and Rhetorical Competence." *CEAF* 20 (1990): 5–13.

Student writers will compose and arrange texts more effectively when taught regularly a sensitivity to readers' expectations.

111. Fagan, William T. "The Writing of Adult Learners: Form and Function." *AdLBEd* 13 (1989): 71–80.

Suggests that Brewer's framework is more useful for understanding why adults write than are Britton and Moffett's child-based theories.

112. Fitzgerald, Jill, and Carol Stamm. "Effects of Group Conferences on First Graders' Revision in Writing." *WC* 7 (January 1990): 96–135.

Reports on an experimental study of the effects of group conferences on first graders' knowledge of revision and revision activity. The extent of revision was related to various student characteristics.

113. Fleckenstein, Kristie S. "Connections: The Cognitive and Affective Links between Expressive Writing and Aesthetic Reading." *DAI* 50 (March 1990): 2875A.

Analyzes five subjects' reading and writing logs. Concludes that affective processes and structures direct aesthetic reading and expressive writing.

114. Flesher, Gretchen. "A Response to 'Throwing Our Voices' [*WE* 2 (Fall 1990)]." *WE* 2 (Fall 1990): 51–54.

Suggests that personal voice be defined more broadly and that the sharp dichotomy between personal and academic discourse be softened.

115. Flower, Linda, Karen A. Schriver, Christina Haas, and John R. Hayes. *Planning in Writing: The Cognition of a Constructive Pro-*

cess. CSW Technical Report, no. 34. Berkeley, Calif.: CSW, 1989. ERIC ED 313 701. 61 pages

> Discusses the executive strategies skilled and unskilled adults use to plan ill-defined writing tasks.

116. Flower, Linda, Victoria Stein, John Ackerman, Margaret J. Kantz, and Kathleen McCormick. *Reading-to-Write: Exploring a Cognitive and Social Process.* New York: Oxford University Press, 1990. 320 pages

> A descriptive study of reading-to-write that examines the task of reading a source, integrating personal ideas, and creating a text.

117. Flynn, Dale. "Ritual of Writing: An Interview with Richard Selzer." *WE* 2 (Fall 1990): 57–68.

> Selzer discusses the origin of his writing career, the teaching of writing, and his own writing process.

118. Fortune, Ron. "Style in Composition Research and Teaching." *Style* 23 (Winter 1989): 508–529.

> A review of recent literature on "style's changing role in composition studies."

119. Foster, David. "Hurling Epithets at the Devils You Know: A Response to Carol Berkenkotter [*JAC* 9 (1989)]." *JAC* 10 (1990): 149–152.

> Argues that, while Berkenkotter and others see a polarity between positivistic empiricism and hermeneutic/social research, the two should be seen as partners rather than as rivals.

120. Fowler, Alastair. "Apology for Rhetoric." *Rhetorica* 8 (Spring 1990): 103–118.

> Argues for a modern rhetoric of postclassical figures, attuned to linguistic theory, especially pragmatics, yet maintaining the normative function of rhetorical criticism.

121. Fulkerson, Richard. "Composition Theory in the Eighties: Axiological Consensus and Paradigmatic Diversity." *CCC* 41 (December 1990): 409–429.

> Composition studies show a growing consensus for a rhetorical axiology as expressivism, formalism, and mimeticism decline. However, disparities continue about procedures, pedagogy, and epistemological concerns.

122. Fulmer, Hal W., and Carl L. Kell. "A Sense of Place, a Spirit of Adventure: Implications for the Study of Regional Rhetoric." *RSQ* 20 (Summer 1990): 225–232.

> Explores theoretical precepts that underscore discussions of regional rhetoric.

123. Gaonkar, Dilip Parameshwar. "Object and Method in Rhetorical Criticism: From Wichelns to Leff and McGee." *WJSC* 54 (Summer 1990): 290–316.

> Studies the fluctuating dialectic between object and method and attempts to reconnect them.

124. Gates, Rosemary L. "Understanding Writing as an Art: Classical Rhetoric and the Corporate Context." *TWT* 17 (Winter 1990): 50–60.

> Outlines the use of *kairos* or appropriateness and *aitia* or cause as tools for business, scientific, and technical writing.

125. Gerring, Sharon A. "Differences in Metacognitive Knowledge and Behavior between Successful and Unsuccessful College Writers." *DAI* 51 (September 1990): 726A.

> Studies the gap between successful and unsuccessful writers' metacognitive awareness and its effect on writing ability.

126. Gleason, Barbara. "Epistemologies of Composition." *DAI* 51 (July 1990): 19A.

> Compares the epistemological implications of Derrida's deconstruction and Husserl's phenomenology and finds that the latter provides an important realist perspective for composition.

127. Gonzalez, Alberto. "Mexican 'Otherness' in the Rhetoric of Mexican Americans." *SCJ* 55 (Spring 1990): 276–291.

Reviews previous studies, then applies dimensions of Mexican otherness to explore critically the rhetorical potential created by Mexican-American writers.

128. Goodwin, Marjorie Harness. "Tactical Uses of Stories: Participation Frameworks within Girls' and Boys' Disputes." *DPr* 13 (January–March 1990): 33–71.

Girls in a black, working-class neighborhood produced stories likely to lead to future conflicts, whereas boys produced stories that continued ongoing arguments.

129. Gowen, Brent. "Archipelago." *WI* 9 (Fall 1989-Winter 1990): 27–34.

Explores "mapping," a process by which writers "act first and justify later," as a metaphor for thinking about composition.

130. Graves, Richard L., ed. *Rhetoric and Composition: A Sourcebook for Teachers and Writers*. 3d ed. Portsmouth, N.H.: Boynton/Cook, 1990. 336 pages

The new edition of this collection of 31 readings, many reprinted from journals, contains approximately 75 percent new material.

131. Greene, Stuart. *Toward a Dialectical Theory of Composing*. CSW Occasional Paper, no. 17. Berkeley, Calif.: CSW, 1990. ERIC ED 317 991. 24 pages

Reviews social theories of knowledge. Argues that a dialectical conception of a cognitive-social epistemic subsumes a family of cognitive and social theories that accounts for how writing gets produced.

132. Greene, Stuart. "Toward a Dialectical Theory of Composing." *RR* 9 (Fall 1990): 149–171.

Proposes a cognitive-social epistemic, in which both social forces and individual cognition are dialectical and inform us of the processes of making knowledge.

133. Gross, Alan G. "Extending the Expressive Power of Language: Tables, Graphs, and Diagrams." *JTWC* 20 (1990): 221–235.

Because the elements of graphic displays are disparate and do not form a natural set, they are unlikely candidates for unitary theoretical description.

134. Haas, Christina. "Composing in Technological Contexts: A Study of Note Making." *WC* 7 (October 1990): 512–547.

Contrasts transcribing and composing. Offers a taxonomy of the types of notes writers made during essay planning. Supports the notion that early planning with pen and paper differs from planning at the computer.

135. Hample, Dale, and Judith M. Dallinger. "Arguers as Editors." *Arg* 4 (May 1990): 153–169.

An empirical investigation identifies three classes of editorial criteria—effectiveness, person-centered concerns, and discourse quality—that people use in deciding whether to say or suppress potential arguments.

136. Harkin, Patricia. "Bringing Lore to Light." *Pre/Text* 10 (Spring-Summer 1989): 55–67.

A "metacommentary" rearguing the assertion that composition studies is potentially postdisciplinary in its production of knowledge.

137. Harshbarger, Scott. " 'Organic Rhetoric': The Growth of a Trope in Modern Composition Theory." Paper presented at the CCCC Convention, Chicago, March 1990. ERIC ED 318 024. 11 pages

Proposes the plant as the paradigmatic metaphor for composition within the New Rhetoric.

138. Haswell, Richard H. "No Title: A Response to Sam Meyer [*JAC* 8 (1988)]." *JAC* 10 (1990): 396–399.

Rebuts Meyer with an informal study of student writing. Finds no connection between writing quality, the author's experience, and whether or not the essay was titled.

139. Haswell, Richard H. "Richard H. Haswell Responds [to Colomb and Williams, *CE* 52 (February 1990)]." *CE* 52 (February 1990): 212–215.

Defends his position on the use of quantitative research: intuition that lacks descriptive support explains little about writing practices.

140. Haugen, Diane. "Coming to Terms with Editing." *RTE* 24 (October 1990): 322–333.

Distinguishes between academic editing, involving one's own work, and editing in the work place, involving the writing of others. Calls for definitions that bridge theory and practice.

141. Heinrich, Judith Ann. "Communication as Productive Understanding: Toward a New Story." *DAI* 51 (October 1990): 1045A.

Argues that interpersonal communication research needs a paradigm shift. Suggests that the information distribution paradigm should change to a more dialectical model.

142. Henderson, Bruce S. "The Effects of College Class Level and Major Area of Study on the Writing Performance of Seniors and Freshmen." *DAI* 50 (June 1990): 3862A.

Investigates the writing of college seniors, examining relationships among types and frequency of writing, major area, and performance on writing tasks.

143. Hoeffler, Judith Savage. "The Myth of Perpetual Youth; The Reality of Age: A Rhetorical Exigency for the Baby Boom and Vietnam Generations." *DAI* 51 (September 1990): 679A.

Uses Burke to analyze the discourse of four public figures representative of the baby boom and Vietnam generations to elucidate issues of gender, economics, war damage, and age.

144. Huston, Nancy. "A Tongue Called Mother." *Raritan* 9 (Winter 1990): 99–108.

Reflections on the roles language plays in the consciousness of women who write.

145. Jambeck, Karen K., and Barbara D. Winder. "Vygotsky, Werner, and English Composition: Paradigms for Thinking and Writing." *WE* 1 (Spring 1990): 68–79.

A process model of conceptual development can help student writers, especially in the planning and focusing stages.

146. Kemper, Susan. "Adults' Diaries: Changes Made to Written Narratives across the Life Span." *DPr* 13 (April–June 1990): 207–223.

Diaries kept over a 70-year period showed increases in structural complexity and decreases in cohesiveness as the number of ambiguous anaphors grew.

147. Keroes, Jo. "But What Do They Say?: Gender and the Content of Student Writing." *DPr* 13 (April–June 1990): 243–257.

Female college students responded to writing assignments with discussions of personal autonomy almost as frequently as did their male counterparts.

148. Killingsworth, M. Jimmie, and Scott P. Sanders. "Complementarity and Compensation: Bridging the Gap between Writing and Design." *TWT* 17 (Fall 1990): 204–221.

Describes a rhetoric designed to reconcile the competing demands of prose and graphics within the same text.

149. Kim, Bohyun. "Piety and Impiety: Two Opposite Attitudes toward Poetic Language." *DAI* 50 (February 1990): 2481A.

Examines the debate between the need for a more poetic or conceptual language and reliance on silence.

150. Kirsch, Gesa, and Duane H. Roen, eds. *A Sense of Audience in Written Communication.* Written Communication Annual, vol. 5. Newbury Park, Calif.: Sage, 1990. 312 pages

Offers theoretical and empirical considerations of audience, including a history of the concept. Sixteen essays survey authorial responses by scholars, attorneys, ESL students, and basic writers to perceived audience demands.

151. Kleine, Michael. "Beyond Triangulation: Ethnography, Writing, and Rhetoric." *JAC* 10 (1990): 117–125.

A radical critique of ethnographic research to "help us understand social construction in terms of what we do ourselves, not just what the 'natives' do."

152. Kneupper, Charles W., ed. *Rhetoric and Ideology: Compositions and Criticisms of Power*. Arlington, Tex.: Rhetoric Society of America, 1989. 228 pages

Collects 25 essays selected from among papers delivered at the Rhetoric Society of America's 1989 conference. Essays are grouped into six sections: rhetoric and critical theories; traditional figures and concepts; rhetoric and feminist theories; history, theory, and pedagogy; and rhetorical criticism. Includes keynote address.

153. Kostelnick, Charles. "The Rhetoric of Text Design in Professional Communication." *TWT* 17 (Fall 1990): 189–202.

Argues that visual design must become a part of the composing process. Outlines a rhetoric of text design.

154. Kraemer, Don. "No Exit: A Play of Literacy and Gender." *JAC* 10 (1990): 305–319.

An analysis of textual responses, especially on exit tests, as the playing of alternate games, cooperative or confrontational, with gendered overtones.

155. Kravinsky, Zell. "A Table of Rhetorical Elements." *DAI* 50 (January 1990): 2064A.

Derives a Table of Rhetorical Elements and applies it to current practices as well as to selected rhetors in belletristic and scriptural literature.

156. Kutz, Eleanor. "Authority and Voice in Student Ethnographic Writing." *A&E* 21 (December 1990): 340–357.

Examines the issues of authority and voice in student ethnographic writing as a relevant means of inquiry.

157. Laib, Nevin. "Conciseness and Amplification." *CCC* 41 (December 1990): 443–459.

Discusses the "companion arts" of conciseness and amplification, giving greater attention to amplification, its neglect, and its history. Includes a taxonomy of amplification.

158. Lang, Jonathan Sanders. "How Is Discourse of the Self Possible?" *DAI* 51 (November 1990): 1641A.

Inquires into the possibility that all writing involves a confessional aspect that cannot be dissociated from what is written.

159. Langston, Diane M. "Engagement in Writing." *DAI* 50 (February 1990): 2302A.

A study of novice and expert writers. Supports the research of Scardamalia, Bereiter, and Csikszentmihalyi by examining the integration of personal goals in writing.

160. Lassner, Phyllis. "Feminist Response to Rogerian Argument." *RR* 8 (Spring 1990): 220–231.

Discusses the conflict between Carl Rogers' theory of argumentation and the attitudes of women writers. Claims that the feminist resents "losing her voice" in detached writing.

161. Leff, Michael, and Andrew Sachs. "Words the Most like Things: Iconicity and the Rhetorical Text." *WJSC* 54 (Summer 1990): 252–273.

Reviews the form/content dichotomy and indicates its relevance for seeing rhetoric as a cultural and ideological formation.

162. Leggo, Carleton Derek. "Search(ing) (for) Voice(s)." *DAI* 50 (May 1990): 3504A.

Explores the concept of voice, concluding that voice cannot be schematized or classified.

163. Leith, Dick, and George Myerson. *The Power of Address: Explorations in Rhetoric*. New York: Routledge, 1990. 320 pages

Offers an approach to exploring diverse forms of language and varieties of spoken and written texts, both literary and nonliterary, including games, riddles, sermons, debate, folk songs, and conversation.

164. Lockridge, Rebecca Bryant. " 'Rhetorical Strategy' and 'Meaning': A Constructivist Approach to the Feminine- and Masculine-Principled Judgments of Photographic Critics." *DAI* 50 (February 1990): 2302A.

Tests George Kelly's constructivist notions that individuals place value-laden constructs over events. Includes David Swanson's matrix for understanding the representation systems of rhetorical critics.

165. Lovejoy, Kim Brian, and Donald M. Lance. "Discourse Analysis Part I: Information Management and Cohesion." Paper presented at the International Systemic Congress, Lansing, Mich., August 1988. ERIC ED 310 383. 59 pages

Proposes a model for analyzing information management and cohesion in written discourse, drawing upon M. A. K. Halliday's functional grammar and theories of the Prague School of linguistics.

166. Lu, Min-zhan. "Representations of the Other: Theodore Dreiser and Basic Writers." *DAI* 50 (May 1990): 3590A.

Examines the production and correction of stylistic "errors" by literary critics and composition theorists. Sees each act of writing as a means for the writer to reposition the self in relation to a range of discursive sites.

167. Makus, Anne. "Stuart Hall's Theory of Ideology: A Frame for Rhetorical Criticism." *WJSC* 54 (Fall 1990): 495–514.

Hall's notion of articulation enables the critic to examine how consciousness is produced in relationships among linguistic structures and social formation.

168. Mao, LuMing. "Persuasion, Cooperation, and Diversity of Rhetorics." *RSQ* 20 (Spring 1990): 131–142.

Draws on Grice and Burke to propose a heuristic model of persuasive discourse,

"one that takes cooperation through identification as a core constituent and provides a dynamic setting that is conducive to rhetorical diversities."

169. Marius, Richard. "On Academic Discourse." *BADE* 96 (Fall 1990): 4–7.

Defines "academic discourse" and explores its deficiencies, hoping that figurative and associative language will reinvigorate it so that it reaches a wider audience.

170. McCleary, Bill. "The Many Uses of Rhetorical Principles in Teaching Writing." *CompC* 3 (December 1990): 7–8.

Explains the use of Kinneavy's principle of authority at various stages of the teaching and writing processes.

171. McClelland, John. "Music with Words: Semiotic/Rhetoric." *Rhetorica* 8 (Summer 1990): 187–212.

Using Handel, the essay argues that music and words relate to each other simultaneously in a variety of ways and degrees, varying according to the semiotic structure of the medium.

172. McClish, Glen. "Some Less-Acknowledged Links: Rhetorical Theory, Interpersonal Communication, and the Tradition of the Liberal Arts." *RSQ* 20 (Spring 1990): 105–118.

Argues "that scholars of interpersonal communication, in an effort to define their discipline in modern terms, have mistakenly cut themselves off from their true roots and from much of the liberal arts tradition."

173. McCornack, Steven Allen. "The Logic behind Lies: A Rational Approach to Deceptive Message Production." *DAI* 51 (October 1990): 1046A.

Provides a conceptual basis for addressing deceptive messages.

174. McCroskey, James C., and Virginia P. Richmond. "Willingness to Communicate: Differing Cultural Perspectives." *SCJ* 56 (Fall 1990): 72–77.

Understanding the cultural impact on individual differences should be a vital component in the study of intercultural communication.

175. McGee, Michael Calvin. "Text, Context, and the Fragmentation of Contemporary Culture." *WJSC* 54 (Summer 1990): 274–289.

Argues that changing cultural conditions have forced writers and speakers as well as readers and audiences to revise roles.

176. McGinley, William James. "The Role of Reading and Writing in the Acquisition of Knowledge: A Study of College Students' Self-Directed Engagements in Reading and Writing to Learn." *DAI* 50 (April 1990): 3196A.

A think-aloud protocol study of seven students composing suggests that reasoning is mediated by specific reading and writing engagements and their purposes.

177. McKendy, Thomas F. "A Comment on the Canadian Issue [*CE* 50 (December 1988)]." *CE* 52 (January 1990): 102–104.

Argues that composition and rhetoric programs in Canadian universities were misrepresented.

178. Meyer, Sam. "Let's Continue to Take It from the Top: A Response to Richard Haswell [*JAC* 10 (1990)]." *JAC* 10 (1990): 400–402.

Critiques Haswell's argument that titles on student papers are less important than Meyer had argued.

179. Miller, Hildy Lucy. "Design for Writing: Image and Metaphor in the Cognitive Processes of Composing." *DAI* 51 (December 1990): 2001A.

Synthesizes interdisciplinary approaches to image and metaphor "to show how narrow linear descriptions of composing processes can be made more comprehensive."

180. Miller, Susan. *Textual Carnivals: The Politics of Composition.* Carbondale, Ill.: Southern Illinois University Press, 1990. 283 pages

A study of the marginal status of composition in English studies and an examination of the uneasy relationship between composition and literature.

181. Mortensen, Peter L. "Authority, Discourse, Community." *DAI* 50 (January 1990): 2042A.

Speculates "on the architecture of authority in writing, that dense network of social actions and relations which make written discourse possible."

182. Muir, Star Aldebaran. "On Kenneth Burke on Technology: Human Symbolism and the Advance of Counter-Nature." *DAI* 51 (November 1990): 1442A.

Examines Burke's dramatism as a reaction against scientism, with implications for understanding and shaping human attitudes and motivations.

183. Mullin, Anne E. "Errors as Discourse of an Other." Paper presented at the CCCC Convention, Chicago, March 1990. ERIC ED 318 032. 16 pages

Proposes that students be led to see their interior thoughts exteriorized in writing as an other, incorporating it in an expanded discourse of a "subject who knows more."

184. Murray, Donald M. *Shoptalk: Learning to Write with Writers.* Portsmouth, N.H.: Boynton/Cook, 1990. 208 pages

Quotations from 450 authors, classic and contemporary, about the writing process. Organized into 16 thematic units, each with an introductory essay.

185. Myers, Greg. "The Rhetoric of Irony in Academic Writing." *WC* 7 (October 1990): 419–455.

Examines the use of ironic quotation in a controversy between researchers in linguistics and artificial intelligence, demonstrating some limitations of psychological and linguistic accounts of irony.

186. Nash, Walter, ed. *The Writing Scholar: Language and Conventions of Academic Dis-*

course. Written Communication Annual, vol. 3. Newbury Park, Calif.: Sage, 1990. 240 pages

Explores linguistically and psychologically what happens when academics write in the Western tradition of scholarship. Essays are metadiscourse analysis, examining the voice and texture of academic prose.

187. Neuliep, James, and Marifran Mattson. "The Use of Deception as a Compliance-Gaining Strategy." *HCR* 16 (Spring 1990): 409–421.

An empirical study finds that the persuasive message behaviors of truthful and deceptive communicators may differ strategically.

188. Newton, Deborah, and Judee Burgoon. "The Use and Consequences of Verbal Influence Strategies during Interpersonal Disagreement." *HCR* 16 (Summer 1990): 477–518.

Discusses six strategies established by empirical research for resolving disagreements between females and males. The predominant interaction pattern is reciprocal.

189. Nystrand, Martin. "Sharing Worlds: The Effects of Readers on Developing Writers." *WC* 7 (January 1990): 3–24.

Contrasts social constructionism and interactionism as models of the relationship between writers and readers. Reviews recent interactionist research on the effects of readers on developing writers.

190. O'Keefe, Daniel J. *Persuasion: Theory and Research*. Current Communication: An Advanced Text Series, vol. 2. Newbury Park, Calif.: Sage, 1990. 272 pages

A survey of communications research concerning the production of persuasive messages and message effects. Treats social judgment theory, cognitive dissonance theory, the theory of reasoned action, and others.

191. Parsons, Gerald Michael. "Constraints on the Multidisciplinary Approach: Uses and Misuses of the Kuhnian Paradigm." Paper presented at the CCCC Convention, Minneapolis, March 1985. ERIC ED 320 157. 19 pages

Argues that using Kuhn's paradigm in composition studies is fraught with problems.

192. Pegg, Barry. "Two-Dimensional Features in the History of Text Format: How Print Technology Has Preserved Linearity." *TWT* 17 (Fall 1990): 223–242.

Analyzes the relation between text and images. Argues that technical writing teachers need to rethink their traditional adherence to linear text.

193. Penrose, Ann M. *Strategic Differences in Composing: Consequences for Learning through Writing*. CSW Technical Report, no. 31. Berkeley, Calif.: CSW, 1989. ERIC ED 310 402. 24 pages

Reports on an experiment with 40 freshmen. Planning and audience awareness were important variables in the relation between writing and learning.

194. Petrey, Sandy. *Speech Acts and Literary Theory*. New York: Routledge, 1990. 192 pages

Combines a study of Austin's speech-act theory with an analysis of the ways it has been used in literary criticism.

195. Plumb, Carolyn. "What Can Technical Writers Learn from Good Conversation?" *JTWC* 20 (1990): 201–209.

Suggests that technical writing can be improved if we use "conversation as a model for our writing and combine that model with real-world personal interaction."

196. Podis, Joanne M., and Leonard A. Podis. "Identifying and Teaching Rhetorical Plans for Arrangement." *CCC* 41 (December 1990): 430–442.

Offers a taxonomy of eight organizational strategies based on readers' needs and expectations.

197. Poole, Marshall Scott. "Do We Have Any Theories of Group Communication?" *ComS* 41 (Fall 1990): 237–247.

Relates research to criteria required for a good theory of metaphors and imagination, puzzles and problems, and real-world significance and outcomes.

198. "Professing the New Rhetorics." *RR* 9 (Fall 1990): 5–35.

A transcript of a 1990 Roundtable discussion of the new rhetoric. Includes participants' opening philosophical statements and their later reflections during a discussion.

199. Putnam, Linda L., and Cynthia Stohl. "*Bona Fide* Groups: A Reconceptualization of Groups in Context." *ComS* 41 (Fall 1990): 248–265.

A critical study of approaches to examining naturalistic groups. Provides a framework for identifying *bona fide* groups and a rationale for researching such groups.

200. Putnam, Linda L., Steve R. Wilson, and Dudley B. Turner. "The Evolution of Policy Arguments in Teachers' Negotiations." *Arg* 4 (May 1990): 129–152.

An ethnographic study of negotiations between teachers and a school board. Bargainers rely on different argument types at different stages of negotiation.

201. Raccah, Pierre-Yves. "Modelling Argumentation and Modelling *with* Argumentation." *Arg* 4 (November 1990): 447–483.

Discusses epistemological and methodological bases of a scientific theory of meaning. Proposes a formal theory of argumentation that is semantic as well as pragmatic.

202. Rankin, Elizabeth. "Taking Practitioner Inquiry Seriously: An Argument with Stephen North." *RR* 8 (Spring 1990): 260–267.

Argues that Stephen North's *The Making of Knowledge in Composition* undercuts the value of practitioner inquiry by lowering the philosophical expectations of writing teachers.

203. Risch-Nichols, Barbara Ann. "Constructing Written Discourse: The Incorporation of Social and Linguistic Knowledge into Writing Strategies." *DAI* 50 (March 1990): 2816A.

Examines the interactions of the social and linguistic dimensions of writing as part of the composing process.

204. Roen, Duane H. "Synthesizing Current Views of Audience: Notes toward a Fuller Understanding of Audience." Paper presented at the CCCC Convention, Chicago, March 1990. ERIC ED 318 018. 19 pages

Surveys current theorists such as Ong, Vygotsky, Trimbur, and Bruffee on the importance of developing discourse communities in the classroom.

205. Rowan, Katherine E. "Cognitive Correlates of Explanatory Writing Skills: An Analysis of Individual Differences." *WC* 7 (July 1990): 316–341.

Quantitative analyses of explanatory texts written by 169 college students for a fifth-grade audience demonstrate the relative importance of topic knowledge, social cognition, and discourse knowledge.

206. Ryan, Charlton. "Theories of Invention, 1960–1987: A Critique of Theory and Practice." *DAI* 51 (December 1990): 2008A.

Analyzes 120 composition textbooks of the 1980s to determine which invention strategies dominate.

207. Schilb, John. "The Ideology of 'Epistemological Ecumenicalism': A Response to Carol Berkenkotter [*JAC* 9 (1989)]." *JAC* 10 (1990): 153–156.

Suggests that, although Berkenkotter calls for "epistemological ecumenicalism," she actually betrays exclusions of her own and ignores issues of ideology.

208. Schilb, John. "On Personally Constructing 'Social Construction': A Response to Richard

Rorty [*JAC* 9 (1989)]." *JAC* 10 (1990): 146–149.

Critiques the ambiguous use of "social constructionism" in composition, several of Rorty's views about composition, and Bruffee's view of Rorty's antifoundationalism.

209. Schreiner, Steven Michael. "The Modernist Legacy in Composition: The Primacy of the Writer." *DAI* 51 (December 1990): 2006A.

Argues that modernist poetics, especially as seen in Eliot and Pound, informs much of the theory behind process composition.

210. Sheldon, Amy. "Pickle Fights: Gendered Talk in Preschool Disputes." *DPr* 13 (January–March 1990): 5–31.

Supports an earlier characterization of gender differences in verbal conflict, with boys' disputes tending to be more competitive and girls' more collaborative.

211. Shuter, Robert. "The Centrality of Culture." *SCJ* 55 (Spring 1990): 237–249.

Argues for a research effort and teaching agenda that returns culture to preeminence in intracultural communication.

212. Siciliano, Richard John. "The Effects of Word-Processing Instruction on the Writing Styles and Achievement in Higher-Level English Courses of Beginning College Writers." *DAI* 51 (October 1990): 1137A.

Focuses on how word processors affected each phase of the writing process for 71 community college freshmen taking English composition.

213. Simons, Herbert W., ed. *The Rhetorical Turn: Invention and Persuasion in the Conduct of Inquiry*. Chicago: University of Chicago Press, 1990. 388 pages

A collection of 14 essays from the 1986 Temple University Conference on the rhetoric of human sciences. Focuses on the rhetoric of inquiry as a way of addressing issues within and across disciplines that are unresolvable by formal proofs. Fields discussed include biology, politics, psy-

choanalysis, decision science, and conversational analysis.

214. Sipiora, Phillip, and Janet Atwill. "Rhetoric and Cultural Explanation: A Discussion with Gayatri Chakravorty Spivak." *JAC* 10 (1990): 293–304.

Spivak discusses some relationships between cultural criticism, composition, rhetoric, epistemology, literary theory, and gender.

215. Sitko, Barbara Mae. "Writers' Cognitive and Decision Processes: Revising after Feedback." *DAI* 51 (August 1990): 439A.

Explores the thinking processes of writers as they revise their texts, having received feedback from members of their intended audience.

216. Smagorinsky, Peter. "The Effects of Different Types of Knowledge on the Writing Process." Paper presented at the CCCC Convention, Chicago, March 1990. ERIC ED 317 992. 32 pages

Contrasts three treatments: the use of models, free thinking, and specific tasks. Results of protocols showed that a combination of models and task-specific procedures had greatest efficacy.

217. Smagorinsky, Peter. "The Effects of Different Types of Knowledge on the Writing Process: A Protocol Analysis." *DAI* 50 (January 1990): 1928A.

Uses protocol analysis to contrast the effects of three instructional treatments on the composing processes of students.

218. Smith, Wendy B. "How Conversation Influences Expository Writing: The Discourse and Grammar of Basic Writers." *DAI* 51 (November 1990): 1599A.

Finds that the academic prose of basic writers resembles the grammatical structures and discourse functions of their speech.

219. Spivey, Nancy Nelson. "Transforming Texts: Constructive Processes in Reading and Writing." *WC* 7 (April 1990): 256–287.

Offers a constructivist analysis of acts of reading and writing involved in composing from sources, with an emphasis on organizing, selecting, and connecting.

220. Spurlin, William J. "A Comment on 'The Construction of Purpose in Writing and Reading' [*CE* 50 (September 1988)]." *CE* 52 (March 1990): 346–348.

Calls for further collaboration between literary theorists and reading and writing empiricists. Notes Flower's exclusive use of expository prose as she illustrates the intentional fallacy.

221. Steinberg, Erwin R. "A Comment on 'Control in Writing: Flower, Derrida, and Images of the Writer' [*CE* 51 (April 1989)]." *CE* 52 (January 1990): 98–100.

Argues that Brooke's reading of Flower posits a false binary concept, generalizes beyond fact, and fails to clarify methodology.

222. Stotsky, Sandra. "On Planning and Writing Plans; or, Beware of Borrowed Theories." *CCC* 41 (February 1990): 37–57.

Suggests that theories borrowed from cognitive psychology may lead to ambiguity about the concept of "plan" in writing research and pedagogy.

223. Stroethoff, Janet Abuhl. "The Effects of Prior Knowledge, Prior Interest, and Learning on Writing." *DAI* 50 (January 1990): 1970A.

This study examined the effects of prior knowledge, learning through writing, and various affective factors on the written product.

224. Sykes, Richard E. "Imagining What We Might Study if We Really Studied Small Groups from a Speech Perspective." *ComS* 41 (Fall 1990): 200–211.

Places communication studies in the broader realm of academic research. Calls for more descriptive research and alternative research designs.

225. Tannen, Deborah. "Gender Differences in Topical Coherence: Creating Involvement in Best Friends' Talk." *DPr* 13 (January–March 1990): 73–90.

Videotapes of girls' conversations showed more intensive discussion of topics, whereas boys preferred talking extensively about a wider range of topics.

226. Targowski, Andrew S. "Beyond a Concept of a Communication Process [response to van Hoorde, *JBC* 27 (Winter 1990)]." *JBC* 27 (Winter 1990): 75–86.

Although agreeing with van Hoorde on several points, Targowski challenges the inclusion of new "links"—for emotion, knowledge/belief, and interest/desire—in the communication model.

227. Tinberg, Howard B. "A Model of Theory Making for Writing Teachers: Local Knowledge." *TETYC* 17 (February 1990): 18–23.

Seeks to bridge the gap between theory and practice by taking an ethnographic view of the writing classroom.

228. Tirrell, Mary Kay, Gordon M. Pradl, John Warnock, and James Britton. "Re-Presenting James Britton: A Symposium." *CCC* 41 (May 1990): 166–186.

Britton is re-presented as a "scholar/practitioner," "collaborating listener," and "teacher" concerned with learners. Britton adds a response.

229. Torgovnick, Marianna. "Experimental Critical Writing." *BADE* 96 (Fall 1990): 8–10.

Defines and promotes experimental critical writing, arguing that if critical writing is aimed at a large audience, it must be more direct and personal.

230. Tracey, Richard M., Jr. "The Rhetoric of Questions in Text." *DAI* 50 (February 1990): 2477A.

Defines six broad categories of questions in texts, taking issue with the widespread application of just one category, the rhetorical.

231. Tremmel, Robert. "Going Back and Paying Attention: Solving the Problem of the Writing Process." *JTW* 9 (Spring-Summer 1990): 71–83.

Warns against turning the writing process into a formula. Emphasizes the idiosyncratic nature of writing and the necessity of building a scaffolding for each writing task.

232. van Hoorde, Johan. "The Targowski and Bowman Model of Communication: Problems and Proposals for Adaptation." *JBC* 27 (Winter 1990): 51–70.

Proposes modifying a prior communication model to overcome its restrictions to cognitive processing and to broaden its application from business to communication in general.

233. Walsh, Stephen Michael. "The Relationship among Three Factors: Writing Apprehension, Composition Quality, and Inclination to Write Voluntarily." *DAI* 51 (August 1990): 404A.

Finds that awareness and consideration of an audience is a vital part of a good attitude toward writing. Highest essay scores went to those who like to write, do so voluntarily, and score between 90 and 99 on the Writing Apprehension Scale.

234. Washington, Gene. *The Self-Referring Text: Strategies and Intentions*. Bloomington, Ind.: ERIC/RCS, 1989. ERIC ED 313 703. 40 pages

Examines the purposes and strategies of authorial reference in written texts.

235. Welch, Kathleen E. "Electrifying Classical Rhetoric: Ancient Media, Modern Technology, and Contemporary Composition." *JAC* 10 (1990): 22–38.

Explores how secondary orality has led to recovering the canon of delivery. Electronic discourse should not be marginalized but should be treated instead through rhetoric, the chameleon discipline.

236. Wiley, Mark L. "Student Authoring in the American Grain." *DAI* 51 (October 1990): 1243A.

Claims that expressivist and social constructionist schools of composition theory can be analyzed in light of Emersonian philosophy, especially Emersonian thinking about literacy.

237. Willard, Charles Arthur. "Authority." *IL* 12 (Winter 1990): 11–22.

Authority-dependence, part of the crisis of modernity, exposes weaknesses in postmodernism. Sensitivity to the sociorhetorical dynamics of expertise has replaced the Greco-Roman model of the informed citizen.

238. Williams, David Cratis. "Kenneth Burke's Philosophy of Rhetoric: Modern, Postmodern, and Beyond." Paper presented at the Eastern Communication Association meeting, Ocean City, Md., May 1989. ERIC ED 311 474. 40 pages

Argues that Burke participates in both modern and postmodern traditions but is marginal to each and thus beyond them.

239. Winnett, Susan. "Coming Unstrung: Women, Men, Narrative, and Principles of Pleasure." *PMLA* 105 (May 1990): 505–518.

Describes an alternative narrative structure that is based on the pleasure experience of a woman's body.

240. Winsor, Dorothy A. "The Construction of Knowledge in Organizations: Asking the Right Questions about the Challenger." *JBTC* 4 (September 1990): 7–20.

Uses insights from the sociology of technology and the new rhetoricians to ask "What does it mean to know something?" and "to pass on information?"

241. Winsor, Dorothy A. "Engineering Writing/Writing Engineering." *CCC* 41 (February 1990): 58–70.

A case study of an engineer's documents, comments on those documents, and paper preparation.

242. Winterowd, W. Ross, and James D. Williams. "Cognitive Style and Written Discourse." *Focuses* 3 (Spring 1990): 3–23.

Studies "measurable ways to assess possible relationships between mental processes and writing performance" using argumentative and narrative tasks. Offers implications for teaching.

243. Wright, Mark Hamilton. "The Role of Identification in Rhetorical Explanation." *DAI* 50 (February 1990): 2305A.

Argues that Burke's treatment of identification has often been misunderstood because it consists of three separate but valid identification types.

244. Wright, Patricia, Audrey Hull, and Deborah Black. "Integrating Diagrams and Text." *TWT* 17 (Fall 1990): 244–254.

Reports statistical findings on the effectiveness of various relations between text and graphics.

245. Wyche-Smith, Susan, and Shirley K. Rose. "Throwing Our Voices: The Effects of Academic Discourse on Personal Voice." *WE* 2 (Fall 1990): 34–50.

This edited transcript of a panel discussion at the 1989 Wyoming Conference discusses differing definitions of personal and academic voice, gender roles, and writer's block.

246. Wylie, Dovie R. "On the Structure of Monologue Discourse in English." *DAI* 50 (February 1990): 2476A.

Identifies and describes organizational units in one type of English monologue. Focuses on the importance of topic and aspect movements.

247. Zeigler, William. "The Circular Journey and the Natural Authority of Form." *RR* 8 (Spring 1990): 208–219.

Provides correspondences between organic and abstract forms using circularity as a meaningful construct for a point of depar-ture and return in academic expository writing.

See also 2, 3, 258, 271, 277, 284, 287, 326, 336, 342, 534, 575, 643, 769, 779, 800, 802, 886, 900, 901, 904, 938, 952, 953, 971, 972, 1052, 1068, 1071, 1079, 1084, 1089, 1096, 1776

2.2 RHETORICAL HISTORY

248. Achinstein, Sharon. "War of Words: Writing in the English Revolution." *DAI* 51 (July 1990): 166A.

A rhetorical analysis of a broad range of writing. Focuses on how writers set up public debates through their works.

249. Anderson, Robert Dale. "Medieval Speculative Grammar: A Study of the *Modistae*." *DAI* 50 (January 1990): 2081A.

Examines the views of certain medieval grammarians (the *modistae*) and determines that many of their views have been misunderstood.

250. Anderson, Vivienne M. "Rhetoric and Cultural Conservatism: An Historical Examination." *DAI* 50 (March 1990): 2875A.

Examines the works of Isocrates, Erasmus, and Richards in terms of their emphasis on cultural literacy and rhetoric as keys to educational reform.

251. Arnold, Paula Elaine. "Fallacies and Persuasion in Four Political Debates in Thucydides." *DAI* 51 (August 1990): 497A.

An analysis of rhetorical fallacies in 10 speeches indicates that the fallacies draw readers into texts, complicate their logic, and show Thucydides' care in constructing the speeches.

252. Barton, Kerri M. "Sophistic Strategies in Platonic Texts: The Naive and Self-Conscious Traditions of Epideictic Rhetoric." *DAI* 50 (March 1990): 2886A.

Discusses "the epideictic tradition in Athens and the way in which the Sophists and Plato worked within it for their own purposes."

253. Beale, Walter H. "Richard M. Weaver: Philosophical Rhetoric, Cultural Criticism, and the First Rhetorical Awakening." *CE* 52 (October 1990): 626–640.

Details the importance of Weaver's philosophy to twentieth-century rhetoric. Suggests that Weaver's work comprises an early version of cultural criticism comparable to Burke's.

254. Benoit, William. "Campbell's *The Philosophy of Rhetoric* and the Advancement of Rhetorical Theory: The Integration of Philosophical Antecedents." *ComS* 41 (Spring 1990): 89–100.

Analyzes Campbell's work as an example of theory development that can serve as a model for integrating cognitive and epistemic approaches to rhetoric.

255. Benoit, William. "Isocrates and Aristotle on Rhetoric." *RSQ* 20 (Summer 1990): 251–259.

Compares the views of Isocrates and Aristotle on the nature of rhetoric, the relationship of rhetoric and knowledge, criticisms of previous rhetoricians, and sources of proof.

256. Berman, Scott J. "Socrates and the Science of Happiness." *DAI* 51 (October 1990): 1253A.

Studies Socrates' arguments about the ethical considerations in attaining happiness.

257. Berquist, Goodwin. "The Rhetorical Travels of Robert T. Oliver." *RR* 9 (Fall 1990): 173–183.

Applauds Oliver's contributions to cultural rhetoric. Includes biographical information and describes works illustrating rhetoric's influence on history in Great Britain, America, and Asia.

258. Bizzell, Patricia, and Bruce Herzberg, eds. *The Rhetorical Tradition: Readings from Classical Times to the Present.* New York: St. Martin's Press, 1990. 1328 pages

An anthology of 54 primary texts on rhetorical theory representing the classical, medieval, Renaissance, enlightenment, and twentieth-century periods. Includes introductions to each section and to each selection.

259. Blair, Carole, and Mary L. Kahl. "Rhetoric and Historiography." *WJSC* 54 (Spring 1990): 148–159.

Discusses revising the history of rhetorical theory.

260. Blakesley, David E. "Kenneth Burke and Rhetorical Inquiry in American Criticism, 1920–1950." *DAI* 51 (July 1990): 162A.

Argues that Burke's rhetorical inquiry is a way of identifying and negotiating the philosophical, political, and critical differences in American criticism between the wars.

261. Brinton, Alan. "The Outmoded Psychology of Aristotle's Rhetoric." *WJSC* 54 (Spring 1990): 204–218.

Concludes that the conceptual framework is alive and well.

262. Broaddus, Dorothy C. "Moral Sense Theory in the History of Rhetoric." *DAI* 50 (April 1990): 3233A.

Argues that the moral sense philosophy of Lord Shaftesbury and Francis Hutcheson was accepted more widely than was Scottish common sense realism.

263. Brown, Margery Lemon. "From Biography to Romance: The 'Letter from Alexander to Aristotle.' " *DAI* 50 (February 1990): 2477A.

Traces the genre known as "the life" by studying the letter as it appears in different versions.

264. Browne, Stephen H. "Shandyean Satire and the Rhetorical Arts in Eighteenth-Century England." *SCJ* 55 (Winter 1990): 191–205.

Presents an alternative approach to assessing eighteenth-century theory and practice.

265. Bunting, Sarah S. "Rhetorical Language in Ovid and Vergil." *DAI* 51 (October 1990): 1217A.

Uma quantitative and qualitative evaluation of rhetorical figures in the *Metamorphoses* and the *Aeneid*.

266. Calhoun, David Harris. "Friendship and Self-Love in Aristotle's Ethics." *DAI* 50 (February 1990): 2517A.

Asserts that Aristotle's friendship is neither a basic recognition of others nor a masked self-interest but rather a necessary combination of the two.

267. Campbell, Charles P. "Technical Communication in Discourse." *DAI* 50 (January 1990): 2033A.

Summarizes the history of technical communication and examines some of its principal dogmas: be objective, consider the audience, and write plainly.

268. Campbell, J. L. " 'It is as if a green bough were laid across the page': Thoreau on Eloquence." *RSQ* 20 (Winter 1990): 61–70.

Sees Thoreau's theoretical version of eloquence as distinct from Emerson's and ultimately incompatible with Whately's rhetoric of good reasons.

269. Carson, David L. "From the Editor's Desk." *JTWC* 20 (1990): 325–327.

Surveys some major changes in technical writing over the past 20 years, noting especially an increased awareness of the need for better technical writing.

270. Casaregola, Vincent G. "Inventions for Voice: Humanist Rhetoric and the Experiments of Elizabethan Prose Fiction." *DAI* 50 (May 1990): 3598A.

Examines how Renaissance rhetorical and educational traditions served as both conceptual and stylistic sources for prose fiction, focusing on the problem of voice.

271. Cleland, Marilyn R. "Sophistic Epideictic Rhetoric: A Classical Theory and a Contemporary Interpretation." *DAI* 50 (April 1990): 2478A.

Develops a theory of sophistic epideictic for the classical period of Greece and outlines a new sophistic rhetoric in which irony is the major trope.

272. Cole, Thomas. *The Origins of Rhetoric in Ancient Greece*. Baltimore: The Johns Hopkins University Press, 1990. 160 pages

Argues that early Greek rhetoric was largely an unsystematic effort to explore, more by example than by precept, all aspects of discourse. Rhetoric of the fifth century B.C. should not be judged by the standards of Plato and Aristotle.

273. Conley, Thomas M. "Aristotle's *Rhetoric* in Byzantium." *Rhetorica* 8 (Winter 1990): 29–44.

Summarizes what can be learned about the Byzantine reception of Aristotle's *Rhetoric* and our response to that reception.

274. Conley, Thomas M. *Rhetoric in the European Tradition*. New York: Longman, 1990. 325 pages

Beginning with Homer and concluding with Habermas, Conley provides "both an overview of the subject and some detailed information about particular authors and texts." Sees rhetoric historically as becoming particularly important to people during times of strife and crisis, which in turn produce distinctive views of what rhetoric is, not a single perspective of some unitary art or discipline.

275. Connors, Patricia E. "The History of Intuition and Its Role in the Composing Process." *RSQ* 20 (Winter 1990): 71–78.

Examines historical uses of the term *intuition*, which at times refers to "a genius theory of creativity" and in other cases suggests "an ordinary rational process."

276. Connors, Robert J. "Overwork/Underpay: Labor and Status of Composition Teachers since 1880." *RR* 9 (Fall 1990): 108–126.

Traces the changes in status of the composition teacher since the Harvard entrance exam of 1874.

277. Corbett, Edward P. J., James Golden, and Goodwin Berquist, eds. *Essays on the Rhetoric of the Western World.* Dubuque, Iowa: Kendall/Hunt, 1990. 464 pages

Twenty-five essays cover major periods and figures from the classical period to the last quarter of the twentieth century. Provides overviews of rhetorical developments and introductions to the work of particular rhetoricians.

278. Craig, Robert T. "The Speech Tradition." *ComM* 57 (December 1990): 309–314.

Historically approaches the question "Are rhetoric and science incompatible?" by narrating the speech tradition.

279. Culliton, Thomas E., Jr. "The Development of Business English at the Collegiate Level." *DAI* 51 (October 1990): 1090A.

Compares twentieth-century business textbooks with nineteenth-century grammar and rhetoric texts. Concludes that all basic writing skills were and still are relevant to business.

280. Davis, Margaret Haigler. "'Thy Maker Is Thy Husband': The Espousal Metaphor in Seventeenth-Century New England." *DAI* 51 (November 1990): 1612A.

Examines seventeenth-century American Puritan rhetoric to determine how males in a logocentric society use discourse to maintain hierarchy and to control women.

281. Dillery, John David. "Xenaphon's Historical Perspectives." *DAI* 50 (February 1990): 2478A.

Tries to validate Xenaphon's *Hellenica* by attributing careful ordering to the omissions. Uses comparative references from Thucydides, Isocrates, and Xenaphon's nonhistorical writing.

282. Dunn, Walter K. " 'To the Gentle Reader': Prefatory Rhetoric in the Renaissance." *DAI* 50 (May 1990): 3578A.

Explores the historical development of prefatory rhetoric in the Renaissance, arguing that the preface is transformed from the locus of authorial marginality to established authority.

283. Eden, Kathy. "The Rhetorical Tradition and Augustinian Hermeneutics in *De Doctrina Christiana.*" *Rhetorica* 8 (Winter 1990): 45–64.

Argues that Augustine interpreted scriptural obscurities in terms of the discrepancy between *scriptum* and *voluntas* and ambiguity, reading them as oppositions (internal/external and literal/spiritual).

284. Enos, Richard Leo, ed. *Oral and Written Communication: Historical Approaches.* Written Communication Annual, vol. 4. Newbury Park, Calif.: Sage, 1990. 264 pages

Eleven essays explore communication across cultures from prehistory to the present. Focuses on how meaning is created within social contexts.

285. Ferreira-Buckley, Linda. "The Influence of Hugh Blair's *Lectures on Rhetoric and Belles Lettres* on Victorian Education: Ruskin and Arnold on Cultural Literacy." *DAI* 51 (December 1990): 2024A.

Discusses how the belletristic rhetorical theory of Blair helped shape Ruskin's and Arnold's theorizing about education, language, and culture.

286. Fournier, Denis Richard. "Rhetoric in Benedictine Monastic Schools: Composition in the Richardton Abbey School, 1900–1936." *DAI* 51 (August 1990): 431A.

Conservatism, adaptability, and a "commitment to classical education" impact textbook selection and the teaching of rhetoric in this school. Links the history of the school to contemporary rhetorical theory.

287. France, Alan W. "Self, Society, and Text in Rhetoric and Composition Theory since 1970." *DAI* 50 (March 1990): 2875A.

Argues that since about 1970 theory has attempted to reincorporate the "vitalist individualism of the earlier decades" while avoiding crucial issues of cultural politics.

288. Gaonkar, Dilip. "Plato's Critique of Protagoras' Man-Measure Doctrine." *Pre/Text* 10 (Spring-Summer 1989): 71–80.

Argues that Plato's critique can succeed only by ascribing to Protagoras views that some scholars insist he could not possibly have held.

289. Gini, Anthony. "Philosophy and Word-Play in the Epistles of Horace." *DAI* 50 (February 1990): 2479A.

Studies linguistic nuances and thematic borrowings that may have inspired Horace's reading of Plato.

290. Glenn, Cheryl Jean. "Muted Voices from Antiquity through the Renaissance: Locating Women in the Rhetorical Tradition." *DAI* 50 (February 1990): 2675A.

Researches the contribution of female participants but finds no female-only traditions. Concludes that women have been systematically and purposefully excluded.

291. Green, Lawrence D. "Aristotelian Rhetoric, Dialectic, and the Traditions of *Antistrophos*." *Rhetorica* 8 (Winter 1990): 5–28.

Using the term *counterpart* to explain Aristotle's view of the relationship between rhetoric and dialectic does not resolve the controversy.

292. Grego, Rhonda C. "The Textual Nature of Memory and Particular Texts: Rediscovering a Lost Canon of Rhetoric." *DAI* 51 (August 1990): 342A.

Examines the classical conception of memory as a capacity for storing perceptual experience and shaping abstract knowledge.

293. Griffin, Susan. "Shaftesbury's Soliloquy: The Development of Rhetorical Authority." *RR* 9 (Fall 1990): 94–106.

Uses this eighteenth-century writer's views on the soliloquy to demonstrate its usefulness to modern composition.

294. Hadot, Pierre. "Forms of Life and Forms of Discourse in Ancient Philosophy." *CritI* 16 (Spring 1990): 483–505.

An article translated by Arnold I. Davidson urges studying the influence of Greek thought on Roman culture. Focuses on the relationship between philosophical theory and the practices of everyday life.

295. Hagge, John. "The First Technical Writer in English: A Challenge to the Hegemony of Chaucer." *JTWC* 20 (1990): 269–289.

Argues that an important tradition of technical writing existed in both the Old and Middle English periods and extended through the English Renaissance.

296. Heisler, Raymond J. "Epictetus on Speech: The Argument." *DAI* 50 (January 1990): 2033A.

A commentary on *On the Faculty of Speech*. Elucidates Epictetus' views and uses of rhetoric and the text's underlying principles of Stoic physics and ethics.

297. Hidalgo-Serna, Emilio. "Metaphorical Language, Rhetoric, and Comprehension: J. L. Vives and M. Nizolio." *P&R* 23 (1990): 1–11.

Explores the philosophico-rhetorical relationship between Vico's precursors Juan Luis Vives and Mario Nizolio, who argue for a rhetoric situated in everyday historic discourse.

298. Horner, Winifred Bryan. "The Roots of Modern Writing Instruction: Eighteenth-and Nineteenth-Century Britain." *RR* 8 (Spring 1990): 322–345.

Traces the development of writing instruction in British universities in the eighteenth and nineteenth centuries, noting remnants of past composition studies dominating the modern disciplines.

299. Hubert, Henry Allan. "The Development of English Studies in Nineteenth-Century Anglo-Canadian Colleges." *DAI* 50 (June 1990): 3875A.

English studies in Anglophone colleges and universities in Canada have returned to a historically normative program featuring both poetics and rhetoric.

300. Jarratt, Susan C. "The Heraclitean *Logos* and Rhetoric." *Pre/Text* 10 (Spring-Summer 1989): 81–86.

Heraclitus and his formulation of a principle of cosmic organization on the word *logos* may be one source for the prefiguration of rhetoric.

301. Jarratt, Susan C. "The Role of the Sophists in Histories of Consciousness." *P&R* 23 (1990): 85–95.

Examines Jean-Pierre Vernant's account of the fifth-century political origins of discourse and consciousness as a mediation of the *mythos/logos* duality through *nomos*.

302. Johnstone, Henry W., Jr. "Invective and Metaphysical Argument: Heraclitus and Parmenides." *Pre/Text* 10 (Spring-Summer 1989): 87–89.

Claims that Heraclitean metaphysical declarations, as opposed to his invective, are not argumentative.

303. Kinsella, Thomas E. "Essays on Eighteenth-Century Dialogue." *DAI* 50 (January 1990): 2064A.

Links the movement toward realistic dialogue to technical and social influences bearing on publishing, authorship, literary conventions, and conversation as an art form.

304. Kirby, John T. "The 'Great Triangle' in Early Greek Rhetoric and Poetics." *Rhetorica* 8 (Summer 1990): 213–228.

Explains how the three concepts of *peitho, bia,* and *eros* unify Greek rhetoric and poetics from Homer to Plato, influencing the structure and content of a work.

305. Kitzhaber, Albert. *Rhetoric in American Colleges, 1850–1900.* SMU Studies in Composition and Rhetoric. Dallas: Southern Methodist University Press, 1990. 290 pages

Traces the history of rhetoric during the period that saw the rise of modern courses in English, a period when nearly every development that was to appear in rhetorical theory and instruction up to the middle 1930s was formulated.

306. Krell, David Farrell. *Of Memory, Reminiscence, and Writing.* Bloomington, Ind.: Indiana University Press, 1990. 352 pages

Traces the history of memory from Plato to the present, discussing the deconstruction of memory in Nietzsche, Heidegger, and Derrida and the refiguration of memory "on the verge of a never present past."

307. Lawrence, Kathleen Ann. "The Domestic Idiom: The Rhetorical Appeals of Four Influential Women in Nineteenth-Century America." *DAI* 51 (September 1990): 680A.

Examines the work of Abigail Adams, Sarah Josepha Hale, Louisa May Alcott, and Victoria Claflin Woodhull—all of whom idealized the home and motherhood as women's contribution to society.

308. Leahy, Susan Beth. "Visual Literacy: Investigation of Visual Literacy Concepts as Historically Developed in the Writings of Selected Western Philosophers from the Pre-Socratics to Comenius." *DAI* 50 (March 1990): 2824A.

Explores the contributions of selected Western philosophers to our current understanding of the concept of visual literacy.

309. Lipson, Carol S. "Ancient Egyptian Medical Texts: A Rhetorical Analysis of Two of the Oldest Papyri." *JTWC* 20 (1990): 391–409.

Demonstrates how major rhetorical formulations revealed in the Smith and Ebers texts "present or encourage innovation while simultaneously adhering to the value placed on tradition."

310. Makus, Anne. "Rhetoric Then and Now: A Proposal for Integration." *WJSC* 54 (Spring 1990): 189–203.

Ideology theory maintains a foundational continuity that extends traditional rhetorical theory, each enriching rather than preempting the other.

311. Matsen, Patricia P., Philip Rollinson, and Marion Sousa, eds. *Readings from Classical Rhetoric*. Carbondale, Ill.: Southern Illinois University Press, 1990. 400 pages

An anthology of rhetorical works by 24 writers arranged chronologically in six sections: early figures, Greek rhetoric, Greco-Roman rhetoric, educational rhetoric, the rhetoric of style, and the rhetoric of later antiquity.

312. McPherson, Elizabeth. "Remembering, Regretting, and Rejoicing: The Twenty-Fifth Anniversary of the Two-Year College Regionals." *CCC* 41 (May 1990): 137–150.

Reflections on the history, current state, and future of writing instruction in two-year colleges.

313. Miller, Thomas P., ed. *The Selected Writings of John Witherspoon*. Landmarks in Rhetoric and Public Address. Carbondale, Ill.: Southern Illinois University Press, 1990. 319 pages

Presents five tracts and sermons on politics and education as well as 32 lectures on moral philosophy and eloquence.

314. Miller, Thomas P. "Where Did College English Studies Come From?" *RR* 9 (Fall 1990): 50–69.

Argues that the proper source of English studies derives not from elite English universities but from the dissenting academies of British cultural provinces.

315. Moberg, Goran George. "The Revival of Rhetoric: A Bibliographic Essay." *JBW* 9 (Fall 1990): 66–82.

Recommends that basic writing teachers examine three intersections of classical and modern rhetoric: the humanist nature of rhetoric, the importance of persuasion, and the value of invention.

316. Moran, Michael G. "John White: Renaissance England's First Important Ethnographic Illustrator." *JTWC* 20 (1990): 343–356.

Describes how the Elizabethan artist John White contributed to technical and scientific communication by adapting his traditional artistic training to ethnographic illustration of native Americans.

317. Murphy, James J., ed. *A Short History of Writing Instruction from Ancient Greece to Twentieth-Century America*. Davis, Calif.: Hermagoras Press, 1990. 241 pages

Seven articles trace the teaching of writing through 25 centuries of Western culture. The final article presents an overview of school and college English from 1890 until 1985.

318. Myers, David Gershom. "Educating Writers: The Beginnings of Creative Writing in the American University." *DAI* 50 (May 1990): 3592A.

Outlines the origins of creative writing.

319. Neeley, Kathryn A. "I. A Genre Study of Histories of Science. II. College Composition Readers, 1878–1988: A History and Critical Analysis." *DAI* 50 (March 1990): 2910A.

A two-part study. Part I examines how a culture's view of science is shaped by the writing of its history. Part II suggests that thematic or content-oriented readers best support effective teaching.

320. Okabe, Roichi. "The Impact of Western Rhetoric on the East: The Case of Japan." *Rhetorica* 8 (Autumn 1990): 371–388.

Looks for Western influences in eight representative Japanese texts published in the tradition of classical rhetoric during the Meijii enlightenment period (1868 to 1912).

321. Peaden, Catherine L. "Language and Rhetoric in Locke, Condillac, and Vico." *DAI* 51 (August 1990): 491A.

Argues for the influence of eighteenth-century language theories on modern rhetorical theory.

322. Pinkus, Karen Elyse. "The *Symbolicae Quaestiones* of Achille Bocchi: Humanist Emblems and Counter-Reformation Communication." *DAI* 51 (November 1990): 1605A.

Sees the Renaissance emblem as a central discursive mode in humanist philological practice. Discusses the importance of visual images for the dissemination of humanist ideology.

323. Porter, James E. "*Divisio* as Em-/De-Powering Topic: A Basis for Argument in Rhetoric and Composition." *RR* 8 (Spring 1990): 191–205.

Examines *divisio* in rhetorical history and theory and in composition pedagogy. Considers dividing practices in rhetoric and composition as em-powering and de-powering forces.

324. Porter, William Malin. "Cicero's *Pro Archia* and the Responsibilities of Reading." *Rhetorica* 8 (Spring 1990): 137–152.

Interprets Cicero's oration as an ethical argument to explain the poetic vocation. Argues that this more responsible reading overcomes some hermeneutical problems.

325. Poulakos, John. "Hegel's Reception of the Sophists." *WJSC* 54 (Spring 1990): 160–171.

Argues that locating sophistical rhetoric under the control of philosophy renders it impotent and ineffective.

326. Poulakos, John. "Interpreting Sophistical Rhetoric: A Response to Schiappa [*P&R* 23 (1990)]." *P&R* 23 (1990): 218–228.

Critiques Schiappa's article for its reliance on a dead Platonism that treats historical facts as a given rather than as constituted.

327. Poulakos, Takis. "The Historical Intervention of Gorgias' *Epitaphios:* The Genre of Funeral Oration and the Athenian Institution of Public Burials." *Pre/Text* 10 (Spring-Summer 1989): 90–99.

Discusses the novelty of Gorgias' oration as conforming to and rebelling against established practice.

328. Poulakos, Takis. "Historiographies of the Tradition of Rhetoric: A Brief History of Classical Funeral Orations." *WJSC* 54 (Spring 1990): 172–188.

Argues that the orations are instances of laudatory discourse designed to fulfill the institutional function of glorifying the state.

329. Prince, Michael Benjamin. "Strains of Enlightenment: Philosophical and Religious Dialogue in England, 1700–1780." *DAI* 51 (November 1990): 1622A.

Traces the development of the dialogue as a central mode of philosophical and religious discourse.

330. Ronald, Kate. "A Reexamination of Personal and Public Discourse in Classical Rhetoric." *RR* 9 (Fall 1990): 36–48.

Argues against the notion that classical rhetoric was solely public and not private. Private concerns voiced publicly combined to form *ethos*.

331. Ronnick, Michele V. "Cicero's *Paradoxa Stoicorum:* A Commentary, an Interpretation, and a Study of Its Influence." *DAI* 51 (October 1990): 1211A.

Argues that the *Paradoxa Stoicorum* had a lasting impact upon literature, philosophy, educational theory, and the history of early printed books.

332. Rouse, Joy. "Positional Historiography and Margaret Fuller's Public Discourse of Mutual Interpretation." *RSQ* 20 (Summer 1990): 233–239.

Uses Fuller's journalism to argue that most histories of rhetoric focus on universities. Exploring alternative sites can explain the diversity of issues and proliferation of public discourse in the nineteenth century.

333. Russell, David R. "Writing across the Curriculum in Historical Perspective: Toward a Social Interpretation." *CE* 52 (January 1990): 52–73.

Traces the evolution of cross-curricular programs during the past century. Suggests that current programs may succeed because of pedagogical reforms within modern university systems.

334. Saillant, John Daniel. "Letters and Social Aims: Rhetoric and Virtue from Jefferson to Emerson." *DAI* 50 (February 1990): 2543A.

Suggests that virtue was meant to promote social unity or self-interest and explains why Emerson later dismissed the concept from his public writings.

335. Schiappa, Anthony Edward, Jr. "Protagoras and *Logos:* A Study in Early Greek Rhetorical Theory." *DAI* 50 (February 1990): 2303A.

Argues that Protagoras' teachings involved *logos* and *arete* instead of rhetoric. Discusses his contributions to philosophy, education, and rhetorical theory.

336. Schiappa, Edward. "Neo-Sophistic Rhetorical Criticism or the Historical Reconstruction of Sophistic Doctrines." *P&R* 23 (1990): 192–217.

Argues for distinguishing between the construction of neo-sophistic rhetorical theory and the historical reconstruction of specific sophistic doctrines concerning discourse.

337. Sousa, Marion Covell. "Literacy and Classical Rhetoric." *DAI* 51 (August 1990): 498A.

Examines literacy practices in ancient Greece and their relevance to the teaching of composition today.

338. Steinberg, Marc W. "Worthy of Hire: Discourse, Ideology, and Collective Action among English Working-Class Trade Groups, 1800–1830." *DAI* 51 (July 1990): 299A.

Discusses ideological discourse in light of the moral rationality of collective action as a constitutive element of working-class culture.

339. Sutton, Jane. "Antiphon's *On the Chorus-Boy:* The Practice of Practical Truth." *Pre/Text* 10 (Spring-Summer 1989): 100–106.

Argues that Antiphon's *On the Chorus-Boy* offers significant insight into sophistical rhetoric's direct link to politics and society.

340. Tebeaux, Elizabeth. "Books of Secrets: Authors and Their Perception of Audience in Procedure Writing of the English Renaissance." *Issues* 3 (Fall–Winter 1990): 41–67.

English Renaissance writers of information books laid the foundation for the emphasis in modern technical writing on audience-based page design, style, and content.

341. Thorpe, Anna Livia Plurabelle. "Prometheus Revised: Socratic Forethought in the *Protagoras.*" *DAI* 50 (June 1990): 3940A.

Explores connections between the design and the content of the *Protagoras,* discussing the relation between what Plato depicts and what he displays.

342. Tordesillas, Alonso. "Chaim Perelman: Justice, Argumentation, and Ancient Rhetoric." *Arg* 4 (February 1990): 109–124.

Examines Perelman's analysis of justice and reviews his rehabilitation of the theory of argumentation. The article is translated from French by Serge Nicolas and Hugh Barton Smith.

343. Ulman, H. Lewis. "Discerning Readers: British Reviewers' Responses to Campbell's Rhetoric and Related Works." *Rhetorica* 8 (Winter 1990): 65–90.

Explains that eighteenth-century reviewers expected rhetorics to be philosophically sound and pedagogically useful, appealing to discerning and general readers as well as accommodating new inquiry and language theory.

344. Vitanza, Victor J. "What's 'at Stake' in the Gorgian Fragment on Seriousness/Laughter." *Pre/Text* 10 (Spring–Summer 1989): 107–114.

Twenty-five content endnotes treat the paradoxes of lack and excess and seriousness and laughter. Explores the problem of the ethical subject in this pre-Socratic fragment.

345. Wagner, Joanne. "Characteristic Curves and Counting Machines: Assessing Style at the Turn of the Century." *RSQ* 20 (Winter 1990): 39–48.

Focuses on a late nineteenth-century debate between Robert Moritz and Thomas Mendenhall over the relationship between scientific methodology and traditional rhetorical assumptions about the nature of writing.

346. Wakefield, Peter Wallace. "On the Separation of Forms." *DAI* 50 (February 1990): 2522A.

Questions whether Plato's forms are "separate" in the damaging sense explained by Aristotle. Proposes an alternative interpretation.

347. Warnick, Barbara. "The Bolevian Sublime in Eighteenth-Century British Rhetorical Theory." *Rhetorica* 8 (Autumn 1990): 349–369.

Discusses the evolution of the Bolevian sublime in the eighteenth century by examining three views of the concept: classicist, scientific, and belletristic.

348. Weir, Vickie E. "Revisioning Traditions through Rhetoric: Studies in Gertrude Buck's Social Theory of Discourse." *DAI* 50 (March 1990): 2876A.

Surveys Buck's major works, focusing on her vision for a progressive society based on a rhetorical theory combining Plato's rhetoric and the Sophists'.

349. Yoos, George E. "Ich gelobe meine Treue dem Banner." *RSQ* 20 (Winter 1990): 5–12.

The editor of *RSQ* reflects on recent developments in rhetoric, especially as reflected in the interdisciplinary, pluralistic character of books published in the field.

See also 12, 13, 14, 23, 45, 55, 120, 172, 236, 357, 368, 376, 418, 424, 440, 448, 460, 487, 496, 613, 670, 683, 687, 715, 730, 734, 862, 1068, 1105

2.3 POLITICAL, RELIGIOUS, AND JUDICIAL RHETORIC

350. Adamczyk, Lawrence Paul. "Rhetoric and Reality: The Form and Meaning of Italy's Role as a Great Power in the Eastern Question and the Congress of Berlin of 1878." *DAI* 51 (November 1990): 1734A.

Examines the manipulation of information and public opinion.

351. Ahlersmeyer, Thomas Richard. "The Rhetoric of 'Reformation': A Fantasy Theme Analysis of the Rhetorical Vision of Robert Harold Schuller." *DAI* 51 (December 1990): 1825A.

Analyzes 12 sermons from 1975 to 1980 and finds three repeated dramatizations, three fantasy types, and a rhetorical vision of reformation that links Schuller with Calvinism.

352. Alexander, Thomas Craig. "Paul's Final Exhortation to the Elders from Ephesus: The Rhetoric of Acts 20:17–38." *DAI* 51 (November 1990): 1645A.

Rhetorically examines this Pauline text by focusing on such features as style, invention, and topics.

353. Asante, Molefi Kete. "The Tradition of Advocacy in the Yoruba Courts." *SCJ* 55 (Spring 1990): 250–259.

Analyzes novels and speeches to demonstrate an extensive system of advocacy based on group consensus.

354. Asbell, Sally L. "Understanding the Rehabilitation Act of 1973: A Rhetorical Analysis of the Legislative Hearings." *DAI* 50 (February 1990): 2300A.

Uses a neo-Aristotelian approach to examine how well the concerns and issues expressed at the original hearings were addressed in the legislation.

355. Baaske, Kevin T. "The Rhetoric of Character Legitimation: Geraldine A. Ferraro and

the 1984 Vice-Presidential Campaign." *DAI* 50 (May 1990): 3411A.

Uses a dramatistic and narrative perspective to examine the impact of Ferraro's discourse.

356. Ball, Moya Ann. "A Case Study of the Kennedy Administration's Decision Making Concerning the Diem Coup of November 1963." *WJSC* 54 (Fall 1990): 4.

Introduces the concept of adhocracy and provides a rhetorical framework for decision making.

357. Bauman, Lisa Passaglia. "Power and Image: Della Rovere Patronage in Late Quattrocentro Rome." *DAI* 51 (December 1990): 1810A.

Examines the rhetoric of art patronage that legitimized the power of the della Rovere family in late quattrocentro Rome.

358. Becerra, Yvonne. "Comparable Worth/ Pay Equity: *Topoi* in the Arguments for Women's Economic Equality." *DAI* 50 (March 1990): 2703A.

Examines the debate between Phyllis Schlafly and the National Committee on Pay Equity and finds that the *topos* of past/ future fact creates rhetorical tension.

359. Bellman, Kathryn A. "Language and Rhetoric in *Brown v. Board of Education*." *DAI* 51 (December 1990): 2003A.

In evoking familiar images, "the court used language to change the focus of public awareness from race to education."

360. Bello-Ogunu, John Okegbe. "Analysis of the Argumentative Validity of the Legal Rulings on the 1979 Nigerial Presidential Elections." *DAI* 51 (October 1990): 1044A.

Uses Toulmin's model of argumentation to analyze court data, warrants, and claims related to the 1979 Nigerian election.

361. Berk-Seligson, Susan. *The Bilingual Courtroom: Court Interpreters in the Judicial Process*. Language and Legal Discourse. Chi-

cago: University of Chicago Press, 1990. 311 pages

An ethnographic study of the role of the court interpreter, specifically Spanish/English interpreters. Analyzes verbal and nonverbal interactions between interpreters and other participants in the courtroom and how interpreters alter pragmatic elements of attorneys' questions and witnesses' answers. Finds that interpreters' linguistic alterations are not inconsequential.

362. Bertelsen, Dale A. "Rhetorical Privation as Cultural *Praxis:* Implicit Rhetorical Theory in Presidential Oratory and Contemporary Hollywood Films." *DAI* 50 (January 1990): 1846A.

Examines the rhetoric that contributed to a cultural dialogue about American relations with the Soviet Union.

363. Bickenbach, Jerome E. "The 'Artificial Reason' of the Law." *IL* 12 (Winter 1990): 23–32.

Making sense of legal reasoning and writing requires seeing it as a Gadamerian hermeneutical act, rather than as a deduction based on decoding. Judges make texts and law.

364. Blyler, Nancy Roundy. "Rhetorical Theory and Newsletter Writing." *JTWC* 20 (1990): 139–152.

Drawing on schema theory, social construction, and audience theory, studies newsletters produced by two political activist organizations and suggests directions for further research.

365. Braithwaite, Charles A. "An Ethnography of Speaking among Vietnam Veterans." *DAI* 50 (February 1990): 2300A.

Asserts that the forms, meanings, and functions of speech among Vietnam veterans constitute a significant dimension of their cultural identity.

366. Brockett, Mary Ann. "A Burkean Analysis of the Use of Islamic Symbols in the Rheto-

ric of Ruhollah Musavi Khomeni: 1963 to 1982." *DAI* 51 (November 1990): 1440A.

Identifies 25 symbols and five strategies that Khomeni used. Shi'ite symbols of martyrdom especially polarized the Iranians.

367. Brown, Penelope. "Gender, Politeness, and Confrontation in Tenejapa." *DPr* 13 (January–March 1990): 123–141.

In courtroom confrontations, Mayan women's speech was less restrained than in other social encounters. They expressed sarcasm through following conventionally polite formulas.

368. Browne, Stephen H. "Generic Transformation and Political Action: A Textual Interpretation of Edmund Burke's *Letter to William Elliot, Esq.*" *ComQ* 38 (Winter 1990): 54–63.

A rhetorical analysis of Edmund Burke's political tract.

369. Burnett, Nicholas F. S. "The Impetus for Rebellion: A Rhetorical Analysis of the Conditions, Structures, and Functions of Conspiracy Argumentation during the American Revolution." *DAI* 50 (May 1990): 3411A.

Examines the use of conspiracy arguments by British, loyalist, and patriot rhetors in pamphlets, speeches, proclamations, newspapers, and the *Declaration of Independence*.

370. Campbell, Douglas Atchison. "The Rhetoric of Righteousness in Romans 3:21–26." *DAI* 50 (March 1990): 2943A.

Posits a new reading of the text that rhetorical analysis can reveal.

371. Carilli, Theresa M. "An Ethnography of Creative Writing: A Study of the Sicilian-American Culture through Creative Writing." *DAI* 51 (September 1990): 678A.

Uses Marcus and Fischer's concept of personhood to explore how creative writing can provide cultural insight.

372. Chasteen, Deborah Lynn. "The Effect of Television Advertising on the 1986 Harriett

Woods U.S. Senate Campaign." *DAI* 51 (October 1990): 1044A.

Discusses the ability of television commercials to influence what the Woods campaign was able to accomplish.

373. Conley, John M., and William M. O'Barr. *Rules Versus Relationships: The Ethnography of Legal Discourse.* Language and Legal Discourse. Chicago: University of Chicago Press, 1990. 222 pages

The language litigants use to describe and analyze their legal problems has two orientations, one governed by rules and the other, by relationships. The legal system shares the rules-oriented perspective but not the relational orientation.

374. Conti, Delia Bloom. "President Reagan's Rhetoric of Trade." *DAI* 51 (November 1990): 1440A.

Examines four strategies President Reagan used to shift from resisting economic protectionist pressure to proposing protectionist legislation.

375. Cunningham, David Scott. "Faithful Persuasion: Prolegomena to a Rhetoric of Christian Theology." *DAI* 51 (November 1990): 1658A.

Classical rhetoric can be appropriated as a methodological tool for Christian theology by understanding theological language as persuasive discourse.

376. Dean, Kevin W. "A Rhetorical Biography of Jonathan Edwards: Beyond the Fires of Hell." *DAI* 50 (June 1990): 3792A.

Finds that Edwards' sermons promoted social change by emphasizing human dependence on a sovereign God.

377. Deeley, Mary Katherine. "The Rhetoric of Memory: A Study of the Persuasive Function of the Memory Commands in Deuteronomy 5–26." *DAI* 50 (February 1990): 2524A.

Examines three "memory clusters" and finds that the Deuteronomist purposefully arranged them so that his argument might be understood.

378. Dei, Sharon. "The International Speech-Making of Yasuhiro Nakasone: A Case Study in Intercultural Rhetoric." *DAI* 50 (May 1990): 3412A.

Examines the effect of culture on rhetoric, finding that Nakasone's discourse is a synthesis of Western and Eastern approaches.

379. Dennis, Valerie Cryer, Lynda Lee Kaid, and Sandra Ragan. "The Impact of Argumentativeness and Verbal Aggression on Communication Image: The Exchange between George Bush and Dan Rather." *WJSC* 54 (Winter 1990): 99–112.

Questions simplistic distinctions among the concepts and their relationships to each other and to other communication variables.

380. De Wet, Johan Christian. "Propaganda and the Concept of Democracy: A Communicological Study." *DAI* 50 (January 1990): 1839A.

Analyzes how propaganda undermines dialogic communication, which is a truly "democratic" form of communication.

381. Dougherty, Edward C. "The Syntax of the Apocalypse." *DAI* 51 (November 1990): 1658A.

A computational syntactic analysis of the Apocalypse. Sees this analysis as the first step in a project to describe systematically the entire New Testament.

382. Dumser, Thomas Edward, II. "A Rhetorical-Critical Analysis of Selected Presidential Addresses to the Southern Baptist Convention, 1971–1987." *DAI* 51 (November 1990): 1647A.

A rhetorical critique that examines the extent to which presidents of the Southern Baptist Convention utilized the rhetorical opportunities afforded by the annual presidential address.

383. Elliott, R. Neil. "The Rhetoric of Romans: Argumentative Constraint and Strategy and Paul's 'Dialogue with Judaism.' " *DAI* 50 (January 1990): 2104A.

Uses a rhetorical-critical approach to examine Romans 1–4. Finds that Paul's message is often misunderstood, especially regarding Judaism.

384. Fabj, Valeria F. "Forgiveness and Tolerance in the Nuclear Age: The Rhetoric of the Nuclear-Weapon-Free Zone Movement in the U.S." *DAI* 50 (February 1990): 2301A.

Uses Burke's notions about the move from guilt to redemption to analyze the rhetoric of the movement, which allows people to cease tolerating nuclear weapons and embrace forgiveness by considering the past finished.

385. Friebel, Kelvin G. "Jeremiah's and Ezekiel's Sign-Acts: Their Meaning and Function as Nonverbal Communication and Rhetoric." *DAI* 50 (March 1990): 2932A.

Analyzes sign-acts in Jeremiah and Ezekiel, concluding that such rhetorical strategies function persuasively.

386. Friedenberg, Robert V. *Theodore Roosevelt and the Rhetoric of Militant Decency.* Great American Orators, no. 9. New York: Greenwood Press, 1990. 232 pages

Analyzes President Roosevelt's use of classical rhetorical method by studying his speeches and primary collections of his manuscripts.

387. Fulmer, Hal W. "Southern Clerics and the Passing of Lee: Mythic Rhetoric and the Construction of a Sacred Symbol." *SCJ* 55 (Summer 1990): 355–371.

Examines the redemptive power of audience unity, the foundation for later mythic discourse on General Lee's life.

388. Gelman, Ruth Samberg. "The Rhetoric of Think Tanks: Representing a Social Reality for Public Policy." *DAI* 50 (January 1990): 2237A.

Analyzes the appraisive rhetoric of think tanks, viewed as fabricators of a social reality, setting problems and rationalizing public policy processes.

389. Gorman, Michael J. "The Self, the Lord, and the Other: The Significance of Reflexive Pronoun Constructions in the Letters of Paul, with Comparison to the 'Discourses' of Epictetus." *DAI* 50 (January 1990): 2095A.

Analyzes reflexive pronoun constructions in Paul's letters and finds such constructions to be self-referential to Paul's own theology and ethics.

390. Gow, Joseph D. " 'America, You're Too Young to Die!': The New Christian Right's Rhetoric of Recruitment." *DAI* 50 (January 1990): 1847A.

Examines a made-for-television recruitment film and finds that it targets viewers already predisposed to the organization's blend of Christianity and conservative politics.

391. Gustainis, J. Justin. "Demagoguery and Political Rhetoric: A Review of the Literature." *RSQ* 20 (Spring 1990): 155–161.

Discusses situations prompting demagoguery, personal characteristics of the demagogue, the focus on enemies, the demagogue's self-proclaimed role as savior, and the rhetorical appeals typical of demagogues.

392. Hamlet, Janice D. "Religious Discourse as Cultural Narrative: A Critical Analysis of the Rhetoric of African-American Sermons." *DAI* 51 (July 1990): 20A.

Uses Asante's Afrocentric metatheory to examine the cultural context and sermonic content of African-American preachers during the Civil Rights Movement.

393. Harris, Scott L. "The Rhetorical Dimensions of a Crisis: A Critical Evaluation of the Iranian Hostage Situation." *DAI* 50 (February 1990): 2301A.

Examines how the media and the Carter administration defined the event as a crisis and how public discourse impacted the administration's efforts to build consensus.

394. Hasan, Jaballa M. "Rhetorical Situation Analysis of U.S.-Syrian Discourse: The Hostage Crisis." *DAI* 50 (February 1990): 2302A.

Uses Bitzer's theory of rhetorical situation to analyze official discourse and finds that neither rhetor achieved the genuine dialogue requisite for nonviolent peacemaking.

395. Hassan, Hassan M. Wageih. "A Linguistic Analysis of Mechanism Underlying Power in International Political Negotiations." *DAI* 50 (May 1990): 3567A.

Argues that international political negotiations must be analyzed from perspectives shaped by linguistics, political science, and international relations.

396. Hindson, Paul. "Burke's Dramatic Theory of Politics." *DAI* 51 (October 1990): 1254A.

Examines the relationship between Burke's use of the dramatic metaphor and his political theory.

397. Hingstman, David Bernard. "The Voice of the Public in Legal Discourse: A Critique of Jurisprudential Argument." *DAI* 51 (December 1990): 1827A.

Examines the rhetorical strategies of three legal scholars—Steven Burton, Duncan Kennedy, and Robert Bork—to see which techniques exclude the public.

398. Howard, Kathryn Michelle. "Failed Hope: A Rhetorical Study of the 1985 Anglo-Irish Agreement." *DAI* 51 (December 1990): 1827A.

Examines the unionist and nationalist communities who drafted the agreement in Northern Ireland. Concludes that it failed because its rhetorical strategy of ambiguity could not conquer obstinancy.

399. Howell, Randolph Allen. "Structured Discourse as Ideology in the American Space Weapons Debate." *DAI* 51 (December 1990): 2070A.

Demonstrates how structured discourse perpetuates the arms race by making military research and development capability seem natural and by masking and transforming contradictions between threat and security.

400. Hurtgen, John E. "Anti-Language in the Apocalypse of John." *DAI* 51 (October 1990): 1276A.

Examines the text of the Apocalypse in John using a theoretical model and discovers a connection between the incidents of anti-language and theocentricity.

401. Iltis, Robert S. "Beyond Devil Tokens: The Style of Huey P. Long." *DAI* 51 (July 1990): 20A.

Examines the stylistic characteristics of Long's rhetoric to assess his contribution to the legacy of Populism.

402. Ingram, Michael Thomas. "A Rhetorical Analysis of the New Christian Right's Arguments against Secular Humanism." *DAI* 51 (October 1990): 1045A.

Evaluates three major rhetorical claims of the social and political movement known as the New Christian Right.

403. Jamieson, Kathleen Hall. "The Cunning Rhetor, the Complicitous Audience, the Conned Censor, and the Critic." *ComM* 57 (March 1990): 73–78.

Explores eloquence's ability to propel social change, sustain it, and reconcile those who contest it when societies confront issues of importance.

404. Jeffers, Stephen L. "The Cultural Power of Words: Occult Terminology in Hebrew, Greek, Latin, and English Bibles." *DAI* 50 (June 1990): 3984A.

Meanings of occult words in various Bibles changed with respect to historical periods and within certain religious and social contexts.

405. Johnson, John J. L. "A Rhetorical Analysis of Robert Marion LaFollette as a Social Movement Leader and Presidential Aspirant, 1897–1924." *DAI* 51 (September 1990): 679A.

Uses Charles J. Stewart and Herbert W. Simons' concept of functional imperative and social movement perspective to examine LaFollette's rhetorical efforts.

406. Jorgensen-Earp, Cheryl R. "The Lady, the Whore, and the Spinster: The Rhetorical Use of Victorian Images of Women." *WJSC* 54 (Winter 1990): 82–98.

Analyzes how a discourse of the dominant culture may be used to force revolutionary change within the culture.

407. Kimaru, Christopher Maina. "An Analysis of U.S. Foreign Assistance to Tropical Africa in the 1980s." *DAI* 51 (December 1990): 2154A.

Contrasts the "rhetoric of aid" with the "empirical reality of U.S. foreign assistance" and examines the extent to which U.S. objectives succeeded.

408. Kitchens, Lester David. "An Examination of the Degree of Effectiveness of Expository Preaching in Obtaining Evangelistic Results." *DAI* 51 (October 1990): 1262A.

Examines how expository preaching might get evangelistic results. Formulates principles of expository preaching.

409. Koch, William Nicholas. "An Unexpected American Apocalypse: Eschatology in the Thought of Thomas Merton and Its Significance for the Myth of America." *DAI* 50 (February 1990): 2543A.

Analyzes the content of Merton's published writings in the context of American religious thought.

410. Koptak, Paul Edward. "Judah in the Biblical Story of Joseph: Rhetoric and Biography in the Light of Kenneth Burke's Theory of Identification." *DAI* 51 (December 1990): 2048A.

Examines both the allegorical and rhetorical strategies of Judah's encouragement of exiles "to maintain their ethnic identity."

411. Lange, Jonathan I. "Refusal to Compromise: The Case of Earth First!" *WJSC* 54 (Fall 1990): 473–494.

Argues that the nature of compromise is determined by the context in which it occurs and the perspective from which it emerges.

412. Leeman, Richard Wendel. "The Rhetoric of Counter-Terrorism: A Strategy of Response." *DAI* 51 (November 1990): 1442A.

Argues that a "democratic rhetoric" or non-reflective response is the more effective response strategy because it privileges deliberation and communication over exhortation and action.

413. Levi, Judith N., and Anne G. Walker, eds. *Language in the Judicial Process*. Law, Society, and Policy, vol. 5. New York: Plenum, 1990. 373 pages

A series of 12 essays that analyze naturally occurring language as used in legal contexts. Based primarily on empirical studies, the essays were originally given as papers for a July 1985 conference held at Georgetown University.

414. Linkugel, Wil A., and Martha Solomon. *Anna Howard Shaw: Suffrage Orator and Social Reformer*. Great American Orators, no. 10. New York: Greenwood Press, 1990. 240 pages

Traces Rev. Shaw's career and work as a public orator.

415. Love, Ira Jeffrey. "Language, Discourse, and the Justification of Political Authority." *DAI* 50 (June 1990): 4083A.

Argues that political practices depend on ability or inability, are determined by values and beliefs, and can be resolved through communicative interactions.

416. Lucaites, John Louis, and Celeste Michelle Condit. "Reconstructing Equality: Culturetypal and Counter-Cultural Rhetorics in the Martyred Black Vision." *ComM* 57 (March 1990): 5–24.

Examines how Martin Luther King, Jr.'s, culturetypal rhetoric and Malcolm X's counter-cultural rhetoric functioned together to construct a revised conception of cultural equality.

417. Mangano, Mark J. "Rhetorical Content in the Amarna Correspondence from the Levant." *DAI* 51 (November 1990): 1593A.

Analyzes the ethical, emotional, and logical appeals found in the text.

418. Marino, Virginia M. "Rhetorical Strategies: A Study of Voltaire's Historiography and Frederick II's 'Antimachiavel.' " *DAI* 50 (May 1990): 3614A.

Explores how "both authors initiate new eras of historiographic practice by emphasizing the rhetorical foundations of power politics—in writing, reading, and 'making' history."

419. McCants, David A. *Patrick Henry: The Orator*. Great American Orators, no. 8. New York: Greenwood Press, 1990. 192 pages

Places Henry's oratory in its political and historical contexts. Also includes texts of six important addresses, a chronology, a bibliography, and an index.

420. McLennan, David Bryan. "Communication and the Revitalization of Public Image." *DAI* 51 (December 1990): 1829A.

Uses the rhetorical strategies of Adolph Hitler, Tom Hayden, and Charles Colson to investigate how public figures revitalize their images.

421. McMannus, Leo. "A Coordinated President." *EngT* 6 (October 1990): 3–6.

Discusses George Bush's style and usage, especially his dependence on the coordinating conjunction.

422. Medhurst, Martin J., Robert L. Ivie, Philip Wander, and Robert L. Scott, eds. *Cold War Rhetoric: Strategy, Metaphor, and Ideology*. Contributions to the Study of Mass Media and Communications, no. 19. New York: Greenwood Press, 1990. 240 pages

Eleven essays critique central texts of the Cold War, including speeches by Presidents Eisenhower and Kennedy, the Murrow-McCarthy confrontation on CBS, the speeches and writings of peace advocates, and the theme of un-Americanism expressed in various media.

423. Mendez-Mendez, Serafin. "Toward an Understanding of Didactic Rhetoric: The Case of Golda Meir, Teacher and Politician." *DAI* 50 (February 1990): 2303A.

Analyzes 40 speeches, concluding that Meir changed her strategies according to her audience and used "teacherly" language.

424. Meyer, Elizabeth Ann. "Literacy, Literate Practice, and the Law in the Roman Empire, A.D. 100–600." *DAI* 50 (May 1990): 3708A.

Studies the use of writing in certain areas of Roman private law.

425. Meyer, John. "Ronald Reagan and Humor: A Politician's Velvet Weapons." *ComS* 41 (Spring 1990): 76–88.

Applies three major theories to show how humor may be used to promote positive feelings and to criticize authority without negative repercussions.

426. Miller, Keith D. "Composing Martin Luther King, Jr." *PMLA* 105 (January 1990): 70–82.

Describes Dr. King's published voice in terms of the "voice-merging" tradition of the black folk pulpit that refuses to treat language as a privately owned commodity.

427. Mooney, Christopher Zimmer. "Pushing Paper: The Flow and Use of Written Information in State Legislative Decision Making." *DAI* 51 (November 1990): 1755A.

Much of the written information legislators use comes from sources outside the legislative process.

428. Mowery, Diane, and Eve Duffy. "The Power of Language to Efface and Desensitize." *RSQ* 20 (Spring 1990): 163–171.

Studies the use of language to efface and desensitize the relationship between human beings and animals, as paralleled by the German/Jew relationship from the mid-1800s through the fall of the Third Reich.

429. Muldoon, Gary. "The Supercalifragilisticexpialidocious Effect; or, How to Talk like a Lawyer." *QRD* 16 (July 1990): 10.

A satirical analysis of the language of lawyers. Emphasizes syntax, diction level, and redundancy.

430. Neal, Janice K. "The Rhetoric of the Reverend Jesse Louis Jackson: A Fantasy Theme Analysis of Selected Speeches during the 1988 Presidential Campaign." *DAI* 50 (January 1990): 1849A.

Uses fantasy theme analysis to examine 10 speeches by Rev. Jackson.

431. Nelson, Jeffrey, and Mary Ann Flannery. "The Sanctuary Movement: A Study in Religious Confrontation." *SCJ* 55 (Summer 1990): 372–387.

Uses Burke's concept of identification to analyze how different scenes operating for two sides motivate opposing rhetorical agencies.

432. Newman, Linda Fahy. "Writing in the Legal Community: Constraints upon the Writing Processes of Lawyers." *DAI* 51 (July 1990): 275A.

Describes the legal writing process as a recursive process of collecting and analyzing data, of transcribing language to comply with context-dependent legal interpretations, and of reconstructing ordinary events as legal events.

433. Odiam, Alan Richard. "The Rhetoric of the Fourth Gospel: A Key to Preaching." *DAI* 50 (March 1990): 2948A.

Rhetorically analyzes the text of the Fourth Gospel and finds that its structures can be applied effectively to sermon construction.

434. Ohmann, Richard. "A Kinder, Gentler Nation: Education and Rhetoric in the Bush Era." *JAC* 10 (1990): 215–230.

A synthetic critique of President Bush's education rhetoric and proposals. Speculates on appropriate roles for composition.

435. Owen, Anna Susan. "Liberalizing Clio: The Rhetoric of Feminist History." *DAI* 51 (August 1990): 344A.

Analyzes rhetorical strategies that construct and promote feminist history. Argues that a "rhetorically sensitive feminist history" informs many academic disciplines.

436. Pfau, Michael, and Henry C. Kenski. *Attack Politics: Strategy and Defense*. New York: Praeger, 1990. 194 pages

Examines the use of "attack messages" in American political advertising, drawing on studies of a 1986 Senate race and the 1988 Presidential campaign to evaluate a defense tactic known as the "inoculation message strategy."

437. Pollock, Mark A. "A Reconsideration of the Prospects for Rhetoric in Hannah Arendt's Political Philosophy." *DAI* 50 (February 1990): 2303A.

Asserts that Arendt's unfinished theory of political judgment fails to examine the specific rhetorical utterances and contexts in which political concepts are used.

438. Procter, David Edward. "Enacting Political Culture: Rhetorical Transformations of Liberty Weekend 1986." *DAI* 50 (March 1990): 2706A.

Examines the rhetorical process by which liberty constructs and sustains American political culture.

439. Pyle, William Texil. "A Burkean Approach to Proclaiming Misunderstanding Sequences in the Fourth Gospel." *DAI* 50 (February 1990): 2541A.

Evaluates Burke's rhetoric as an analytical and generative methodology.

440. Reid, Ronald F. *Edward Everett: Unionist Orator*. Great American Orators, no. 7. New York: Greenwood Press, 1990. 304 pages

Addresses the historical and oratorical paradoxes that have influenced perceptions of Everett's career, reconstituting the role of epideictic rhetoric from the end of the Revolutionary War to the eve of the Civil War.

441. Salvador, Michael. "Coming to Terms with Consumption: The Rhetoric of American Consumer Unrest." *DAI* 50 (March 1990): 2690A.

Analyzes patterns in consumer protest language and their relationship to cultural conflict.

442. Smith, Abraham. "The Social and Ethical Implications of the Pauline Rhetoric in I Thessalonians." *DAI* 51 (August 1990): 531A.

Rhetorically analyzes the text of I Thessalonians to discover the social and ethical makeup of the Pauline community described.

443. Smith, Herb. "Technical Communications and the Law: Product Liability and Safety Labels." *JTWC* 20 (1990): 307–319.

Describes what technical communicators should know about the law of product liability and safety labels. Offers some sources of additional information.

444. Smith, John Webster. "A Dramatistic Analysis of William Lucas' 1986 Gubernatorial Campaign." *DAI* 50 (February 1990): 2304A.

Uses Kenneth Burke and Horatio Alger to examine Lucas' political failure and its implications for future black voters.

445. Smith, Larry David. "Convention Oratory as Institutional Discourse: A Narrative Synthesis of the Democrats and Republicans of 1988." *ComS* 41 (Spring 1990): 19–34.

Discusses the rhetoric of coalition formation, the theoretical significance of strategic activities, and the utility of narrative synthesis as a critical tool.

446. Smith, Ruth L. "Order and Disorder: The Naturalization of Poverty." *CCrit* 14 (Winter 1989–1990): 209–229.

Examines American society's conception of the poor as those who exist far from the ordered and rational norm.

447. Smith, Walter Jesse. "The Dissolution of Citizenship." *DAI* 51 (December 1990): 2147A.

Finds in the *Federalist Papers* a "classical republican rhetoric" without "true republican substance."

448. Spradlin, Anna Lenell. "Elise Boulding and the Peace Movement: A Study of Leadership Rhetoric and Practice within Social Movement Organizations." *DAI* 51 (December 1990): 1831A.

A descriptive case study using rhetorical criticism and qualitative methodologies to "distill the essence of Boulding as a rhetor and leader" in the peace movement.

449. Stoller, Martin. "The Greenhouse Effect and the Destruction of the Ozone Shield: Implications for Rhetoric and Criticism." *DAI* 51 (July 1990): 21A.

Argues that, for policy making, traditional rhetoric is not appealing anymore. A new crisis-oriented rhetoric for the environmental problem must be constructed.

450. Stratman, James F. "The Emergence of Legal Composition as a Field of Inquiry: Evaluating the Prospects." *RER* 60 (Spring 1990): 153–235.

Argues for granting disciplinary status to the field of legal composition.

451. Stygall, Gail. "Trial Language: Contrasts in the Discourse Processing of Lawyers and Jurors in an Indiana Court." *DAI* 50 (June 1990): 3936A.

Concludes that "legal and common varieties of English are different linguistic and conceptual systems, a matter of serious consequence for legal theorists assuming shared language."

452. Tremaine, Richard Rene. "The *Ethos* of Jesse Jackson in the 1984 Presidential Primaries: Rhetorical Strategies to Address Image Problems and Enhance Credibility." *DAI* 51 (September 1990): 683A.

Analyzes campaign speeches and other documents for elements of character, competence, and dynamism used to construct an *ethos*.

453. Tyson, John Nelson, Jr. "Paradigms of Religious Expression: An Analysis of Religious Broadcasting." *DAI* 51 (December 1990): 1831A.

Examines "closed system ideological discourse" in televised religious broadcasts. Focuses on narcissism, techniques of cinema verite, the use of a "collegial paradigm," and syncretistic rhetoric.

454. University of Washington Discourse Analysis Group. "The Rhetorical Construction of a President." *D&S* 1 (October 1990): 189–200.

A discourse analysis of President Bush's inaugural speech reveals audience manipulation.

455. Vogel, Robert A. "Against Your Brother: Conflict Themes and the Rhetoric of the Gospel According to Matthew." *DAI* 50 (May 1990): 3414A.

Uses exegetical and rhetorical methods to analyze the prominent conflict enacted between Jesus and Jewish leaders.

456. Ward, James W. "Judges' Attitudes toward Standard English and Black English in the State of Texas." *DAI* 50 (January 1990): 1850A.

Finds that judges favor Standard English in their courts, a possible explanation for the disproportionate incarceration of blacks.

457. Warner, Martin, ed. *The Bible as Rhetoric: Studies in Biblical Persuasion and Credibility*. New York: Routledge, 1990. 224 pages

A collection of interdisciplinary papers that explore how the persuasive strategies of biblical texts relate to concerns about religious and historical truths. Contributors are not indexed separately in this volume.

458. Westen, Peter. *Speaking of Equality: An Analysis of the Rhetorical Force of Equality in Moral and Legal Discourse*. Princeton, N.J.: Princeton University Press, 1990. 318 pages

Argues that "equality arguments" draw some of their rhetorical force from masking the standards of comparison on which they are based.

459. Wilson, John. *Politically Speaking: The Pragmatic Analysis of Political Language.* Oxford, England: Basil Blackwell, 1990. 203 pages

Uses data from speeches, interviews, press conferences, and other writings in an analysis of political language in the U.S., Britain, and other countries.

460. Winfield, Betty Houchin. *FDR and the News Media.* Urbana, Ill.: University of Illinois Press, 1990. 276 pages

Analyzes how President Roosevelt's "news-management" tactics differed during major crises.

461. York, John O. "The Rhetorical Function of Bi-Polar Reversal in Luke." *DAI* 50 (January 1990): 2101A.

Examines the Aristotelian notion of reversal of fortune in Luke. Concludes that many reversals function thematically and argumentatively.

462. Zernicke, Paul Haskell. "Presidential Roles and Rhetoric." *DAI* 50 (March 1990): 3050A.

Analyzes presidential descriptions of the office, conceptualized in terms of presidential roles, in the rhetoric of three presidents.

See also 54, 59, 155, 329, 342, 482, 536, 608, 716, 1001, 1019, 1030, 1041

2.4 COMPUTER AND LITERACY STUDIES

---

463. Allen, Bryce. "Knowledge Organization in an Information Retrieval Task." *IPM* 26 (1990): 535–542.

The way people organize their knowledge of a topic influences the way they interact with new information. An experiment applies data to computer retrieval tasks.

464. Alterman, Richard, and Lawrence A. Bookman. "Some Computational Experiments in Summarization." *DPr* 13 (April–June 1990): 143–174.

A program called Nexus makes possible analyses of explicit and implicit information, producing summaries sensitive to the level of detail in the original narrative.

465. Alvarado, Sergio Jose. "Understanding Editorial Text: A Computer Model of Argument Comprehension." *DAI* 50 (February 1990): 3566B.

Describes OpEd, a prototype editorial comprehension and question-answering system, and its operation on texts within a particular domain.

466. Balajthy, Ernest. "Computers in Curricula Program for Networked College-Level Writing Process Instruction: A First-Year Report." Paper presented at the College Reading Association, Philadelphia, November 1989. ERIC ED 309 455. 25 pages

Reports on advantages and disadvantages of using local-area networks and describes ESL and developmental writing applications at one site.

467. Baldursson, Stefan. "Technology, Computer Use, and the Pedagogy of Writing." *DAI* 50 (March 1990): 2763A.

Argues that the problems associated with computers in education are pedagogic ones.

468. Baron, Dennis. *The English-Only Question: An Official Language for Americans?* New Haven, Conn.: Yale University Press, 1990. 248 pages

Explores the philosophical, legal, political, sociological, and educational implications of the official-English movement, tracing the 200-year history of American attitudes toward English and minority languages.

469. Batson, Lorie Goodman. "Feeling Deaf and Dumb: The Costs of Literacy." *FEN* 18 (Spring 1990): 27–30.

A discussion of literacy that includes a feminist perspective.

470. Bolter, Jay David. *Writing Space: The Computer, Hypertext, and the History of Writing*. Hillsdale, N.J.: Erlbaum, 1990. 258 pages

A study of the computer as a new technology for reading and writing. Bolter integrates introductory, historical, illustrative, and theoretical material in support of his claim that the computer will carry literacy into a new age, the age of electronic text that will emerge from the age of print that is now passing.

471. Botstein, Leon. "Damaged Literacy: Illiteracies and American Democracy." *Daedalus* 119 (Spring 1990): 55–84.

Analyzes the political and cultural consequences of illiteracy among the affluent and privileged as well as the poor and disadvantaged.

472. Brady, Laura. "Overcoming Resistance: Computers in the Writing Classroom." *CC* 7 (April 1990): 21–33.

Once teachers accepted CAI, they were more inclined to use it, especially if they had a stake in its design.

473. Brandt, Deborah. *Literacy as Involvement: The Acts of Writers, Readers, Texts*. Carbondale, Ill.: Southern Illinois University Press, 1990. 174 pages

Examining the cultural and social roots of reading and writing, Brandt questions whether literacy is a natural development or a radical shift from orality.

474. Campbell, William P. "A Comment on 'On the Subjects of Class and Gender in the Literacy Letters' [*CE* 51 (February 1989)]." *CE* 52 (March 1990): 345–346.

Describes Brodkey's style as "sludge" and O'Reilley's as "clear and bubbly," arguing for more of the latter, particularly in research articles.

475. Chisman, Forrest P. *Leadership for Literacy: The Agenda for the 1990s*. San Francisco: Jossey-Bass, 1990. 302 pages

Eleven essays examine shortcomings in the field of adult literacy, including federal policy, the literacy profession, funding sources, and research and development. The authors recommend strategies to enable public and private groups cooperatively to combat adult literacy problems.

476. Christensen, Larry C., and Michael R. Bodey. "A Structure for Creating Quality Courseware." *CollM* 8 (August 1990): 201–209.

Addresses the issue of assuring quality software used in CBI. Provides a structure by which authors and developers can create quality courseware.

477. Cohen, Robin. "A Processing Model for the Analysis of One-Way Arguments in Discourse." *Arg* 4 (November 1990): 431–446.

Describes a computational model for analyzing arguments in discourse, in particular the processes necessary for interpreting one uninterrupted argument from a speaker.

478. Coles, Janice. "Literacy Learning: A Case Study in Intervention." *DAI* 50 (March 1990): 2782A.

Describes the acquisition of literacy for a self-described "at risk" reader.

479. Croft, Vaughn Earl. "A National Study to Determine the Characteristics of Technological Literacy for High School Graduates." *DAI* 51 (November 1990): 1531A.

Identifies 24 consensus items to be used as minimum characteristics of technological literacy.

480. Csikszentmihalyi, Mihaly. "Literacy and Intrinsic Motivation." *Daedalus* 119 (Spring 1990): 115–140.

Calls for greater emphasis on stimulating the enjoyment of learning as the answer to the literacy problem.

481. Damon, William. "Reconciling the Literacies of Generations." *Daedalus* 119 (Spring 1990): 33–53.

Contrasts perceptions of functional literacy held by today's youth and adults. Advocates respect for children in order to communicate mature values to them.

482. Daniels, Harvey A., ed. *Not Only English: Affirming America's Multilingual Heritage.* Urbana, Ill.: NCTE, 1990. 135 pages

Twelve essays examine the nature and origins of the English-only movement, describe problems caused by such laws, and explore the deeper causes and consequences of the English-only sentiment. Offers possible responses to calls for making English the sole official language of the U.S.

483. DiPardo, Anne, and Mike DiPardo. "Towards the Metapersonal Essay: Exploring the Potential of Hypertext in the Composition Class." *CC* 7 (August 1990): 7–22.

Describes how exploring hypertext for classroom use also requires collaboration, especially from technical experts initially.

484. Eller, Rebecca Gaeth. "Teacher Resistance and Educational Change: Toward a Critical Theory of Literacy in Appalachia." *DAI* 50 (May 1990): 3460A.

An ethnographic study of teachers' attitudes towards critical literacy and of the factors that have led to these attitudes.

485. Ferdman, Bernardo M. "Literacy and Cultural Identity." *HER* 60 (May 1990): 181–204.

Sees in cultural diversity significant implications for literacy acquisition. Contends that in a multiethnic society, the type and content of literacy education can influence cultural identity.

486. Giray-Saul, Eren. "Jula Oral Narratives in Bobo-Dioulasso: Continuity, Recreation, and Transcultural Communication." *DAI* 50 (February 1990): 2607A.

Studies the oral narrative tradition in Bobo-Dioulasso in southwestern Burkina Faso.

487. Graubard, Stephen R. "Doing Badly and Feeling Confused." *Daedalus* 119 (Spring 1990): 257–279.

Traces the history of literacy in the U.S. and argues that providing meaningful literacy to all requires a social revolution.

488. Graves, William H., ed. *Computing across the Curriculum: Academic Perspectives.* EDUCOM Strategies Series on Information Technologies. McKinney, Tex.: Academic Computing, 1989. 450 pages

Describes efforts to improve instructional computing at nine institutions, examining the effects of technology on faculty, curricula, and institutional missions.

489. Haas, Christina. *How the Writing Medium Shapes the Writing Process: Effects of Word Processing on Planning.* Pittsburgh: Carnegie Mellon University Center for Educational Computing in English, 1988. ERIC ED 309 408. 43 pages

An experimental study finds that word processing affects the planning process of novices differently from that of experienced writers.

490. Halio, Marcia Peoples. "Maiming Reviewed [response to Young, Kaplan and Moulthrop, and Slatin *et al.*, *CC* 7 (August 1990)]." *CC* 7 (August 1990): 103–107.

Defends her article as descriptive research.

491. Halio, Marcia Peoples. "Student Writing: Can the Machine Maim the Message?" *Academic Computing* 4 (January 1990): 16–46.

Reports on an experiment to determine how the user-interface designs of IBM and Macintosh word processors influence students' writing.

492. Harper, Helen. "Theory into Practice: Literacy and the State: A Comparison of Hirsch, Rosenblatt, and Giroux." *EQ* 22 (1990): 169–175.

Examines the validity of Hirsch's cultural literacy, Rosenblatt's liberal ideas, and Giroux' radical ideas in the classroom. Raises doubts about Hirsch's theories meeting the needs of a democratic society.

493. Hawkins, David. "The Roots of Literacy." *Daedalus* 119 (Spring 1990): 1–14.

Sets forth an extended definition of literacy and traces the roots of literacy to the elementary school years.

494. Heslop, Yvonne, ed. *Literacy: Focus on Asia and the Pacific*. Canberra, Australia: Asian South Pacific Bureau of Adult Education, 1989. ERIC ED 313 579. 135 pages

Collects 16 essays and a list of literacy materials to commemorate the 1990 International Literacy Year.

495. Hornberger, Nancy H. "Bilingual Education and English-Only: A Language-Planning Framework." *Annals* 508 (March 1990): 12–26.

Examines the English-only movement and bilingual education as examples of issues in language planning, defined as "the authoritative allocation of resources to language."

496. Houston, R. A. *Literacy in Early Modern Europe: Culture and Education, 1500–1800*. New York: Longman, 1988. 288 pages

Discusses education, literacy, and popular culture during a 300-year period and describes the relationship education and literacy have to political, economic, and social structures.

497. Huffman, G. David. "Semi-Automatic Determination of Citation Relevancy: User Evaluation." *IPM* 26 (1990): 295–302.

Users evaluated software for ranking database bibliographic citations by relevancy as ideal in 22 percent of cases, 23 percent better than random, and four percent poorer than random.

498. Imhoff, Gary. "The Position of U.S. English on Bilingual Education." *Annals* 508 (March 1990): 48–61.

Sets out objections to bilingual education voiced by U.S. English, an organization whose "goal is to maintain the blessings of a common language—English."

499. IRA and NCTE. *Cases in Literacy: An Agenda for Discussion*. Newark, Del.: IRA, 1989. ERIC ED 311 403. 46 pages

Presents 14 case studies designed to increase awareness of the range of meanings embraced by the term *literacy*.

500. Kamel, M., B. Hadfield, and M. Ismail. "Fuzzy Query Processing Using Clustering Techniques." *IPM* 26 (1990): 279–293.

A prototype computer program carefully overlaps related queries to solve the problem of processing fuzzy queries to a data base.

501. Kaplan, Nancy, and Stuart Moulthrop. "Other Ways of Seeing [response to Halio, *Academic Computing* 4 (January 1990)]." *CC* 7 (August 1990): 89–102.

Describes weaknesses in Halio's observations and inferences. Suggests exploring technology's influence on education and the impact of graphics on writing.

502. Kellog, Ronald T., and Suzanne Mueller. "Cognitive Tools and Thinking Performance: The Case of Word Processors and Writing." Paper presented at the annual meeting of the Psychonomic Society, Atlanta, November 1989. ERIC ED 311 455. 30 pages

Reports on a quasi-experimental study, finding that word processing restructured the composing process but failed to improve writing performance.

503. Kirby, Peggy C. "Computers in Schools: A New Source of Inequity." *CompEd* 14 (1990): 537–541.

Suggests measures to redress the growing gap in educational resources available to economically disadvantaged students. Includes a study describing computer usage in one Southern state.

504. Krendl, Kathy A., and Russell B. Williams. "The Importance of Being Rigorous: Research on Writing to Read." *JCBI* 17 (Summer 1990): 81–86.

Flawed research on the computer program Writing to Read raises questions about its effectiveness. The authors argue for process-based writing as a viable alternative.

505. LeBlanc, Paul. "Competing Ideologies in Software Design for Computer-Aided Composition." *CC* 7 (April 1990): 7–19.

Software programs reflect professionals' views of writing and learning, yet they are given little credence—and their developers even less—in academe.

506. LeBlanc, Paul Joseph. "The Development of Computer-Aided Composition Software and Its Implications for Composition." *DAI* 51 (September 1990): 771A.

Assesses the design and development of computer-aided composition software from theoretical and pedagogical perspectives, noting the rise of cognitively based development programs.

507. Lunsford, Andrea A., Helene Moglen, and James Slevin, eds. *The Right to Literacy*. New York: MLA, 1990. 306 pages

Twenty-nine essays discuss what literacy is, what keeps people from attaining it, and how they can be helped to achieve it. The essays were originally presented at the 1988 Right to Literacy Conference in Ohio.

508. Madrid, Arturo. "Official English: A False Policy Issue." *Annals* 508 (March 1990): 62–65.

Argues against the English-only movement's claim that bilingual education weakens the social fabric. Maintains instead that literacy ought to be the policy goal.

509. Markel, Mike. "The Effect of the Word Processor and the Style Checker on Revision in Technical Writing: What Do We Know and What Do We Need to Find Out?" *JTWC* 20 (1990): 329–342.

Concludes that research on text editing and style checking as aids to revision is presently inconclusive. Suggests a research agenda for the future.

510. Mulcahy-Ernt, Patricia I. "The Writer's Choice: On-Line Versus Hard-Copy Documentation for the Twenty-First Century." *TWT* 17 (Spring 1990): 167–175.

Provides a methodology for determining the appropriate use of on-line and hard-copy documentation formats.

511. "No Official Language." *Time* (19 February 1990): 82.

Reports on a federal judge's striking down Arizona's official English law, which was found to violate First Amendment guarantees.

512. Ogbu, John U. "Minority Status and Literacy in Comparative Perspective." *Daedalus* 119 (Spring 1990): 141–168.

Asserts that minorities perceive and respond differently to educational institutions and thus have varying degrees of success in becoming literate.

513. Paice, Chris D. "Constructing Literature Abstracts by Computer: Techniques and Prospects." *IPM* 26 (1990): 171–186.

Although computer programs can extract key information sentences from a text, none can yet construct a coherent abstract.

514. Papa, Michael J. "Communication Network Patterns and Employee Performance with New Technology." *ComR* 17 (June 1990): 344–368.

Finds significant positive relationships between diversity, size, and activity on computer networks and employee productivity with new technology.

515. Peyton, Joy Kreeft. "Technological Innovation Meets Institution: Birth of Creativity or Murder of a Great Idea?" *CC* 7 (April 1990): 15–32.

Discusses how two Gallaudet teachers used an ENFI network in different and evolving ways and explains what real-time written interaction seems to offer a program.

516. Reichman, R. "Modeling Human Dialogue with Computers." *Arg* 4 (November 1990): 415–430.

Presents a formal analysis of everyday conversation and sketches a computerized model designed for human being-machine discourse interaction.

517. Resnick, Daniel P. "Historical Perspectives on Literacy and Schooling." *Daedalus* 119 (Spring 1990): 15–32.

Asserts that low expectations about literacy have roots in archaic models. Argues for curricular revisions based on higher-order thinking, not basic competences.

518. Resnick, Lauren B. "Literacy in School and Out." *Daedalus* 119 (Spring 1990): 169–185.

Calls for literacy apprenticeships outside the schools as the way to change general levels of literacy.

519. Rizzoni, Maria B. "Logic Grammars and Pronominal Anaphora." *DAI* 50 (April 1990): 4622B.

Develops a sequence of grammar formalisms that can handle pronominal reference in natural language.

520. Rose, Shirley K. "Reading Representative Anecdotes of Literacy Practice; or, 'See Dick and Jane Read and Write!' " *RR* 8 (Spring 1990): 244–258.

Applies Burke's language philosophy to student and professional literacy autobiographies. Investigates the "literacy myths of postsecondary educational culture," focusing on gender-related differences.

521. Salomon, Gavriel. "Cognitive Effects with and of Computer Technology." *ComR* 17 (February 1990): 26–44.

Argues that the quality of effects with computer programs depends on the setting, the user's goals, and engagement with the activity.

522. Siann, G., H. MacLeod, P. Glissov, and A. Durndell. "The Effects of Computer Use on Gender Differences in Attitudes to Computers." *CompEd* 14 (1990): 183–191.

Concerned with attitudes about computers before and after intensive use in primary schools. Raises questions for future research and practice.

523. Simpson, Mark D. "Shaping Computer Documentation for Multiple Audiences: An Ethnographic Study." *DAI* 51 (August 1990): 491A.

The writing group in the study identified at least three audience roles and four text attributes in preparing computer documentation.

524. Slatin, John M. "Reading Hypertext: Order and Coherence in a New Medium." *CE* 52 (December 1990): 870–883.

Compares hypertext to traditional notions of text and explicates the new rhetoric necessary to the study of hypertextual production.

525. Slatin, John, and others. "Computer Teachers Respond to Halio [*Academic Computing* 4 (January 1990)]." *CC* 7 (August 1990): 73–79.

Reports on a group discussion over a Bitnet loop. Twenty teachers agree that Halio's article was flawed by methodological and interpretive errors. They regard the author and journal irresponsible.

526. Snyder, Benson R. "Literacy and Numeracy: Two Ways of Knowing." *Daedalus* 119 (Spring 1990): 233–256.

Reports on a 25-year longitudinal study of 51 undergraduates, concluding that literacy and numeracy must be balanced for adaptation to a changing, complex world.

527. Spilka, Rachel. "Orality and Literacy in the Workplace: Process- and Text-Based Strategies for Multiple-Audience Adaptation." *JBTC* 4 (January 1990): 44–67.

A qualitative study of seven engineers in a large corporation revealed that orality, more than literacy, led to rhetorical success.

528. Stairs, Arlene. "Questions behind the Question of Vernacular Education: A Study in Literacy, Native Language, and English." *EQ* 22 (1990): 103–123.

Studies the writing proficiency of Inuit students in Canada to explore questions of cultural identity and school language policy.

529. Steen, Lynn Arthur. "Numeracy." *Daedalus* 119 (Spring 1990): 211–231.

Asserts that because numeracy leads to inequality of opportunity in technological society, schools face the challenge of achieving appropriate levels of numeracy for all students.

530. Stotsky, Sandra. "On Literacy Anthologies and Adult Education: A Critical Perspective." *CE* 52 (December 1990): 916–923.

Critiques several adult literacy texts, especially their theoretical and practical implications.

531. Stuckey, J. Elspeth. *The Violence of Literacy*. Portsmouth, N.H.: Boynton/Cook, 1990. 140 pages

A critique of literacy as a system that justifies disenfranchising people, often by violent means. The real issues confronting people are economic, not pedagogic.

532. Sumali, Pin-Ngern. "A Lexical Data Base for English to Support Information Retrieval, Parsing, and Text Generation." *DAI* 51 (December 1990): 2995B.

Describes the construction of an English lexical data base designed for information retrieval, language understanding, and text generation.

533. Suttles, Arles L. "Word Processing: Overview of a Changing Technology." *DAI* 50 (February 1990): 2380A.

Examines word processing's origins, key stages and modifications, and current and future applications for business and professional writing as well as writing instruction.

534. Taylor, Charles T. "HAAS: A Computational Model for the Analysis of Hierarchical Argumentative Discourse." *DAI* 51 (November 1990): 2468B.

Examines HAAS, a computational model for processing human argument. Discusses the system's strengths and limitations.

535. Turner, Judith Axler. "Use of Computers Can Improve Students' Writing Ability, Study Shows." *CHE* 37 (7 November 1990): A13, A15.

Results of a three-year study of 1695 students at 15 institutions show that those scoring in the top and bottom fifths on a pretest improved most.

536. U.S. Congress. *Eliminating Illiteracy: Hearings on Examining Proposed Legislation*. Washington, D.C.: Senate Committee on Labor and Human Resources, 1989. ERIC ED 313 528. 369 pages

Reports on testimony given at three Congressional hearings on eliminating illiteracy.

537. Venezky, Richard L., Daniel A. Wagner, and Barrie S. Ciliberti, eds. *Toward Defining Literacy*. Newark, Del.: IRA, 1989. ERIC ED 313 677. 89 pages

Collects nine papers on literacy in America.

538. Weinstein-Shr, Gail. *Literacy and Social Process: A Community in Transition*. Washington, D.C.: ERIC/FLL, 1989. ERIC ED 313 930. 43 pages

Studies Hmong refugees in Philadelphia, noting community resources available for literacy transmission.

539. Weinstein-Shr, Gail, and Nora E. Lewis. *Language, Literacy, and the Older Refugee in America: Research Agenda for the 90s*. Washington, D.C.: ERIC/FLL, 1989. ERIC ED 313 928. 29 pages

A research review that stresses the literacy requirements for older refugees.

540. Wiebe, Janyce M. "Recognizing Subjective Sentences: A Computational Investigation of Narrative Text." *DAI* 51 (September 1990): 1369B.

Computationally investigates the ways in which a reader recognizes subjectivity within particular kinds of sentence structures.

541. Williams, James D., and Grace Capizzi Snipper. *Literacy and Bilingualism*. New York: Longman, 1990. 162 pages

Analyzes the mechanisms and issues in literacy as they relate to bilingualism. Synthesizes current theories and research to give teachers the theoretical framework and resources for developing reading and writing skills among bilingual students.

542. Williams, Noel, and Patrik Holt, eds. *Computers and Writing*. Norwood, N.J.: Ablex, 1990. 176 pages

A collection of 10 essays that report on research and development in the design of computational models and tools for teaching writing.

543. Young, Steven. "Computers and Student Writing: Maiming the Macintosh [response to Halio, *Academic Computing* 4 (January 1990)]." *CC* 7 (August 1990): 81–88.

Finds Halio's article based on poor experimental design and filled with questionable logic and evidence. Also explains why the Macintosh is useful for writing instruction.

544. Zubrow, David Michael. "Gender Differences and Learning to Compute: A Socialization Perspective." *DAI* 51 (October 1990): 1415A.

Uses socialization theory to study gender and computer use. Finds evidence that social roles affect students' abilities to use computers.

See also 1, 20, 25, 250, 308, 424, 927, 930,

981, 1284, 1286, 1294, 1327, 1331, 1364, 1464, 1793

2.5 ADVERTISING, PUBLIC RELATIONS, AND BUSINESS

545. Abbuhl, Phyllis Rae. "Communicative Action in the Corporate Setting: An Analysis of Validity Claims in Use by Managers." *DAI* 51 (November 1990): 1679A.

Investigates upper-level corporate managers' basic assumptions about participatory management relative to communication in a hierarchical structure.

546. Ajirotutu, Cheryl Seabrook. "Communicative Competence in Employment Interviews." *DAI* 50 (June 1990): 3996A.

Investigates the communicative behavior of African-Americans in employment interviews.

547. Amariglio, Jack, Stephen Resnick, and Richard Wolff. "Division and Difference in the 'Discipline' of Economics." *CritI* 17 (Autumn 1990): 108–137.

Investigates how the discipline of economics is formed from a shifting field of different discourses.

548. Artz, Nancy Campbell. "Numeric and Verbal Information: Implications for Persuasion." *DAI* 50 (May 1990): 3663A.

Examines the implications of numeric and verbal presentation formats in persuasive communications.

549. Barge, J. Kevin, David W. Schlueter, and Gregory Duncan. "Task Structure as a Moderator of Task and Relational Skills." *ComS* 41 (Spring 1990): 1–18.

Examines how managerial communication affects the attitudes and performances of subordinates.

550. Bauerly, Ronald John. "An Experimental Investigation of Humor in Television Advertising: The Effects of Product Type, Program Context, and Target of Humor on Selected

Consumer Cognitions." *DAI* 50 (June 1990): 4017A.

Examines the effects of three independent factors within humorous advertising upon various consumer cognitions.

551. Bell, Hanan Samuel. "A New Approach to Incentives for Information Creation and Distribution." *DAI* 50 (January 1990): 2163A.

Examines alternative incentive structures for creating and distributing information.

552. Blount, Brian Carson. "The Role of Communication Media in Decision Making: A Study of Selected North Carolina Agribusiness Chief Administrators and Their Perceptions of Communication Media." *DAI* 51 (October 1990): 1054A.

Examines how the prior use of communication media affects the perceptions of chief administrators of agribusiness. Finds that young, educated administrators were more likely to use media.

553. Broes, Igor. "Communication in the Marketing of Magazines as Advertising Vehicles." *DAI* 50 (March 1990): 2983A.

Discusses the rhetoric, creativity, and semiology of messages used in the marketing communication process.

554. Butler, Susan Lowell. "What's Ahead for Communicators in the Nineties." *PC* 10 (Spring 1990): 16–17, 22.

Notes trends in demographics, the work force, the economy, and education, analyzing their implications for communications professionals.

555. Byun, Young Hoon. "Takeover Announcements, Information Asymmetry, and Market Microstructure: An Empirical Study." *DAI* 50 (January 1990): 2177A.

Investigates if specialists on the New York Stock Exchange can detect insider trading.

556. Caricaburu, Linda. "Personal Communication in an Impersonal World." *PC* 10 (Summer 1990): 23, 27.

Etiquette expert Letitia Baldridge discusses how to increase personal communication.

557. Cornett-Devito, Myrna M. "The Relationship between Four Communication Processes and Merger Effectiveness in Four Financial Institutions." *DAI* 51 (October 1990): 1044A.

Examines communication processes and institutional mergers. Supports Nadler's and Devine's crisis management theories.

558. Gwin, Louis Marion, Jr. "Speak No Evil: The Promotional Heritage of Nuclear Risk Communication." *DAI* 51 (August 1990): 634A.

Critiques the effectiveness of required emergency communications by nuclear utilities.

559. Hawkins, Scott Alfred. "Information Processing Strategies in Riskless Preference Reversals: The Prominence Effect." *DAI* 50 (February 1990): 2572A.

Argues that the constructive nature of preference implies that consumers will be sensitive to a number of variations in the marketing environment.

560. Hensley, Connie Spector. "Survival and the Fine Art of Billing." *PC* 10 (Spring 1990): 11, 14.

Suggests billing strategies for freelance communications professionals.

561. Hirst, Russel Keith. "Using Visual Mnemonics to Make Instructions Easier to Remember." *JTWC* 20 (1990): 411–423.

Argues that classical mnemonic theory can guide technical communicators in creating illustrations or instructions that will help users memorize steps quickly and thoroughly.

562. Hobgood-Brown, Lucy. "Crisis Communications—after the Quake." *PC* 10 (Spring 1990): 8–10.

San Francisco Bay Area communicators discuss what they learned about crisis communications in the aftermath of the October 1989 earthquake.

563. Holguin-Wright, Mary E. "Valuing Diversity." *PC* 10 (Winter 1990): 9.

    Steve Hanamura suggests how professional communicators can identify cultural differences and learn to value diversity.

564. Indjejikian, Raffi J. "The Impact of Information on the Extent of Agreement among Investors: A New Perspective on Firm Disclosures." *DAI* 50 (January 1990): 2140A.

    Examines the role of firm disclosures in a market setting where investors use the information to make portfolio decisions.

565. Jacobs, Liz. "Networking in the Nineties." *PC* 10 (Summer 1990): 21, 27.

    Discusses how to develop personal contacts that can broaden outlooks, provide educational and personal resources, and lead to new job opportunities.

566. Kacmar, Karen Michele. "Relational Communication and Mutual Influence in the Employment Interview." *DAI* 51 (November 1990): 1683A.

    Examines employment interviews from a relational communication perspective, especially the influence that the applicant's "impression management tactics" have on the interviewer's communication.

567. Kalaja, Paula M. "Service Encounters: Towards Successful Negotiations from the Perspective of Customers." *DAI* 50 (May 1990): 3570A.

    Shows that linguistics can be applied to solve everyday communication problems in the service setting of airline companies.

568. Kanetkar, Vinay. "The Effects of Television Advertising on Consumer Price Sensitivity: An Investigation of Frequently Purchased Products." *DAI* 50 (June 1990): 4019A.

    Studies whether household price sensitivity increases or decreases as the number of exposures to television advertising increases.

569. Keller, Merily H., Susan Combs, Danee Crouch, and Kay Sharp. "Hungry for Communication and Change." *PC* 10 (Winter 1990): 20–21, 24.

    Reports on a two-week Texas/Soviet Women's Summit involving a 15-member delegation. Discusses Soviet journalism, advertising, and women's issues.

570. Kim, Young Ho. "Public Diplomacy and Cultural Communication: The International Visitor Program." *DAI* 51 (November 1990): 1769A.

    Examines the communicative processes of Korean journalists, analyzing their attitude changes and communication functions during visits to the U.S.

571. Kreshel, Peggy Jean. "Toward a Cultural History of Advertising Research: A Case Study of J. Walter Thompson, 1908–1925." *DAI* 50 (January 1990): 2202A.

    Challenges the "common lore" explanation that research emerged during the Great Depression in an effort to bring rationality to an uncertain marketplace.

572. Lang, James L. "Commentary: Question Your Assumptions." *JTWC* 20 (1990): 321–323.

    Argues that technical writers' sensitivity to assumptions, overt or implied, is the key to their ability to convey difficult concepts clearly.

573. Lay, Mary M., and William M. Karis, eds. *Collaborative Writing in Industry: Investigations in Theory and Practice*. Amityville, N.Y.: Baywood, 1990. 286 pages

    Twelve essays study the benefits of and obstacles to collaborative writing, examine case studies of collaboration in industry, discuss strategies that enable students to collaborate effectively, and articulate current industry concerns about gathering, verifying, and editing information.

574. Lenowitz, Joan. "The Information Content of Dividends and the Precision of Prior Beliefs." *DAI* 50 (February 1990): 2593A.

Examines the "information effect" as an explanation for the market's response to dividend announcements.

575. Lunsford, Andrea A., and Lisa Ede. "Rhetoric in a New Key: Women and Collaboration." *RR* 8 (Spring 1990): 234–241.

Examines collaborative writing in the business and professional worlds. Explains differences between hierarchical and dialogic modes and discusses sociological and pedagogical antipathy.

576. Manning, Alan D. "Abstracts in Relation to Larger and Smaller Discourse Structures." *JTWC* 20 (1990): 369–390.

Argues that "problematic properties of abstracts can be explained in terms of the general discourse contrast between general and specific information."

577. McCathrin, Zoe. "Small Group Meetings." *PC* 10 (Spring 1990): 6–7, 10.

Suggests ways to improve corporate communications and increase productivity by introducing interactive programs for employees and supervisors. Offers guidelines for successful group leadership.

578. McIsaac, Claudia Monpere, and Mary Ann Aschauer. "Proposal Writing at Atherton Jordan, Inc." *MCQ* 3 (May 1990): 527–560.

Analyzes the proposal-writing strategies of seven engineers at a firm that does government work. Considers the methods the organization uses to facilitate collaborative writing.

579. McKenzie, Susan. "Operation Just Cause and the War with Words." *PC* 10 (Summer 1990): 16–17.

Describes the author's work for the U.S. Army's Fourth Psychological Operations Group, which produced propaganda supporting the American invasion of Panama.

580. Mehta, Abhilasha. "Celebrity Advertising: A Cognitive Response Approach." *DAI* 51 (October 1990): 1311A.

Studies the effectiveness of celebrity advertisements by using the elaboration likelihood model and a repeated-measures experimental design.

581. Michel, Susan L. "Writing and Learning to Write in a Bicultural, Corporate Setting." *DAI* 51 (August 1990): 399A.

A discourse-based study of the rhetorical choices writers make in business communication, especially in addressing the audience. Suggests that writers also consider the culture-specific preferences of their readers.

582. Mikulecky, Larry. "Basic Skills Impediments to Communication between Management and Hourly Employees." *MCQ* 3 (May 1990): 452–473.

Argues that designing a variety of training programs will help workers of various literacy levels to comprehend communications.

583. Miller, Katherine I., Beth Hartman Ellis, Eric G. Zook, and Judith S. Lyles. "An Integrated Model of Communication, Stress, and Burnout in the Workplace." *ComR* 17 (June 1990): 300–326.

Results show that social support and participation in decision making have an impact on perceived workplace stress, burnout, satisfaction, and commitment.

584. Mirel, Barbara. "Expanding the Activities of In-House Manual Writers." *MCQ* 3 (May 1990): 496–526.

In-house writers must use two strategies to produce manuals, conducting audience analysis and acting as liaisons in their work places.

585. Mualla, Naji D. Saleh. "Message Variation and Source Credibility in Advertising." *DAI* 51 (October 1990): 1311A.

Examines empirical research on the effects of source credibility and message variation on persuasive communication.

586. Mynatt, Patricia Graff. "The Information Content of Financial Statement Releases." *DAI* 50 (February 1990): 2558A.

Investigates the conditions under which releasing annual financial statements conveys new information useful to investors.

587. Nik Yacob, Nik Rahimah. "An Empirical Examination of Product Symbolism from an Ethnic Subcultural Perspective." *DAI* 51 (October 1990): 1311A.

Identifies and assesses determinants of product symbolism and creates a model for cross-cultural interactions in information processing.

588. North, Ernest John. "Multistep Research on Children in Advertising." *DAI* 50 (January 1990): 2160A.

Investigates the portrayal of children as models in magazine and television advertisements.

589. Northey, Margot. "The Need for Writing Skill in Accounting Firms." *MCQ* 3 (May 1990): 474–495.

Explores the kinds of writing that professional accountants do and discusses the extent to which firms encourage good writing.

590. Papa, Michael J., and Wendy H. Papa. "Perceptual and Communicative Indices of Employee Performance with New Technology." *WJSC* 54 (Winter 1990): 21–41.

A field study assessing why five perceptual attributes of a new technology and three types of messages should affect productivity with that technology.

591. Peltier, James Warren. "The Effects of Schema-Congruent and Schema-Incongruent Character Usage in Advertisements on Processing and Memory." *DAI* 51 (November 1990): 1691A.

Used free recall, aided recall, and recognition tests to explore the effect of context on memory for characters, products, brands, and claims in magazine advertisements.

592. Porter, Lynnette Raye. "Technical Writing with Computers: A Study of the Documentation-Production Process of Technical Com-

municators in Industry." *DAI* 50 (February 1990): 2285A.

Describes the composing processes of 16 technical writers in three manufacturing companies. Suggests ways technical writing teachers can use computers to "develop a computerized text-creation process."

593. Rich, Steven Paul. "Corporate Investment Announcements and Informational Asymmetries: An Empirical Study." *DAI* 50 (January 1990): 2145A.

Examines the impact of capital spending announcements on stock prices.

594. Rogers, Priscilla S. "A Taxonomy for the Composition of Memorandum Subject Lines: Facilitating Writer Choice in Managerial Contexts." *JBTC* 4 (September 1990): 21–43.

An analysis of 483 items indicates that subject lines in memos are typically "neutral" but alternatively "directed."

595. Russman, Linda deLaubenfels. "The Real Reason Women Leave Corporations." *PC* 10 (Summer 1990): 20, 27.

An 18-month survey of 100 professionals suggests that the reason for high turnover rates among professional women is the search for career growth opportunities.

596. Russman, Linda deLaubenfels. "WICI Job and Salary Survey Results." *PC* 10 (Spring 1990): 18–21.

Reports the results of a survey of more than 2500 full-time professional women communicators.

597. Schaper, Norvin Henry. "A Survey of the Use of Oral Communication Skills in Meetings by High-Level Executives." *DAI* 50 (May 1990): 3661A.

Suggests that executives can improve their meetings with enhanced oral communication skills.

598. Schlueter, David W., J. Kevin Barge, and Diana Blankenship. "A Comparative Analysis of Influence Strategies Used by Upper- and

Lower-Level Male and Female Managers."
WJSC 54 (Winter 1990): 42–65.

Assesses whether structure, socialization, or some combination of strategies accounts best for the relationships among gender, power, and influence.

599. Seyyed, Fazal Jawad. "Information Content of Bond Ratings." *DAI* 50 (January 1990): 2136A.

Attempts to ascertain the information content of bond ratings.

600. Shuy, Roger W., and David G. Robinson. "The Oral Language Process in Writing: A Real-Life Writing Session." *RTE* 24 (February 1990): 88–108.

Analyzes a collaborative business writing session involving a male executive, his secretary, and a male state official.

601. Sivaramakrishnan, Konduru. "Information Content of Earnings Components, Reporting Choice, and Long-Term Contracts." *DAI* 50 (February 1990): 2559A.

Investigates the role of financial reports in performance evaluation.

602. Spotts, Harlan Earl. "An Investigation into the Impact of Human Age on Persuasion and Advertising." *DAI* 51 (December 1990): 2099A.

Examines differences between elderly and young adults in information processing recall and the response to advertising copy.

603. Strong, James Thomas. "Threat Appeals in Marketing and Mass Communication: A Theoretical Framework and Empirical Findings." *DAI* 51 (September 1990): 934A.

Provides a conceptual framework for studying appeals to fear and describes the persuasive impact of five increasingly threatening advertisements on beliefs, attitudes, and intentions about buying sunscreens.

604. Tang, Michael Tzung-I. "A Study of Managers' Perceptions of the Effectiveness of Computer Graphics in Small Businesses." *DAI* 51 (September 1990): 930A.

Finds a significant relationship between demographic variables and the perceived effectiveness of computer graphics. No relationship is found between their effectiveness and the task, software, or environment.

605. Taylor, Paul S. "The Language of Business Interviewing: A Study in Cross-Cultural Communication." *DAI* 51 (October 1990): 1216A.

Analyzes the differences in language use among English, French, and West German native speakers. Treats cultural determination in business interviews.

606. Twomey, Cordelia Ryan. "Word Processing and the Office, 1964–1987: A Thematic Analysis." *DAI* 50 (March 1990): 2760A.

Examines the history of word processing in the business office.

607. Weiss, Edmond H. "Visualizing a Procedure with Nassi-Schneiderman Charts." *JTWC* 20 (1990): 237–254.

Argues that using Nassi-Schneiderman charts "to diagram human procedures eliminates prose ambiguities and provides most of the advantage of decision tables and trees."

608. Whalen, Susan A. "The Institutionalization of Relations of Power through Practices of Speech: A Theoretical Inquiry." *DAI* 51 (December 1990): 1832A.

Examines oral histories of laborers in the United Steelworkers of America, especially their descriptions of the grievance process.

609. Winegarden, Alan D. "A Burkean Analysis of the 1982 and 1986 Tylenol Poisoning Tragedies." *DAI* 50 (January 1990): 1850A.

Uses Burke's dramatistic analysis of human motives to examine corporate crisis communication.

610. Woodhouse, Linda. "Equipping Ourselves for the Knowledge Society." *PC* 10
(Summer 1990): 12–13, 22.

> Discusses the growing need for a better
> educated workforce and the decline of ba-
> sic skills among entry-level workers.

611. Young, Richard O. "Cognitive Processes
in Argumentation: An Exploratory Study of
Management Consulting Expertise." *DAI* 50
(February 1990): 3764B.

> Examines problem-solving operators and
> rhetorical impact in statements by experts
> and novices. The expert argues rhetori-
> cally, winning client agreement.

612. Zachlod, Craig Edward. "Theory and
Practice in the Selection and Education of
U.S. Managers for Overseas Assignment: A
Study in Communicative Competence and the
Organizational Experience of Overseas Per-
sonnel." *DAI* 51 (November 1990): 1534A.

> Questions appropriate practice in light of
> new organizational theories that emphasize
> people and their language as the essence of
> organizations.

See also 94, 279, 427, 436, 443, 890, 941,
1020, 1043, 1058

2.6 LITERATURE, FILM, AND THEATER

613. Akers, Stanley W. "The Role of Rhetoric
in American Cinema in the U.S. Intervention-
ist Movement, 1936–1945." *DAI* 51 (December 1990): 1481A.

> Analyzes speeches, films, and government
> documentaries to examine their roles in
> shifting policy.

614. Ashley, Kathleen M. *Victor Turner and
the Construction of Cultural Criticism: Between Literature and Anthropology.* Bloomington, Ind.: Indiana University Press, 1990.
224 pages

> Eleven essays examine anthropologist
> Turner's concepts and their implications

for studying a variety of texts and critical
practices.

615. Baker, William. "Recent Work on Critical
Theory." *Style* 24 (Winter 1990): 564–583.

> Reviews 93 recent essays on semiotics,
> narratology, rhetoric, and language sys-
> tems; structuralism and deconstruction;
> feminism; psychoanalytic criticism; histor-
> ical criticism; postmodernism; reader re-
> sponse; and phenomenology.

616. Beeman, Susan E. " 'Nothing Goes by
Luck in Composition . . . The Best You Can
Write Will Be the Best You Are': Style and
Structure in Thoreau." *DAI* 51 (December
1990): 2015A.

> Argues for four stylistic techniques in *Wal-
> den* and in two historical essays. These
> techniques create a structure fulfilling Tho-
> reau's literary aim of transcendence.

617. Bender, Daniel Robert. "Singing High and
Low: Shakespearean Comedy and the Rhetoric of Variety." *DAI* 51 (November 1990):
1617A.

> Emerging from the humanist emphasis on
> deliberation, choice, and character devel-
> opment, Shakespeare's stage characters
> function to stimulate the audience to exer-
> cise powers of prudent choice.

618. Benjamin, Helen Spencer. "The Aristotelian Tradition in the Novels of Alice Walker:
A Contemporary Application of the Five Canons." *DAI* 51 (September 1990): 847A.

> In the three novels studied, Aristotelian
> persuasion informs Walker's descriptions
> of African-American women.

619. Bensel-Myers, Linda. "Empowering the
Audience: The Rhetorical Poetics of Renaissance Drama." *Style* 23 (Winter 1989): 70–
86.

> When we read Renaissance drama, espe-
> cially Shakespeare's plays, as a cultural
> artifact, we view the plays as products of
> humanist rhetoric and discover the drama-
> tists' ethical purposes.

620. Bergonzi, Bernard. *Exploding English: Criticism, Theory, Culture*. New York: Oxford University Press, 1990. 240 pages

Examines the state of contemporary English studies, discussing changes and developments in the U.S. and England since 1959.

621. Bialostosky, Don H. "Dialogics, Narratology, and the Virtual Space of Discourse." *JNT* 19 (Winter 1989): 167–173.

Discusses the dialogic nature of discourse regarding the discipline of narratology. Focuses on Gerald Prince, Shlomith Rimmon-Kenan, Michael Holquist, and W. J. T. Mitchell.

622. Bineham, Jeffery L. "Pedagogical Justification for a Theory-Method Distinction in Rhetorical Criticism." *ComEd* 39 (January 1990): 30–45.

Stresses practical criticism over theory. Illustrates the approach by using Burke's pentad to study motive in Francis Schaeffer's *A Christian Manifesto*.

623. Blaeser, Kimberly M. "Gerald Vizenor: Writing in the Oral Tradition." *DAI* 51 (September 1990): 849A.

Argues that Vizenor's writing includes techniques of Native American literature and reader-response aesthetics.

624. Blake, Robert W., ed. *Reading, Writing, and Interpreting Literature: Pedagogy, Positions, and Research*. New York State English Council Monographs. Schenectady, N.Y.: New York State English Council (distributed by NCTE), 1989. 244 pages

Eighteen essays explore the roles that different skills play in students' formation of meanings in literature. Areas studied include hearing and oral literature, reading and the ability to print, critical analyses and creative writing, and various interpretative stances toward literature.

625. Blumenthal, Anna Sabol. "The Ambivalence of Stance in Edward Arlington Rob-

inson's Early Poems and Letters." *Style* 23 (Winter 1989): 87–112.

Robinson's oblique style in early letters and poems helps him come to terms with the relationship of the individual to the surrounding community.

626. Bonnefoy, Yves. "Lifting Our Eyes from the Page." *CritI* 16 (Summer 1990): 794–806.

An article translated by John Naughton argues that reading is a temporal experience, not an escape from time. Interruption is the key reading experience because it acknowledges the reader's own life.

627. Britton, Bruce K., and A. D. Pellegrini, eds. *Narrative Thought and Narrative Language*. Hillsdale, N.J.: Erlbaum and the University of Georgia Cognitive Studies Group and Institute for Behavioral Research, 1990. 296 pages

Ten essays describe empirical investigations into the relationship between stories and cognition. Philosophical, linguistic, anthropological, and psychological perspectives on narratives are used as a mirror to human cognition.

628. Brooke-Rose, Christine. "Whatever Happened to Narratology?" *PT* 11 (Summer 1990): 283–293.

Answers that narratology, which purports to explain texts by naming their structures, is simply another narrative, a postmodern text, a rhetoric characteristic of its time.

629. Brummett, Barry. "How to Propose a Discourse: A Reply to Rowland [*ComS* 41 (Summer 1990)]." *ComS* 41 (Summer 1990): 128–135.

Discusses the creative use of categories. Assesses and critiques Rowland's categorization of mythic discourse and his attempt to guide mythic criticism.

630. Burrison, John A., ed. *Storytellers: Folktales and Legends from the South*. Athens, Ga.: University of Georgia Press, 1990. 384 pages

Selected tales from more than 20 years of recorded interviews conducted in the lower Southeast by folklore students. Brings together stories told in voices of African-American, Anglo-Saxon, and Native American descent.

631. Butler, Susan Lowell. "What Do Women Really Want?" *PC* 10 (Fall 1990): 12–13.

Sara Paretsky, mystery novelist and creator of female private investigator V. I. Warshawski, discusses her work, her women readers, and portrayals of women in mysteries today.

632. Campbell, Andrew S. "A Dramatistic Analysis of John Grierson's Rhetoric in the British Documentary Film Movement, 1929–1939." *DAI* 50 (February 1990): 2300A.

Uses Burke's concept of symbolic action to examine Grierson's notion of a "public-servant cinema" stimulating social action.

633. Carlson, Marvin. *Theatre Semiotics: Signs of Life*. Bloomington, Ind.: Indiana University Press, 1990. 144 pages

Studies how theater signs are produced and how they are received and interpreted by audiences.

634. Chatman, Seymour. "What Can We Learn from Contextualist Narratology?" *PT* 11 (Summer 1990): 309–328.

Argues that contextualist narratology's orientation toward act rather than structure is misguided in embracing Labov's sociolinguistic models but helpful in its borrowings from Grice.

635. Christensen, Jerome. "From Rhetoric to Corporate Populism: A Romantic Critique of the Academy in an Age of High Gossip." *CritI* 16 (Winter 1990): 438–465.

Literary criticism tells us most about our everyday professional practice. Discusses Paul De Man's anti-Semitic writings.

636. Clifford, John, ed. *The Experience of Reading: Louise Rosenblatt and Reader-Response Theory*. Portsmouth, N.H.: Boynton/Cook, 1990. 232 pages

Thirteen essays by current reader-response theorists explore Rosenblatt's work, discussing the contemporary implications of her study, *Literature as Exploration* (1938).

637. Cohn, Dorrit. "Fictional Versus Historical Lives: Borderlines and Borderline Cases." *JNT* 19 (Winter 1989): 3–24.

Examines relationships between history and fiction and between first-person and third-person narratives. Argues that biography is the common ground between fiction and history.

638. Corrigan, Elena. "Patterns of Communication in Poetry: The Theoretical Work of Osip Madel'stam and T. S. Eliot." *DAI* 51 (October 1990): 1220A.

Discusses the theoretical debate about what is communicated in poetry.

639. Crowley, Sharon. "Jacques Derrida on Teaching and Rhetoric: A Response [to Olson, *JAC* 10 (1990)]." *JAC* 10 (1990): 393–396.

"The advantage of deconstruction is that it permits us to oppose tradition to its suppressed alternatives" and thus generate others.

640. Curtis, Paul Marion. "Rhetorical Indirection and the Self in the Poetry of Lord Byron." *DAI* 51 (October 1990): 1044A.

Examines narrative progression in Byron and discusses how the concept of self disrupts the linear sequence in the narrative in order to create knowledge.

641. Cutrofello, Andrew Fred. "Hegel and Derrida's Conceptions of Textual Interpretation." *DAI* 50 (February 1990): 2518A.

Argues that texts are equivocal for both Hegel and Derrida but that Hegel presents a more promising account of communication.

642. Damon, Maria. "Tell Them about Us." *CCrit* 14 (Winter 1989–1990): 231–257.

Focuses on poems written by three female GED students from South Boston. Reads them as artifacts of subversion and resistance.

643. Davis, Emory. "An Interview with Amy Tan: Fiction—'The Beast That Roams.' " *WE* 1 (Spring 1990): 96–111.

Tan discusses teaching writing, her writing process, and her own work.

644. Eco, Umberto. *The Limits of Interpretation.* Advances in Semiotics. Bloomington, Ind.: Indiana University Press, 1990. 256 pages

Theoretical essays on the problem of limiting the interpreter's domination of texts.

645. Edwards, Barry Michael. "Wordsworth's Preface to *Lyrical Ballads,* M. H. Abrams' *The Mirror and the Lamp,* and the Question of Rhetoric." *DAI* 50 (March 1990): 2905A.

Argues that the dominant ideology underpinning the Preface is rhetorically rooted.

646. Edwards, Lee R. "Schizophrenic Narrative." *JNT* 19 (Winter 1989): 25–30.

Distinguishes between schizophrenia in narrative and schizophrenia as narrative. Analyzes schizophrenic narrative and its relationship to contemporary critical theory.

647. Elsky, Martin. *Authorizing Words: Speech, Writing, and Print in the English Renaissance.* Ithaca, N.Y.: Cornell University Press, 1989. 232 pages

Discusses the impact of linguistic theory on textual practice in English Renaissance writing, especially in the work of Bacon, Burton, and Herbert.

648. Enright, D. J. *Fields of Vision: Essays on Literature, Language, and Television.* New York: Oxford University Press, 1988. 256 pages

A collection of cultural essays covering literature, language, and television. Includes notes on usage, etymologies, and misappropriations.

649. Farquhar, Dion N. "The Novel as Political Theory." *DAI* 51 (August 1990): 625A.

Argues, from a Marxist, feminist, deconstructionist view of politics, that fiction is an ignored and resisted but effective medium for expanding political theory.

650. Farrell, Kathleen L. "Literary Integrity and Political Action: The Public Argument of James T. Farrell." *DAI* 50 (February 1990): 2301A.

Examines Farrell's role as an advocate of literary independence during the controversies between political radicals and American writers in the 1930s.

651. Foley, Barbara. "Subversion and Oppositionality in the Academy." *CollL* 17 (June–October 1990): 64–79.

Explores the "rhetoric of subversion" and "the implications this rhetoric carries for a politically oppositional practice in the academy."

652. Foss, Sonja K. *Rhetorical Criticism: Exploration and Practice.* Prospect Heights, Ill.: Waveland Press, 1989. 420 pages

Ten chapters offer a theoretical foundation for rhetorical criticism, a guide to constructing and writing critical studies, and a survey of critical methodologies for conducting rhetorical analyses of film and visual art as well as speeches and other discourses.

653. Gabler-Hover, Janet. *Truth in American Fiction: The Legacy of Rhetorical Idealism.* Athens, Ga.: University of Georgia Press, 1990. 320 pages

Addresses a nineteenth-century belief in rhetorical idealism, the truth-telling power of language, by examining works by Hawthorne, Twain, James, Melville, and Brown. Challenges deconstructionism on the open-endedness of texts and argues that nineteenth-century American novels often invite readings that offer closure.

654. Gergen, Kenneth J. "Textual Considerations in the Scientific Construction of Human Character." *Style* 24 (Fall 1990): 365–379.

Suggests that the attempts by scientific psychologists to reconstruct human character require the same type of literary technique critics use to interpret literary character.

655. German, Kathleen M. "Frank Capra's *Why We Fight* Series and the American Audience." *WJSC* 54 (Spring 1990): 237–248.

Analyzes Capra's portrayal of fundamental American values through the visual contrast techniques of parallel editing and deep focus.

656. Gerrig, Richard J., and David W. Allbritton. "The Construction of Literary Characters: A View from Cognitive Psychology." *Style* 24 (Fall 1990): 380–391.

Uses Ian Fleming's James Bond novels to examine the cognitive processes readers use to analyze literary events and characters.

657. Giroux, Henry A. "Rethinking the Boundaries of Educational Discourse: Modernism, Postmodernism, and Feminism." *CollL* 17 (June–October 1990): 1–50.

Introduces "some of the central assumptions that govern the discourses of modernism, postmodernism, and postmodern feminism" and discusses their impact upon pedagogy.

658. Glynn, Marie. "Corneille: Within and beyond Rhetoric." *DAI* 51 (December 1990): 2036A.

Argues that history, society, and politics are inseparable from a hermeneutical approach in Corneille's *Le Cid, Cinna,* and *Nicomede.*

659. Goldberg, Jonathan. *Writing Matter: From the Hands of the English Renaissance.* Stanford, Calif.: Stanford University Press, 1990. 349 pages

Discusses literacy and the material act of writing in the Elizabethan era.

660. Goodwin, Donald W. *Alcohol and the Writer.* New York: Penguin, 1990. 208 pages

Examines connections between alcohol and creativity in the work of Faulkner, Fitzgerald, Hemingway, Lowry, O'Neill, Poe, Simenon, and Steinbeck.

661. Graham, Kenneth J. E. "The Performance of Conviction: Wyatt's Antirhetorical Plainness." *Style* 23 (Fall 1989): 374–394.

Examines Wyatt's stylistic plainness as emblematic of his desire for "trouth" and his reaction against rhetorical skepticism.

662. Graham, Robert J. "Literary Theory and Curriculum: Rethinking Theory and Practice in English Studies." *EQ* 22 (1990): 20–29.

Explores the relationship between literary theory and curriculum practice.

663. Green, Shelly Rae. "Radical Juxtaposition: The Films of Yvonne Rainer." *DAI* 51 (September 1990): 661A.

Examines Rainer's techniques, including the use of disjunctive language, speech, repetition, and interrelated texts.

664. Grunst, Robert Charles. "Faraway Business: Stories and Essays about Problematics in Storytelling." *DAI* 50 (May 1990): 3588A.

A selection of stories with commentaries and an analysis of how storytellers manipulate language.

665. Gutierrez, Nancy. "*Beware the Cat:* Mimesis in a Skin of Oratory." *Style* 23 (Winter 1989): 46–69.

William Baldwin's *Beware the Cat* is a declamation through dialogue, an interdependent communicative activity between the author, audience, and text, which creates a moral reader.

666. Halion, Kevin Joseph. "Speech-Act Theory and Deconstruction: A Defence of the Distinction between Normal and Parasitic Speech Acts." *DAI* 50 (May 1990): 3619A.

Argues that speech-act theory does not account for metaphorical uses and fictional promises of language.

667. Hamilton, Donna B. "Defiguring Virgil in *The Tempest*." *Style* 23 (Fall 1989): 352–373.

Claims that traditional source studies are inadequate for Shakespearean texts. Demonstrates a different method with *The Tempest*, showing its relation to the *Aeneid* in terms of *imitatio*.

668. Haney, David P. "Catachresis and the Romantic Will: The Imagination's Usurpation in Wordsworth's *Prelude* Book 6." *Style* 23 (Winter 1989): 16–31.

In the apostrophe to "Imagination," in *The Prelude* Book 6, the trope of catachresis reveals the paradoxical connection between imagination and loss.

669. Henkel, Jacqueline. "Linguistic Models and Recent Criticism: Transformational-Generative Grammar as Literary Metaphor." *PMLA* 105 (May 1990): 448–463.

Describes the recent history of critical theories rooted in linguistics.

670. Hewett, Gregory G. "A Rhetoric of Androgyny: The Composition, Teaching, and Ethics of Gender." *DAI* 50 (February 1990): 2476A.

Studies texts from Plato to Kristeva to promote androgyny as a unifying subject and as the overriding metaphor for composition, teaching, and ethics.

671. Hobbs, Jerry R. *Literature and Cognition*. Center for the Study of Language and Information Lecture Notes. Stanford, Calif.: Center for the Study of Language and Information (distributed by University of Chicago Press), 1990. 180 pages

Because literature is discourse, a cognitive analysis of discourse can be applied to it. Presents a theory of discourse interpretation and metaphor interpretation.

672. Hoffman, Nicole Tonkovich. "Scribbling, Writing, Author(iz)ing: Nineteenth-Century Women Writers." *DAI* 51 (November 1990): 1613A.

Discusses the importance in an author's development of family and class, education in "writerly conventions," reviewers and editors, and the author's response to social boundaries.

673. Holt, Sandra Waters. "A Rhetorical Analysis of Three Feminist Themes Found in the Novels of Toni Morrison, Alice Walker, and Gloria Naylor." *DAI* 50 (April 1990): 3224A.

Applies an Aristotelian theory of modes of proof and types of discourse to the novels. Identifies the authors' target audiences.

674. Horne, Dee Alyson. "The Role of the Journal in the Writing of Virginia Woolf, Elizabeth Smart, and Sylvia Plath." *DAI* 51 (October 1990): 1225A.

Examines the role of journal writing in the works of three women authors. A concluding chapter analyzes how the creative writing process for these and other women differs from that of men.

675. Huffer, Lynn R. "The (En)Gendered Text: Collette and the Problems of Writing." *DAI* 50 (January 1990): 2078A.

Centers on Collette's narrative strategies, outlining the theoretical implications her work raises for women's writing in general.

676. Hughes, Helen Muriel. "Changes in Historical Romance, 1890s to the 1980s: The Development of the Genre from Stanley Weyman to Georgette Heyer and Her Successors." *DAI* 50 (May 1990): 3603A.

Discusses the changing functions of historical romance by analyzing a range of authors.

677. Jeffrys, Mark Edwin. "T. S. Eliot's *Athenaeum* Reviews: Rhetoric, Drama, and the Critical Point of View." *DAI* 51 (November 1990): 1620A.

Examines how Eliot's literary dicta meshed with his rhetorical strategies for establishing literary authority.

678. Johns, Donald. "An Interview with Gary Snyder: 'Language Is Wild.' " *WE* 2 (Fall 1990): 100–112.

Snyder discusses his own writing, his teaching career, and the connections between writing and the oral tradition.

679. Johnstone, Barbara. *Stories, Community, and Place: Narratives from Middle America.* Bloomington, Ind.: Indiana University Press, 1990. 192 pages

An ethnographic study of the uses of narrative to create, perpetuate, and manipulate social roles and relations.

680. Kahn, Lorraine Susan. "Cinematic Collaborations: Production System and Film Structure in Documentary." *DAI* 51 (December 1990): 1809A.

Suggests that the collaborative nature of filmmaking shapes the film-text and the experiences of spectators.

681. Kahn, Victoria. "Habermas, Machiavelli, and the Humanist Critique of Ideology." *PMLA* 105 (May 1990): 464–476.

Describes the rhetorical turn in literary theory in terms of the critique of ideology developed in the humanist tradition.

682. Kayes, Jamie Barlowe. "Reading against the Grain: The Power and Limits of Feminist Criticism of American Narratives." *JNT* 19 (Winter 1989): 130–140.

Compares the ideological principles, theoretical views, and agendas of Judith Fetterly, Nina Baym, and Jane Tompkins.

683. Kegl, Rosemary. "The Rhetoric of Concealment: Figuring Gender and Class in Renaissance Literature." *DAI* 50 (March 1990): 2908A.

Analyzes selected works of George Puttenham, Philip Sidney, and Andrew Marvell and discusses the "recurrent rhetorical gesture's" participation in struggles over class and gender.

684. Kirstj-Gundersen, Karoline Paula. "Walter Benjamin's Theory of Narrative." *DAI* 50 (May 1990): 3608A.

Investigates Benjamin's theory of the narrative and his defamiliarization effect.

685. Knapp, John V. "Self-Preservation and Self-Transformation: Interdisciplinary Approaches to Literary Character." *Style* 24 (Fall 1990): 349–364.

Argues that critics have focused too much on Freud, ignoring the possible contributions of mainstream psychology to the analysis of literary character.

686. Kochhar-Lindgren, Gray Meredith. "Narcissus Transformed: Textuality and the Self in Psychoanalysis and Literature." *DAI* 51 (November 1990): 1608A.

Using the myth of Narcissus, considers how the self is written and whether it might be transformed by rewriting itself in the context of otherness.

687. Kwok, Wai-Leung. "The Laws of Reading: Rhetoric in the Age of Revolutions: A Study of the Relationships between Reading, History, and Institutions in the Writings of John Locke, Joseph Addison, Edmund Burke, and William Wordsworth." *DAI* 51 (December 1990): 2025A.

Examines four authors' perceptions of reading as possible ways to confront the institutional and historical grounds of being.

688. Lamarque, Peter. "Reasoning to What Is True in Fiction." *Arg* 4 (August 1990): 333–346.

Critiques David Lewis' "Truth in Fiction." Narrative requires readers to construe rather than simply accept meaning; thus, truth in fiction is relative to an interpretation.

689. Langford, Larry L. "The Ethics of Mimesis: Postmodernism and the Possibility of History." *DAI* 50 (June 1990): 3947A.

Suggests that representations of the past are literary re-creations, as much the projection or transference of desire as they are objective description and analysis.

690. Law, Marita. "*Piers Plowman:* The Influence and the Effects of Sermon Structure and

Rhetoric in the B Text." *DAI* 51 (October 1990): 1223A.

Compares the structure of *Piers Plowman* with sermon structures.

691. Leckie, Ross Creighton. "A New Knowledge of Reality: Wallace Stevens' Use of Metaphor and Syntax as Modes of Perception." *DAI* 51 (October 1990): 1403A.

Argues that Stevens' poetry used techniques that allowed him to posit a central metaphorical landscape and simultaneously to undermine it as a transitory, dependent mode of experience.

692. Long, David Andrew. "Authorial Politics: Poe and the Conservative *Ethos* in Antebellum American Culture." *DAI* 50 (June 1990): 3954A.

Places Poe among his contemporaries as magazine authors seeking to control the social and psychological problem of the mob through conservative paradigms of union.

693. Manduzik, Roseann Marie. "History in Our Own Language: The Rhetorical Functions of Women's Documentary Film for the Contemporary Women's Movement." *DAI* 51 (August 1990): 344A.

Studies the rhetorical effectiveness and rhetorical strategies of 12 documentary films made by women, categorizing the films as imagistic, experiential, and argumentative.

694. Margolin, Uri. "The What, the When, and the How of Being a Character in Literary Narrative." *Style* 24 (Fall 1990): 453–468.

Argues that literary character is determined by theory. Examines three varieties of literary character in current poetics: the synthetic, thematic, and mimetic.

695. McNichols, Melvin D., and Margaret Enright Wye. "A Discussion with Jacques Derrida." *WI* 9 (Fall 1989–Winter 1990): 7–18.

"An edited transcript of a discussion held in April 1989 at the University of Southern California between Derrida and a group of students and professors."

696. Mead, Dana Gulling. "From *Topoi* to Dialectic: The Progression of Invention Techniques in the Poetry of William Blake." *DAI* 50 (March 1990): 2909A.

Surveys possible rhetorics in Blake's thinking and relevant criticism of Blake's works.

697. Mead, Gerald. "The Representation of Fictional Character." *Style* 24 (Fall 1990): 440–452.

Uses a "representational stylistics" to explain why we recognize and understand fictional characters differently from how we understand real people.

698. Meeker, Robert G. "A Descriptive Analysis of the Kinds of Essays in Johnson's *Rambler*." *DAI* 51 (August 1990): 513A.

Argues that Johnson's own words may best categorize the kinds of essays he wrote.

699. Meyerson, Gregory Dean. "The Dialectic of Defeat: Domination and Liberation in Contemporary Critical Theory." *DAI* 50 (May 1990): 3620A.

Analyzes the work of major critical theorists of the last 30 years.

700. Miall, David S. "Education, Authority, and Literary Response: A New Model." *EQ* 22 (1990): 7–19.

Proposes a model for the structure of literary response that clarifies the spheres of authority of both teacher and student.

701. Moore, Gerian Steven. "Modes of Black Discourse in the Narrative and Structure of James Baldwin's Fiction." *DAI* 50 (March 1990): 2952A.

Offers a theoretical framework and method of analysis for addressing Baldwin's fiction.

702. Moran, Charles, and Elizabeth F. Penfield. *Conversations: Contemporary Critical*

Theory and the Teaching of Literature. Urbana, Ill.: NCTE, 1990. 237 pages

Explores alternative approaches to literary criticism. Includes teachers' reactions to recent theoretical developments and their thoughts on connecting theory and practice in their classrooms.

703. Mowat, Barbara A. " 'A Local Habitation and a Name': Shakespeare's Text as Construct." *Style* 23 (Fall 1989): 335–351.

Argues against earlier critics' portrayal of Shakespeare as highly original in his poetic and rhetorical invention by tracing the character Theseus through other works.

704. Murray, Joel K. "How to Stop Writing: In Search of Heterotopia." Paper presented at the SCA meeting, San Francisco, November 1989. ERIC ED 313 704. 13 pages

Speculates about the writing processes of playwrights.

705. Myers, Stephen Wilson. "Yeats' Book of the Nineties: Poetry, Politics, and Rhetoric." *DAI* 51 (December 1990): 2027A.

Traces Yeats' theories of poetry, politics, and occultism in his early poetry, a prelude to the "political propaganda" of the 1890s.

706. Neel, Jasper. " 'Where Have You Come from, Reb Derissa, and Where Are You Going?': Gary Olson's Interview with Jacques Derrida [*JAC* 10 (1990)]." *JAC* 10 (1990): 387–392.

Despite what Derrida says, we cannot just let deconstruction happen because it implies and demands a certain fundamentalism.

707. Neverow-Turk, Vara Suzanka. "The Diacritics of Desire: Virginia Woolf and the Rhetoric of Modernism and Feminism." *DAI* 50 (March 1990): 2910A.

Analyzes Woolf's rhetoric as a vehicle for expressing modernist and feminist ideas.

708. Novak, Matthew S. "Sir Joshua Reynolds and Composition Theory: The Value of the

Discourses for the Modern Professional Writer." *DAI* 50 (June 1990): 3963A.

Explores Reynold's technical approach to communicating artistic theory as an interdisciplinary and timeless one because the process of creation is alike for all the arts.

709. Olson, Gary A. "Jacques Derrida on Rhetoric and Composition: A Conversation." *JAC* 10 (1990): 1–21.

Derrida supports the literary canon, respect for tradition, and reading for authorial intent before deconstructing. He wishes to guard against "rhetoricism."

710. Olson, Nadine Faye. "Decoding the Cultural Context: An Ethnographic and Sociolinguistic Analysis of Selected Spanish-Language Feature Films." *DAI* 50 (April 1990): 3172A.

Demonstrates how a systematic analysis of a film's content, themes, and linguistic and visual symbols illuminates many elements of the cultural context.

711. Osborn, Michael. "In Defense of Broad Mythic Criticism: A Reply to Rowland [*ComS* 41 (Summer 1990)]." *ComS* 41 (Summer 1990): 121–127.

Argues that too rigid an approach to mythic criticism may diminish the importance of the critical method and impoverish the perception of rhetorical artifacts.

712. Owens, Derek Vincent. "Resisting Writings (and the Boundaries of Composition)." *DAI* 50 (June 1990): 3938A.

Teachers and consequently students frequently interpret writing and literature from a restricted perspective, overlooking discourse methodologies from ethnic, feminist, third world, and contemporary communities.

713. Panzer, Mary Caroline. "Romantic Origins of American Realism: Photography, Arts, and Letters in Philadelphia, 1850–1875." *DAI* 50 (January 1990): 2121A.

Discusses changes in conventions that prepared audiences and artists to accept photographs as art.

714. Papoulis, Irene. "How 'Interpretation' Can Disempower Students: Learning from Susan Sontag." *CEAF* 20 (1990): 13–15.

A writing teacher is guided by "Against Interpretation" to help students avoid simplistic readings of essays in Bartholomae and Petrosky's *Ways of Reading*.

715. Payne, Paula H. "Tracing Aristotle's *Rhetoric* in Sir Philip Sidney's Poetry and Prose." *RSQ* 20 (Summer 1990): 241.

Examines Sidney's exposure to Aristotle, his use of Aristotelian concepts, and his "questionable" alignment with Ramus.

716. Pieschel, Bridget Smith. "The Rhetoric of Degeneration from Bradford to Cooper." *DAI* 50 (February 1990): 2489A.

Explores the rhetoric of "countertheology" as an expression of religious fears, enlightenment theories, and racial and familial prejudices.

717. Plantinga, Carl Rendit. "A Theory of Representation in the Documentary Film." *DAI* 51 (July 1990): 3A.

Argues that a documentary film is not a representation of reality but a rhetorical construct.

718. Poster, Mark. *The Mode of Information: Poststructuralisms and Contexts*. Chicago: University of Chicago Press, 1990. 200 pages

Explores the differences between electronic communications and ordinary speech and writing. Uses theoretical perspectives of Baudrillard, Foucault, Derrida, and Lyotard to open new interpretive strategies for critical social theory in relation to these differences.

719. Prince, Gerald. "On Narrative Studies and Narrative Genres." *PT* 11 (Summer 1990): 271–282.

Reviews previous work in narrative studies and proposes classes of features for identifying the potentially unlimited set of theoretical narrative genres.

720. Quigley, Michael Dennis. "'The Germ of the Common Cause': History, Rhetoric, and Ideology in the Essays of E. B. White." *DAI* 50 (March 1990): 2899A.

Examines rhetorical and artistic dimensions of White's essays, focusing on *ethos* and *logos*.

721. Quigley, Peter S. "The Ground of Resistance: Nature and Power in Emerson, Melville, Jeffers, and Snyder." *DAI* 51 (December 1990): 2020A.

Finds an opposition to logocentrism in Emerson, male usages of metaphor in Melville, and neofoundational, ecofeminine rhetoric in Jeffers and Snyder.

722. Reaume, Mary Ellen. "The Use of Rhetorical Figures and Tropes in Elizabethan and Jacobean Revenge Drama." *DAI* 51 (October 1990): 1241A.

Claims that, for the Elizabethan and Jacobean playwright, rhetoric is one means of implementing a vision of reality.

723. Rimmon-Kenan, Shlomith. "How the Model Neglects the Medium: Linguistics, Language, and the Crisis of Narratology." *JNT* 19 (Winter 1989): 157–166.

Examines why narratology has ceased to be a flourishing discipline.

724. Riquelme, J. P. "The Transformations of Romantic Tropes in T. S. Eliot's 'Rhapsody on a Windy Night.'" *Style* 23 (Winter 1989): 1–15.

In "Rhapsody on a Windy Night," Eliot twists Romantic tropes, challenges Romantic notions toward aesthetic creation, and presents writing as a disfiguring process.

725. Rowland, Robert C. "On a Limited Approach to Mythic Criticism: Rowland's Rejoinder [response to Brummett, Osborn, Rushing, and Solomon, *ComS* 41 (Summer 1990)]." *ComS* 41 (Summer 1990): 150–160.

Suggests that his definition of mythic criticism should allow the critic to distinguish the genuinely mythic from other narrative forms and guide critical practice.

726. Rowland, Robert C. "On Mythic Criticism." *ComS* 41 (Summer 1990): 101–116.

Argues for a narrow functional and structural approach to mythic criticism grounded in research on the character of myth in primitive and modern societies.

727. Rushing, Janice Hocker. "On Saving Mythic Criticism: A Reply to Rowland [*ComS* 41 (Summer 1990)]." *ComS* 41 (Summer 1990): 136–149.

Argues that Rowland's definition imposes its own mythic world view, encourages a sterile form of criticism, and reduces the interpreter to a passive recorder of events.

728. Ryan, Frank L. "Theoretical and *Then* Critical Thinking." *Leaflet* 89 (Winter 1990): 39–47.

Argues that theoretical thinking is an essential prelude to critical thinking and presents paradigms of literary theory.

729. Shahin, Kimary N. "Argument as a Formulation-Decision-Decision . . . Sequence." *Arg* 4 (August 1990): 363–373.

Adapts J. Bilmes' account of the notions of formulation and decision to describe relations of opposition in informal argument in an Agatha Christie play.

730. Shiff, Jonathan I. "Rhetoric at Play: Pastoral Entertainments at the Banquets of Doge Marino Grimani, 1595–1605." *DAI* 50 (April 1990): 3247A.

Explores the Grimani playwrights' lucid use of rhetoric, especially in connection with the Sienese game model.

731. Solomon, Martha. "Responding to Rowland's Myth; or, In Defense of Pluralism: A Reply to Rowland [*ComS* 41 (Summer 1990)]." *ComS* 41 (Summer 1990): 117–120.

Critiques underlying features of Rowland's argument and comments on his attitude toward critical practice in general.

732. Stevenson, Jean Myers. "The Writing Processes of Theodore Taylor and Jane Yolen." *DAI* 51 (September 1990): 741A.

Describes the writing processes of two writers of children's books.

733. Sullivan, Dale. "The Prophetic Voice in Jeremy Rifkin's *Algeny*." *RR* 9 (Fall 1990): 134–147.

Explicates the basis for placing *Algeny* in the genre of European Jeremiad because of its pessimism, secularism, and rejection of a teleological perspective.

734. Suppan, Steven Robert. "*Translatio Imperii et Studii:* The Project and Limits of Spanish Humanism (1492–1580)." *DAI* 51 (December 1990): 2012A.

Uses a "technical study of humanist grammar, rhetoric, and poetics" to study prosody, discourse types, and *translatio imperii et studii* in selected Spanish Renaissance humanists.

735. Tahir, Laura. "The Development of a Point of View in Young George Bernard Shaw." *DAI* 50 (May 1990): 5350B.

A cognitive case study of Shaw's developing questions and arguments. Organizing knowledge is seen as a process of constructive opposition to provoke solutions.

736. Taylor, Bryan C. "*Reminiscences of Los Alamos:* Narrative, Critical Theory, and the Organizational Subject." *WJSC* 54 (Summer 1990): 395–419.

Integrates sites of symbolic activity that structure human experience and social action by examining autobiographical narratives of three wartime scientists.

737. Taylor, John W. "From Pulpstyle to Innerspace: The Stylistics of American New Wave Science Fiction." *Style* 24 (Winter 1990): 611–627.

Argues that the stylistic devices of anaphora, pleonasm, and onomastics in new wave science fiction derive from the work of the new journalists.

738. Tolliver, Joyce. "Discourse Analysis and the Interpretation of Literary Narrative." *Style* 24 (Summer 1990): 266–283.

Suggests that discourse analysis provides a more useful model for analyzing narratives than sentence-level linguistic models. Analyzes "Mi Suicidio" by Emilia Pardo Bazan.

739. Travis, Molly Abel. "Subject on Trial: The Displacement of the Reader in Modern and Postmodern Fiction." *DAI* 50 (June 1990): 3947A.

Constructs a reader-response theory that ties the reading subject's response to theories of subjectivity.

740. Trimbur, John. "Essayist Literacy and the Rhetoric of Deproduction." *RR* 9 (Fall 1990): 72–86.

Traces the history of essayist literacy and the rhetoric of deproduction as related to school texts. Argues that students need to read texts more critically.

741. Trimmer, Joseph F. "We've Done It Again: Taking the Fun out of Reading Nonfiction." *JTW* 9 (Spring-Summer 1990): 115–121.

A review essay treating *Literary Nonfiction: Theory, Criticism, Pedagogy*. Warns about overtheorizing and overanalyzing nonfiction.

742. Vice, Susan. "Self-Consciousness in the Work of Malcolm Lowry: An Examination of Narrative Voice." *DAI* 51 (December 1990): 2031A.

Uses Bakhtin's theory of the dialogic novel to show how Lowry's peculiar species of discourse frees the fictional characters from their narrator.

743. Walker, Cheryl. "Feminist Literary Criticism and the Author." *CritI* 16 (Spring 1990): 551–571.

In considering poetry criticism, concludes that an author's individual experience is absent from a text.

744. Wallerstein, Nicholas Perry. "Poetic Quarrel: The Rhetoric of Antithesis in Modern Poetry." *DAI* 50 (March 1990): 2894A.

Traces, analyzes, and evaluates the use of the conjunctions *but* and *yet* in the formation of antithesis.

745. Ward, Jean M. G. "Women's Responses to Systems of Male Authority: Communication Strategies in the Novels of Abigail Scott Duniway." *DAI* 50 (May 1990): 3414A.

Examines Duniway's serialized novels and finds that they reveal the condition of women and call for a transformation of social, political, and economic systems.

746. Ward, Kathleen Martha. "Dear Sir or Madam: The Epistolary Novel in Britain in the Nineteenth Century." *DAI* 50 (June 1990): 3966A.

Considers the epistolary method as a form with a continuous history, not restricted to one historical period or to a limited number of themes or subjects.

747. Washington, Edward T. "Beyond Cultural Stereotypes: The Dramatic Meanings of Shakespeare's Black Characters." *DAI* 51 (October 1990): 1243A.

Examines the literary meanings of blackness in Shakespeare and under what circumstances Shakespeare used stock Renaissance racial types in his dramas.

748. Weiss, Allen S. "Subject Construction and Spectatorial Identification: A Revision of Contemporary Film Theory." *DAI* 51 (August 1990): 321A.

Finds contemporary film theory concerning audience in error because it confuses the "ideal" audience with the combination of responses found in actual audiences.

749. White, Hayden. *The Content of the Form: Narrative Discourse and Historical Represen-*

tation. Baltimore: The Johns Hopkins University Press, 1990. 264 pages

> Argues that the only meaning history can have is the kind that a narrative imagination can give it. Our narrative capacities transform the present into a fulfillment of a past from which we wish to have descended.

750. Willinsky, John. "Matthew Arnold's Legacy: The Powers of Literature." *RTE* 24 (December 1990): 343–361.

> Reconsiders Arnold's practice of cultural literacy as a foundation for the inclusion of literature in educational curricula.

751. Winter, Kari Joy. "Subjects of Slavery, Agents of History: Women and Power in Female Gothic Novels and Slave Narratives, 1790–1865." *DAI* 51 (December 1990): 2009A.

> Examines patriarchal and feminist rhetoric, comparing nominally free women to slaves to locate moments of escape from patriarchal domination in nineteenth-century American gothic fiction.

752. Winterowd, W. Ross. *The Rhetoric of the "Other" Literature*. Carbondale, Ill.: Southern Illinois University Press, 1990. 159 pages

> Advocates including nonfiction works in the literary canon. Writers discussed include Truman Capote, Irving Stone, Peter Matthiessen, Gay Talese, Hunter Thompson, and Tom Wolfe.

753. Yardley, Marion Jeanne. "Writing the Great War: Language and Structures in English-Canadian Prose Narratives of World War I." *DAI* 50 (May 1990): 3584A.

> Traces a shift in the narrative techniques of works written immediately after the war and those written later.

754. Zavarzadeh, Maslud, and Donald Morton. "(Post)Modern Critical Theory and the Articulations of Critical Pedagogies." *CollL* 17 (June–October 1990): 51–63.

> Seeks a New Critical Pedagogy "that reveals the merely localizing and re-formist (not trans-formist) character of both tradi-

tional pedagogical and (post)structuralist pedagogical practice."

See also 36, 155, 180, 184, 194, 209, 214, 236, 239, 265, 270, 282, 285, 303, 331, 362, 390, 760, 897, 915, 1042, 1057, 1101

2.7   READING

755. Afflerbach, Peter P. "The Influence of Prior Knowledge on Expert Readers' Main Idea Construction Strategies." *RRQ* 25 (Winter 1990): 31–46.

> Expert readers used three methods: automatic construction, a draft-and-revision strategy, and a topic-comment strategy.

756. Balota, David A., and James I. Chumbley. "Where Are the Effects of Frequency in Visual Word Recognition Tasks? Right Where We Said They Were! Comment on Monsell, Doyle, and Haggard [*JEPG* 118 (March 1989)]." *JEPG* 119 (June 1990): 231–237.

> Continues the debate about the relationship between lexical identification and word frequency.

757. Bar-Shalom, Eva Greenwald. "Comprehension and Production of Relative Clauses and Passives by Good and Poor Readers." *DAI* 51 (December 1990): 2002A.

> Supports the view that "poor readers' comprehension problems arise from an underlying phonological deficit that creates a bottleneck in working memory."

758. Bauer, Dale. "Jenny Holzer and the Rhetoric of Violence." *Reader* 23 (Spring 1990): 10–22.

> Analyzes Holzer's use of "truisms" and "inflammatory essays" to challenge "rational violence" and teach others to recognize it.

759. Becker, Jane. "The Relationship between Field Dependence, Success in Reading, and the Processes Students Employ in Reading and Comprehending Texts." *DAI* 50 (January 1990): 1997A.

Identifies and compares the thought processes developmental students used when reading.

760. Bogdan, Deanne, and Stanley B. Straw, eds. *Beyond Communication: Reading, Comprehension, and Criticism.* Portsmouth, N.H.: Boynton/Cook, 1990. 384 pages

Fourteen essays consider the connection between reading comprehension theory and reader-response criticism. Presents a rationale for integrating the two approaches at all grade levels.

761. Connine, Cynthia M., John Mullennix, Eve Shernoff, and Jennifer Yelen. "Word Familiarity and Frequency in Visual and Auditory Word Recognition." *JEPL* 16 (November 1990): 1084–1096.

Discusses technical problems in describing visual and auditory word recognition. Suggests that understanding reading and listening will require understanding postlexical components of language processing.

762. Crowley, Rosalind A., and Rosemary J. Stevenson. "Reference in Simple Sentences and in Titles." *JPsyR* 19 (1990): 191–210.

University students' text comprehension was linked to subject comprehension and subject retrieval in both single sentences and texts. Topic comprehension was less significant.

763. Dee-Lucas, Diana, and Jill H. Larkin. "Organization and Comprehensibility in Scientific Proofs; or, 'Consider a Particle p. . . .' " *JEdP* 82 (1990): 701–714.

Undergraduate nonphysics majors had more difficulty identifying and remembering important information in a proof-first text arrangement than in a principle-first text arrangement.

764. Ferreira, Fernanda, and John M. Henderson. "Use of Verb Information in Syntactic Parsing: Evidence from Eye Movements and Word-by-Word Self-Paced Reading." *JEPL* 16 (July 1990): 555–568.

Describes the roles of verbs in initial syntactic parsing of sentences. Disagrees with Ford and Kaplan on the ways verbs function in reading.

765. Fishbein, Harold D., Thomas Eckart, Erika Lauver, Rachel Van Leeuwen, and Daniel Langmeyer. "Learners' Questions and Comprehension in a Tutoring Setting." *JEdP* 82 (March 1990): 163–170.

Adult learners understood better when allowed to ask questions while carrying out an activity than when being taught how to carry it out.

766. Fletcher, Charles R., John E. Hummel, and Chad J. Marsolek. "Causality and the Allocation of Attention during Comprehension." *JEPL* 16 (March 1990): 233–240.

Tests the idea that a sentence followed by causal antecedents remains the focus of a reader's attention while the same sentence followed by causal consequences does not.

767. Garrod, Simon, Edward J. O'Brien, Robin K. Morris, and Keith Rayner. "Elaborative Inferencing as an Active or Passive Process." *JEPL* 16 (March 1990): 250–257.

Investigates the relationship among reading comprehension, explicitly stated information, unstated inferences, and elaborative inferences to develop a model of reading comprehension.

768. Gibbs, Raymond W., Jr. "Comprehending Figurative Referential Descriptions." *JEPL*16 (January 1990): 56–66.

Examines the relative difficulty in processing metaphoric and metonymic referential descriptions and investigates how repetition affects comprehension.

769. Giles, Timothy D. "The Readability Controversy: A Technical Writing Review." *JTWC* 20 (1990): 131–138.

Concludes that while some authorities recommend using readability formulas, others ignore them because they are misleading and can lead to stilted prose.

770. Gulgoz, Sami. "Revising Text to Improve Learning: Methods Based on Text Processing Models, Expertise, and Readability Formulas." *DAI* 51 (September 1990): 1527B.

Examines four versions of a history text for recall and recognition. Finds that, when inferences were provided in the text, subjects recalled more and read faster.

771. Hollingsworth, Paul M., and D. Ray Reutzel. "Prior Knowledge, Content-Related Attitude, Reading Comprehension: Testing Mathewson's Affective Model of Reading." *JEdR* 83 (March–April 1990): 194–199.

Prior attitudes toward content seem to have had no effect on reading comprehension.

772. Hussein, Ali Ahmed. "The Impact of Visual-Verbal Relationships on Native-Nonnative English Speakers' Reading Processes and Comprehension." *DAI* 51 (November 1990): 1561A.

A comparative investigation of readers of different language backgrounds and their responses to expository texts.

773. Jared, Debra, and Mark S. Seidenberg. "Naming Multisyllabic Words." *JEPH* 16 (February 1990): 92–105.

Extends studies of how readers process words to consider multisyllabic words, drawing implications for reading and dyslexia. Finds that frequency and spelling-sound correspondences affect naming.

774. Karnes, Saundra Parker. "Comprehension Performance of Average Readers Using a Summarization Strategy with Test Patterns Varied." *DAI* 50 (January 1990): 1919A.

Examines the effect of summarization strategies on the comprehension of average readers.

775. Kirsch, Irwin, and Peter B. Mosenthal. "Exploring Document Literacy: Variables Underlying the Performance of Young Adults." *RRQ* 25 (Winter 1990): 5–30.

Using relational grammar and analyses of documents, researchers identified three groups of variables: document, task, and process variables.

776. Kroll, Judith F. "Recognizing Words and Pictures in Sentence Contexts: A Test of Lexical Modularity." *JEPL* 16 (September 1990): 747–759.

Determines that verbal context influences both word and picture recognition. Suggests that relationship is important for future research in language processing.

777. Langer, Judith A. "The Process of Understanding: Reading for Literary and Informative Purposes." *RTE* 24 (October 1990): 229–260.

Analyses of reading protocols identify various recursive stances and horizons of possibilities in readers, depending on their purpose.

778. Leigh, Lorrayne Lynn. "The Effects of Metacognitive Strategy Training on the Reading Comprehension Levels of Hispanic College Women." *DAI* 50 (January 1990): 1999A.

Metacognitive strategy training significantly improved the reading comprehension levels of Hispanic college women as measured by a reading test.

779. McCarthey, Sarah J., and Taffy E. Raphael. *Alternate Perspectives of Reading-Writing Connections*. Occasional Paper, no. 130. East Lansing, Mich.: Michigan State University Institute for Research on Teaching, 1989. ERIC ED 314 730. 47 pages

Sketches three perspectives on the relationship between reading and writing: information processing, social constructivism, and Piagetian naturalism.

780. Monsell, Stephen. "Frequency Effects in Lexical Tasks: Reply to Balota and Chumbley [*JEPG* 119 (June 1990)]." *JEPG* 119 (September 1990): 335–339.

Continues the debate about the relationship between lexical identification and word frequency.

781. Morris, Carl Craig. "Retrieval Processes Underlying Confidence in Comprehension Judgments." *JEPL* 16 (March 1990): 223–232.

Investigates why readers' predictions about how much they have comprehended have so little relationship to how they score on comprehension tests.

782. O'Brien, Edward J., Pamela S. Plewes, and Jason E. Albrecht. "Antecedent Retrieval Processes." *JEPL* 16 (March 1990): 241–249.

Experimentally considers how readers use various kinds of information to learn when and how to best present information that readers will need later.

783. Ormrod, Jeanne Ellis. "Comparing Good and Poor Spellers of Equal Reading and Verbal Abilities." *PMS* 71 (October 1990): 432–434.

Good spellers spelled unknown words more accurately. They produced more phonetically correct spellings of misspelled words and spelled more common letter patterns correctly.

784. Pressley, Michael, Elizabeth S. Ghatala, Vera Woloshyn, and Jennifer Pirie. "Sometimes Adults Miss the Main Ideas and Do Not Realize It: Confidence in Responses to Short-Answer and Multiple-Choice Comprehension Questions." *RRQ* 25 (Summer 1990): 232–249.

Young adults felt more confident that their answers to thematic questions were correct, even when the answers were wrong, leading to "gross" comprehension problems.

785. Rasinski, Timothy V. "Effects of Repeated Reading and Listening-While-Reading on Reading Fluency." *JEdR* 83 (January–February 1990): 147–150.

Both methods increased reading speed and word-recognition accuracy. No significant differences between methods were detected.

786. Roller, Cathy M. "Commentary: The Interaction between Knowledge and Structure Variables in the Processing of Expository Prose." *RRQ* 25 (Spring 1990): 79–89.

When subject matter is relatively unknown to readers, the structure of the text helps readers construct relations between concepts in the text.

787. Sadoski, Mark, and Zeba Quast. "Reader Response and Long-Term Recall for Journalistic Text: The Roles of Imagery, Affect, and Importance." *RRQ* 25 (Fall 1990): 256–272.

A study of 54 college students reading three feature articles from popular magazines revealed that imagery most helped the students recall the material.

788. Siegel, Donna Farrell. "The Literacy Press: A Process Model for Reading Development." *JEdR* 83 (July–August 1990): 336–347.

Of nine variables representing home, school, and extracurricular involvement, all are statistically significant indicators of reading ability in young adults.

789. Silver, N. Clayton, Glenn R. Phelps, and William P. Dunnlop. "Baddeley's Grammatical Reasoning Test: Active Versus Passive Processing Differences Reexamined." *LT* 6 (December 1989): 178–198.

Active and passive are equally difficult to process in negative sentences; active is easier in positive sentences.

790. Sinatra, Gale M. "Convergence of Listening and Reading Processing." *RRQ* 25 (Spring 1990): 115–130.

In an experiment with 40 college students, researchers discovered that listening and reading converged at the word level.

791. Smith, M. Cecil. "A Longitudinal Investigation of Reading Attitude Development from Childhood to Adulthood." *JEdR* 83 (March–April 1990): 215–219.

Although childhood measures seem to be poor predictors of adult attitude, evidence suggests that reading attitudes over time remain stable.

792. Wirth, Arthur G. "Basal Readers—'Dominant but Dead' Versus Gadamer and Language for Hermeneutic Understanding." *JT* 24 (Fall–Winter 1989): 4–19.

Advocates resisting the current positivistic, testing mentality because the dialogic nature of language and practical wisdom dictate doing so.

See also 101, 113, 116, 478, 899, 950

2.8   LINGUISTICS, GRAMMATICAL THEORY, AND SEMANTICS

793. Ainsworth-Vaughn, Nancy. "The Acquisition of Sociolinguistic Norms: Style Switching in Very Early Directives." *LangS* 12 (1990): 22–38.

Analyzes 15 videotapes of nine children, ages one to three and a half, to see how they negotiate interactions with parents and an unfamiliar adult.

794. Allen, Mike, Jerold Hale, Paul Mongeau, Sandra Berkowitz-Stafford, Shane Stafford, William Shanahan, Philip Agee, Kelly Dillon, Robert Jackson, and Cynthia Ray. "Testing a Model of Message Sidedness: Three Replications." *ComM* 57 (December 1990): 275–291.

A meta-analysis found that two-sided refutational messages were more persuasive than one-sided messages or than two-sided nonrefutational messages.

795. Andresen, Julie Tetel. *Linguistics in America, 1769–1924: A Critical History.* New York: Routledge, 1990. 320 pages

Proposes that three developments capture a significant portion of American linguistic activity: the study of American Indian languages, the emergence of a distinctive Anglo-American thought accompanied by the "defense and illustration" of American English, and the influence of European linguistic theories on American scholarship.

796. Baker, Adria Lee. "Sociolinguistic Competence in English among Foreign University Students." *DAI* 51 (December 1990): 2002A.

Finds that cultural groups differ significantly in speech acts of requesting, especially in relation to time spent studying English.

797. Banks, David. "Agents and Instruments in Scientific Writing." *IRAL* 28 (November 1990): 336–345.

A study of 11 academic articles in the field of oceanography shows that the distribution of passive *by* phrases corresponds to fairly well defined semantic categories.

798. Baynham, Michael J. "Narrative and Narrativity in the English of a First-Generation Migrant Community." *DAI* 50 (February 1990): 2470A.

Relates narrative to report, generalizing, and autobiographical discourses, showing how men active in community life opted for different strategies than did women or other men.

799. Beach, Cheryl Marguerite. "Duration and Pitch Combine to Represent Grammatical Structure in Temporarily Ambiguous Spoken Sentences." *DAI* 50 (April 1990): 4798B.

Investigates models of syntactic processing, or parsing. Finds that prosodic information influences the identification of syntactic structures for sentences with temporary ambiguities.

800. Beach, Richard, and Susan Hynds, eds. *Developing Discourse Practices in Adolescence and Adulthood.* Advances in Discourse Processes, vol. 39. Norwood, N.J.: Ablex, 1990. 440 pages

Argues that language use is socially motivated. Sixteen essays analyze discourse development from social, textual, institutional, and field perspectives and provide a framework for designing instruction and assessment in college and adult literacy programs.

801. Beason, Larry Wayne. "Tracing the Causes of Writing Errors: A Revision of Error-Analysis Procedures and Assumptions." *DAI* 50 (April 1990): 3170A.

Proposes a model using a variety of procedures and sources for grammatical and rhetorical descriptions of error by analyzing nonstandard uses of *in which*.

802. Bennett, Jeremy, producer and director. *The Story of Writing*. New York: Filmakers Library, 1990. 29 minutes

A videotape tracing the history of written communication from the beginnings to the present. Also considers the roles of the printing press, fountain pen, and typewriter and explains the contributions of various cultures.

803. Bergeron, David. "Heteronyms." *EngT* 6 (October 1990): 39–44.

Discusses the lexical ambiguity of heteronyms and classifies them into four categories.

804. Bernstein, Basil. *The Structuring of Pedagogic Discourse*. New York: Routledge, 1990. 235 pages

A study of the language of education.

805. Bickerton, Derek. *Language and Species*. Chicago: University of Chicago Press, 1990. 297 pages

Examines what language has done for our species and how it has made us different from other species. Discusses the inner world, from an individual's consciousness of the self to the construction of complex knowledge systems, and the outer world of our relationships with one another.

806. Birch, Barbara Mary. "The Psychology of Names, Nouns, and Verbs." *DAI* 50 (April 1990): 3215A.

Offers a theory for how the lexicon is organized and discusses the properties of concepts and conceptual structure.

807. Bolinger, Dwight. "The Doolittling of English." *EngT* 6 (April 1990): 25–28.

Discusses current trends in English toward hypercorrect pronunciation and indifference to grammar.

808. Carson, Joan Eisterhold, Patricia L. Carrell, Sandra Silberstein, Barbara Kroll, and Phyllis A. Kuehn. "Reading-Writing Relationships in First and Second Language." *TESOLQ* 24 (Summer 1990): 245–266.

Indicates that L1 reading skills transfer to L2 but that L1 writing skills may not transfer at advanced levels. Studies Chinese and Japanese adult learners.

809. Chen, Selma. "The Effects of L1 Word Order and English Proficiency on Non-English Speakers' Sentence Processing." *DAI* 50 (May 1990): 3569A.

Results reveal a significant difference across five syntactic constructions.

810. Christophersen, Paul. "The Germanic Legacy." *EngT* 6 (July 1990): 3–7.

Assesses the influence of Anglo-Saxon, Low German, and the Scandinavian languages on the development of English.

811. Coates, Jennifer, and Deborah Cameron, eds. *Women in Their Speech Communities*. New York: Longman, 1989. 208 pages

A collection of essays describing current research on women and language and focusing on a variety of speech communities, linguistic events, and settings. Contributors are not indexed separately in this volume.

812. Cooper, Robert L. *Language Planning and Social Change*. Cambridge, England: Cambridge University Press, 1989. 216 pages

Describes how political, religious, and other leaders try to influence language use. Discusses examples such as the revival of Hebrew as a spoken language, the creation of writing systems for unwritten languages, and feminist campaigns to eliminate sexual bias in language.

813. Coupland, Nikolas. "The Social Differentiation of Functional Language Use: A Sociolinguistic Investigation of Travel Agency Talk." *DAI* 50 (May 1990): 3575A.

Uses Labov's methods of studying sociolinguistic variation to analyze the speech of travel agents in Cardiff, Wales.

814. Croft, William. *Syntactic Categories and Grammatical Relations: The Cognitive Organization of Information*. Chicago: University of Chicago Press, 1991. 343 pages

Offers an explanation for the structure of the clause in natural language. Views the clause as a significant unit for organizing information as well as a natural division of information itself.

815. Crowley, Tony. *Standard English and the Politics of Language*. Urbana, Ill.: University of Illinois Press, 1989. 302 pages

Uses the work of Foucault, Bakhtin, and Volosinov to trace the history of the study of the English language. Sees the objectification of language, including concepts such as "the standard language," as serving particular social and rhetorical purposes.

816. Davis, Brent. "Regression Model of Coarticulation Effects in Naturalized American English." *DAI* 51 (October 1990): 1045A.

Studies the effectiveness of mathematical models in explaining the linguistic variables in Native American English.

817. Deely, John. *Basics of Semiotics*. Bloomington, Ind.: Indiana University Press, 1990. 168 pages

An exposition and synthesis of major semiotic theories.

818. Deibler, Timothy A. "A Philosophical Semantic Intentionality Theory of Metaphor." *DAI* 50 (June 1990): 3978A.

Investigates philosophical theories of metaphor and proposes a semantic intentionality theory that explains how metaphor works.

819. De Vincenzi, Marcia. "Syntactic Parsing Strategies in a Null Subject Language." *DAI* 50 (June 1990): 5900B.

Tests the parsing of Italian to examine the psycholinguistic question of whether syntactic strategies are universal or tied to a specific language.

820. Di Marco, Chrysanne. "Computational Stylistics for Natural Language Translation." *DAI* 51 (November 1990): 2454B.

Describes a computational model of goal-directed stylistics that can help preserve style in French-to-English translation.

821. "Doublespeak and the Invasion of Panama." *QRD* 16 (April 1990): 1.

Provides examples of doublespeak used by the Bush administration when discussing the invasion of Panama.

822. "Doublespeak Here and There." *QRD* 16 (January 1990): 4–12.

Notes examples of doublespeak in business, education, foreign countries, the government, the military, and miscellaneous categories.

823. "Doublespeak Here and There." *QRD* 16 (April 1990): 1–8.

Notes examples of doublespeak in business, education, foreign countries, the government, the military, and miscellaneous categories.

824. "Doublespeak Here and There." *QRD* 17 (October 1990): 1–9.

Notes examples of doublespeak in business, education, foreign countries, the government, medicine, the military, and miscellaneous categories.

825. Drost, Mark P. "An Adverbial Theory of Mental Imagery." *DAI* 51 (September 1990): 883A.

Develops a structured predicate version of an adverbial theory to express mental imagery correctly.

826. Durmusuglu, Gul. "The Notion of 'Parallel Texts' and Its Place in Contrastive and Applied Linguistics." *DAI* 51 (July 1990): 152A.

Attempts to define "parallel texts" and sets up a model of analysis applicable to contrastive and applied linguistics.

827. "Education Doublespeak Thrives." *QRD* 16 (July 1990): 8–9.

Cites examples of doublespeak used in memos received by Joseph Hernandez, chancellor of schools for New York City.

828. Escalante, Fernando. "Voice and Argument Structure in Yaqui." *DAI* 51 (November 1990): 1595A.

A description, analysis, and functional interpretation of the construction types and their discourse functions.

829. Ferguson, K. Scott, and Frank Parker. "Grammar and Technical Writing." *JTWC* 20 (1990): 357–367.

Arguing that earlier work has been too theoretical, these authors attempt to illustrate how "insights from linguistics can be applied to technical writing."

830. Fisher, Cynthia Lee. "Syntax/Semantics Links in the Verb Lexicon." *DAI* 50 (March 1990): 4205B.

Suggests strong and subtle links between syntax and semantics in English. Through correlation, speakers infer meaning from form.

831. Gachelin, Jean-Marc. "Is English a Romance Language?" *EngT* 6 (July 1990): 8–14.

Presents the case for English as a hybrid European language and a hybrid global language.

832. Garrison, Peggy L. "Language in Field Education Site Supervisors' Reports: Are There Gender Differences?" *DAI* 51 (July 1990): 152A.

Uses ethnolinguistic analysis and semantic differentiation to determine the language differences between male and female divinity students.

833. Gozzi, Raymond, Jr. *New Words and a Changing American Culture*. Columbia,

S.C.: University of South Carolina Press, 1990. 136 pages

Uses new words generated by American culture between 1961 and 1986 to describe cultural changes and concerns raised by the words. The new words reveal a culture preoccupied with technology but increasingly mystified by it.

834. "Guidelines for Orwell and Doublespeak Awards." *QRD* 16 (July 1990): 4.

Encourages nominations and provides guidelines for the Orwell and Doublespeak awards.

835. Gusewelle, C. W. "Perils Still Abound— Only Their Names Are Gentler." *QRD* 16 (July 1990): 7–8.

Provides examples of nonpejorative language and argues that it avoids giving offense by blunting reality. Reprinted from the *Kansas City Star*.

836. Hahn, Martin. "Intentionality, Direct Reference, and Individualism." *DAI* 51 (October 1990): 1254A.

Explores the conflict between individualism and semantic theories of direct reference.

837. Hawthorne, James Allen. "A Semantic Theory for Partial Entailments and Inductive Inferences." *DAI* 50 (January 1990): 2084A.

Proposes a semantic theory for inductive logic, using Rudolf Carnap's probabilistic logic as a model.

838. Hayakawa, S. I., and Alan R. Hayakawa. *Language in Thought and Action*. 5th ed. San Diego: Harcourt Brace Jovanovich, 1990. 350 pages

An introduction to semantics that covers the functions of language, the interaction of language and thought, the nature of prejudice, co-optation of language, the nature of advertising, and the language of television.

839. Hinkelman, Elizabeth A. "Linguistic and Pragmatic Constraints on Utterance Interpretation." *DAI* 51 (December 1990): 2004A.

Proposes a method of speech-act interpretation applicable to a wider range of cases.

840. Hislop, William L. "The Relative Clause in College Freshman Writing: A Quantitative Developmental Study." *DAI* 50 (March 1990): 2880A.

Examines relative clauses in the papers of eight basic writers and eight others, exploring possible shifts in students' uses of several clausal features.

841. Horgan, John. "Free Radical: A Word (or Two) about Linguist Noam Chomsky." *SAm* 262 (May 1990): 40–42, 44.

Presents an introduction to Chomsky's generative grammar.

842. Hughes, Geoffrey. "What Is Register?" *EngT* 6 (April 1990): 47–51.

Analyzes levels of formality in English usage.

843. "I Don't Doubt Your Word." *QRD* 16 (July 1990): 12.

Points out the meaninglessness of the common phrase "I don't doubt your word."

844. Iggers, Jeremy. "PR Gimmickry Debases the Language." *QRD* 17 (October 1990): 11–12.

Explains how question-begging, euphemism, and hyperbole twist language. Argues for treating language use as an ethical issue.

845. Ivy, Carrie Anne. "An Investigation of Textual Cohesion in the Narrative Writing of Learning-Disabled and Normal Adolescents." *DAI* 50 (May 1990): 3589A.

Uses the theoretical framework of Halliday and Hasan to examine textual cohesion in narrative writing.

846. Kane, Kathleen. "Representations of Multiply Suffixed Words: Implications for Grammatical and Psychological Models of the Lexicon." *DAI* 50 (May 1990): 3570A.

Argues for a system that is both rule-governed and analogical.

847. Kasten, Wendy C. "Oral Language during the Writing Process of Native American Students." *EQ* 22 (1990): 149–158.

Examines oral language as it accompanied the writing process of children observed over two years.

848. Kline, Susan L., Cathy L. Hennen-Floyd, and Kathleen M. Farrell. "Cognitive Complexity and Verbal Response Mode Use in Discussion." *ComQ* 38 (Fall 1990): 350–360.

Stiles' discourse analysis system was used to determine differences in the way individuals use utterances to establish understanding with others.

849. Langsdorf, Lenore. "On the Uses of Language in Working and Idealized Logic." *Arg* 4 (August 1990): 259–268.

Argues that logical analysis in natural language contexts requires interpretive strategies appropriate to the linguistic situation of statements.

850. Lee, Jinkyu. "Morphological Development in Student Writing." *DAI* 51 (September 1990): 771A.

Examines 60 samples of writing using three independent variables, concluding that morphological complexity appears more often in persuasive than in explanatory writing.

851. Livingston, Howard. "The Study of Doublespeak in England." *QRD* 16 (July 1990): 3–4.

Reports high interest but few materials for teaching about doublespeak. Requests materials, offering to collect and forward them.

852. Luizza, Roy Michael. "New Wine in Old Bottles: The Twelfth-Century Texts of the West-Saxon Gospels." *DAI* 50 (May 1990): 3581A.

Discusses why the interpretation of spellings in a historical text must consider all levels of linguistic structure.

853. Maitland, Karen. "Why Choose Me? The Pragmatics of English Pronouns." *DAI* 51 (August 1990): 494A.

Argues that people may manipulate pronominal systems for communicative purposes, especially for the communication of affect.

854. Martin, James Edward. "Towards a Theory of Textuality for Contrastive Rhetoric Research." *DAI* 50 (May 1990): 3572A.

Examines the constituent textual features and textual characteristics of five L1 and L2 texts.

855. McAndrew, Donald A. "Handwriting Rate and Syntactic Fluency." *JBW* 9 (Spring 1990): 31–39.

This research report concludes that students with slower handwriting speeds tended to produce writing that was "syntactically less complex, showing less embedding and branching."

856. McArthur, Tom. "English in Tiers." *EngT* 6 (July 1990): 15–20.

Analyzes the complex layering of the vocabulary that English has inherited from Germanic, Romance, and Greek languages.

857. McCarthy, Colman. "Euphemistic Language Makes the Gruesome Palatable." *QRD* 16 (July 1990): 7.

Cites examples of doublespeak associated with animals and argues for honesty in language.

858. Melara, Robert D., and Lawrence E. Marks. "Dimensional Interactions in Language Processing: Investigating Directions and Levels of Crosstalk." *JEPL* 16 (July 1990): 539–554.

Findings in the study of language processing and the study of dimensional interaction prompt a call for more research on interactive processing.

859. Melrose, Robin. "A Systemic-Functional Approach to Communicative Course Design in English Language Teaching." *DAI* 50 (April 1990): 3172A.

Examines four models of systemic linguistics and proposes a new model that analyzes social system choices and treats discourse as a dynamic process.

860. Mettler, Sally K. "The Reactions of Listeners to the Discourse of Nonnative Speakers of English." *DAI* 50 (June 1990): 3935A.

A study focusing on language use, language comprehension, and nonlinguistic responses evoked when native or near-native English speakers listened to the discourse of nonnative speakers.

861. Meyers, Miriam Watkins. "Current Generic Pronoun Usage: An Empirical Study." *AS* 65 (Fall 1990): 228–237.

A study that documents the well-established usage of singular *they* in writing. Variables include education, age, gender, the urban or rural residence of the writers, and region.

862. Morrell, Kenneth Scot. "Studies on the Phrase Structure of Early Attic Prose." *DAI* 50 (June 1990): 3931A.

Analyzes words within constituent structures, positing an underlying hierarchical structure and describing types of movement that account for the surface structure.

863. Murphy, Sally Katherine. "Saying Your Piece: The Role of Topic Management in Conversation." *DAI* 51 (October 1990): 1046A.

Discusses how speakers in initial interaction manage topics of conversation.

864. Nayak, Nandini P., and Raymond W. Gibbs, Jr. "Conceptual Knowledge in the Interpretation of Idioms." *JEPG* 119 (September 1990): 315–330.

Examines how people determine the contextual appropriateness of idioms.

865. Nemy, Enid. "What's Said Isn't Always What's Meant." *QRD* 16 (July 1990): 11.

Lists eight examples of language that says one thing but means another.

866. Nunberg, Geoffrey. *The Linguistics of Punctuation*. Center for the Study of Language and Information Lecture Notes. Stanford, Calif.: Center for the Study of Language and Information (distributed by University of Chicago Press), 1990. 150 pages

Argues that punctuation is a linguistic subsystem whose systematic nature may be obscured if analyzed contrastively with reference to spoken-language devices with which it has some functional overlap.

867. Pederson, Lee, ed. *Linguistic Atlas of the Gulf States, Volume 4: Regional Matrix*. Linguistic Atlas of the Gulf States. Athens, Ga.: University of Georgia Press, 1990. 552 pages

Studies speech variations in Georgia, Florida, Alabama, Tennessee, Mississippi, Louisiana, Arkansas, and eastern Texas. Draws on 5000 hours of taped interviews with 1100 individuals in urban and rural areas, recording contrastive evidence in geographical sector maps and giving characteristics of the informants.

868. Peng, Lim Ho. "Ambiguity and ESL Students: A Pilot Experiment." *IRAL* 28 (August 1990): 248–256.

Forty Malaysian ESL students, graduate and undergraduate, had greatest difficulty in determining ambiguity in English sentences when confronted with derived structure ambiguity.

869. Pixton, William H. "On Refining the Free Modifier." *RSQ* 20 (Spring 1990): 119–129.

Seeks to bring grammatical precision to the term *free modifier* by identifying two types, the word modifier and the sentence modifier.

870. "Presidential Doublespeak." *QRD* 16 (April 1990): 8–9.

Cites examples of doublespeak used by the Bush administration in its dealings with China and Soviet President Gorbachev and in discussing German reunification.

871. *QRD* 16 (January 1990): 1–4.

Announces 1989 Orwell and Doublespeak awards, giving nominations for each category and the text of William Lutz's speech announcing the awards.

872. Quirk, Sir Randolph. "Language Varieties and Standard Language." *EngT* 6 (January 1990): 3–10.

Provides a taxonomy of varieties of English and argues for the importance of Standard English.

873. Richardson, Judith Alice. "Testing the Use of Reference in the Assessment of Language Change with Age." *DAI* 51 (December 1990): 3168B.

Investigates tasks involving retold narratives, retold instructions, and personal narratives. Assessing discourse processing may help detect subtle linguistic difficulties.

874. Rimmer, Sharon E. "Sociolinguistic Variability in Oral Narrative." *DAI* 51 (October 1990): 1215A.

A qualitative examination of linguistic variables in four occupational groups—nurses, chefs, hairdressers, and taxi drivers—in Liverpool and Birmingham, England.

875. Ross, Philip E. "Overview: Dead Sea Scrolls; Will Their Editors Perish before Publishing?" *SAm* 263 (November 1990): 36, 38.

Examines how unfamiliar idioms and colloquial grammar are slowing the translation of the Dead Sea Scrolls.

876. Roy, Cynthia B. "A Sociolinguistic Analysis of the Interpreter's Role in the Turn Exchanges of an Interpreted Event." *DAI* 50 (May 1990): 3573A.

Demonstrates that the interpreter's role is active and "governed by social and linguistic knowledge of the entire communicative situation."

877. Rutledge, Kay Ellen. "Analyzing Visual Doublespeak: The Art of Duck Hunting." *QRD* 16 (July 1990): 1–2.

Advocates using Burke's pentad and Rank's schema for propaganda analysis in teaching how to detect and analyze visual doublespeak.

878. Ryan, Frank L. "A Note on the 'Wholeness' of Language in Speech and in Poetry." *Leaflet* 89 (Spring 1990): 30–37.

Argues that metaphorical structure in language is evidence of a unified world.

879. Ryder, Mary Ellen. "Ordered Chaos: A Cognitive Model for the Interpretation of English Noun-Noun Compounds." *DAI* 50 (June 1990): 3936A.

Investigates how English speakers interpret novel noun-noun compounds. One way is productive; the other is unpredictable.

880. Ryder, Mary R. "Feminism and Style: Still Looking for the Quick Fix." *Style* 23 (Winter 1989): 530–544.

Reviews recent discussions about nonsexist language and claims that "traditional linguistic studies, which focus solely on structure, are no longer adequate for confronting sexist assumptions."

881. Sadock, Jerrold M. *Autolexical Syntax: A Theory of Parallel Grammatical Representations*. Chicago: University of Chicago Press, 1990. 266 pages

Hypothesizes that natural language expressions are organized along a number of simultaneous informational dimensions. In each dimension the allowable structural patterns form a system that can be specified by a set of explicit rules.

882. Saraoreh, Mohammed Atawi. "Some Lexical and Syntactic Problems in English-Arabic Translation." *DAI* 51 (October 1990): 1216A.

Discusses a theoretical framework for quality English-Arabic translations.

883. Savion, Leah. "Semantics for Belief Attributions." *DAI* 50 (May 1990): 3621A.

Examines the major semantic theories of belief attributions and proposes an alternative semantic theory to account for belief sentences.

884. Schiller, Janis L. "Writing in L1, Writing in L2: Case Studies of the Composing Processes of Five Adult Arabic-Speaking ESL Writers." *DAI* 50 (March 1990): 2883A.

Finds no significant differences between L1 and L2 composing behaviors for four of the five writers. All five displayed striking similarities between L1 and L2 patterns of composing.

885. Schleppegrell, Mary Josephine. "Functions of *Because* in Spoken Discourse." *DAI* 50 (May 1990): 3574A.

Discusses the distinguishing characteristics of subordinating and a paratactic *because*.

886. Senner, Wayne M., ed. *The Origins of Writing*. Lincoln, Neb.: University of Nebraska Press, 1989. 245 pages

Eleven essays discuss the genesis of the world's major writing systems.

887. Shepherd, Valerie. *Language Variety and the Art of the Everyday*. New York: Pinter Publishers (distributed by Columbia University Press), 1990. 256 pages

Argues that regional dialects and language variations are not inferior to Standard English. Discusses purposeful uses of nonstandard English in speech and writing.

888. Slutsky, Harvey. "Serial, Parallel, and Delay Strategies in the Processing of Structurally Ambiguous Language Constructions." *DAI* 50 (May 1990): 5301B.

Uses a self-paced syntactic-decision task to determine which of three strategies is employed in parsing transitive and verb-complement sentences.

889. Switzer, Jo Young, Virginia H. Fry, and Larry D. Miller. "Semiotics and Communication: A Dialogue with Thomas A. Sebeok." *SCJ* 55 (Summer 1990): 388–401.

Discusses Sebeok's views on the relationships among communication and semiotics, language and communication, signs and symbols, theory and method, and rhetoric and semiotics.

890. Tannen, Deborah. "Cross Talk: Women and Men Talking." *PC* 10 (Fall 1990): 6–7, 19.

Discusses the implications that gender differences in language use and conversational styles can have for office interactions and formal presentations.

891. Urdang, Laurence. "On Observing World English." *EngT* 6 (January 1990): 11–16.

Discusses accents and dialects of British and American English as well as problems with English as a world language.

892. Vangelisti, Anita L., Mark L. Knapp, and John A. Daly. "Conversational Narcissism." *ComM* 57 (December 1990): 251–274.

Six studies suggest that conversational narcissism is determined interactively by the needs and conversational goals of both participants.

893. Williams, Malcolm P. "A Comparison of the Textual Structures of Arabic and English Written Texts: A Study in the Comparative Orality of Arabic." *DAI* 50 (April 1990): 3218A.

Shows that characteristics "of an oral language are still present in Arabic [written texts] to a degree not true of English."

894. Wilson, David B. "The Language of Dc-based Values." *QRD* 16 (July 1990): 11.

Analyzes the use of "acceptable" and argues that it is one way a "value-free society" avoids moral judgments.

895. Witnyasspan, Sompong. "A Theory of Syntactic Compounding in English." *DAI* 51 (October 1990): 1216A.

Advances the claim that word formation takes place in the syntax.

896. Xu, George Qiaoqi. "An *Ex Post Facto* Study of Differences in the Structure of Standard Expository Paragraphs between Written Compositions by Native and Nonnative

Speakers of English at the College Level." *DAI* 51 (December 1990): 1942A.

A study of native and nonnative graduate and undergraduate students that finds "no significant difference between compositions by native and nonnative speakers."

897. Youmans, Gilbert. "Measuring Lexical Style and Competence: The Type-Token Vocabulary Curve." *Style* 24 (Winter 1990): 584–599.

Analyzes samples of literary texts by 13 authors according to the number of words (tokens) and the number of distinct vocabulary words (types) they contain. Draws inferences about lexical style and competence.

898. Zucchi, Alessandro. "The Language of Propositions and Events: Issues in the Syntax and the Semantics of Nominalization." *DAI* 50 (June 1990): 3937A.

Suggests that a theory of nominalization should specify the relation between noun meaning and verb meaning.

See also 17, 18, 29, 93, 165, 185, 186, 218, 249, 361, 451, 456, 468, 516, 519, 528, 541, 567, 605, 627, 633, 648, 669, 710, 764, 920, 928, 931, 943, 945, 970, 1015, 1104, 1108, 1441, 1515, 1543, 1551, 1711, 1847

2.9 PSYCHOLOGY

899. Allen, Philip A., and David J. Madden. "Evidence for a Parallel Input Serial Analysis Model of Word Processing." *JEPH* 16 (February 1990): 48–63.

Discusses ways of studying experimentally reading and related ideas in proofreading, especially as these concepts are reflected in word recognition and letter detection studies.

900. Bavelas, Janet Beavin. "Behaving and Communicating: A Reply to Motley [*WJSC*

54 (Winter 1990)]." *WJSC* 54 (Fall 1990): 593–602.

Separates two propositions on behavior and communication, suggests that they be treated as hypotheses, not axioms, and outlines empirical tests for both.

901. Beach, Wayne A. "On (Not) Observing Behavior Interactionally [response to Motley, *WJSC* 54 (Winter 1990)]." *WJSC* 54 (Fall 1990): 603–612.

Juxtaposes speech-act theory and conversation analysis dialectic with Motley's case study of definitional, conceptual, and theoretical issues.

902. Bean, Manya Maria. "The Poetry of Countertransference." *DAI* 50 (April 1990): 4762B.

An analyst-poet and her poems become heuristic tools for exploring countertransference through an experiential and cognitive record subjected to scrutiny and analysis.

903. Beebe, John. "A Response to Charles Sides' 'Psychological Types and Teaching Writing' [*WE* 1 (Spring 1990)]." *WE* 1 (Spring 1990): 41–43.

Points out a tendency to be unconsciously influenced by one's own psychological type.

904. Benoit, William L., and Pamela J. Benoit. "Aggravated and Mitigated Opening Utterances." *Arg* 4 (May 1990): 171–183.

Aggravated (face-threatening) opening utterances are less likely to be perceived as appropriate or effective than mitigated (face-saving) opening utterances are.

905. Bierschenk, Inger. "Language as Carrier of Consciousness." Cognitive Science Research, no. 30. Paper presented at the European Congress of Psychology, Amsterdam, July 1989. ERIC ED 312 645. 23 pages

Introduces "perspective text analysis," which treats language as an expression of intention and morality. Maintains that consciousness is bound to syntax.

906. Bock, Kathryn, and Helga Loebell. "Framing Sentences." *Cognition* 35 (April 1990): 1–39.

Three studies of 96 undergraduate students show a syntactic construction process that is separable from certain meanings that sentences convey.

907. Booth-Butterfield, Melanie, and Steven Booth-Butterfield. "The Mediating Role of Cognition in the Experience of State Anxiety." *SCJ* 56 (Fall 1990): 35–48.

Studies the interrelationship among thoughts, affect, and personality traits.

908. Bovens, Luc. "Reasons for Preferences." *DAI* 51 (October 1990): 1253A.

A psychological study of how people determine preferences.

909. Bruner, Jerome. "Culture and Human Development: A New Look." *HD* 33 (November–December 1990): 344–355.

Describes how and when "folk psychology" becomes the basis for children's early acquisition of narrative forms.

910. Burleson, Brant R., and Wendy Samter. "Effects of Cognitive Complexity on the Perceived Importance of Communication Skills in Friends." *ComR* 17 (April 1990): 165–182.

Studies the value that college students place on their friends' communication skills and how these evaluations vary as a function of social-cognitive development.

911. Castille, Cathy O. "Ambiguity and Sexuality: The Effects of Advance Organizers on Memory of an Ambiguous Text." *DAI* 50 (February 1990): 3686B.

Finds that when a title or descriptive sentence with a sexual theme precedes an ambiguous text, the interpretation is sexual, regardless of gender or prior experience.

912. Cayton, Mary Kupiec. "What Happens When Things Go Wrong: Women and Writing Blocks." *JAC* 10 (1990): 321–337.

Informal case studies of logs kept by male and female students in an interdisciplinary program suggest special gendered sources of writer's block.

913. Cessna, Kenneth N., and Rob Anderson. "The Contributions of Carl R. Rogers to a Philosophical *Praxis* of Dialogue." *WJSC* 54 (Spring 1990): 125–147.

Argues that Rogers is not sufficiently credited for his work and that his work is often misunderstood.

914. Cohen, Asher, Richard I. Ivry, and Steven W. Keele. "Attention and Structure in Sequence Learning." *JEPL* 16 (January 1990): 17–30.

Analyzes relationships among attention, awareness, and learning in complex motor tasks, drawing implications for understanding speaking and writing.

915. Coles, Robert. *The Call of Stories: Teaching and the Moral Imagination.* Boston Houghton Mifflin, 1990. 256 pages

Explains students' ability to learn about the moral imagination and examines their psychological reactions to books by Tolstoy, Cheever, Olsen, Chekhov, Williams, and others.

916. DeToye, Lela Margaret. "Student Writing Apprehension as a Function of Teacher Writing Apprehension and Teacher Attitudes toward Instruction in Written Composition." *DAI* 50 (March 1990): 2814A.

Teachers' attitudes about gender and the amount of writing performed are influential sources of student apprehension.

917. Donald, Janet G. "University Professors' Views of Knowledge and Validation Processes." *JEdP* 82 (1990): 242–249.

Interviews with 36 professors revealed important differences in how English teachers and faculty members in other disciplines regard validation processes and truth criteria.

918. Donnelly, Daniel A. "A Comparison of Verbal and Written Catharsis." *DAI* 51 (December 1990): 3127B.

Suggests that, when emotional expression in a cathartic procedure is extended to four days, written expression is as effective as psychotherapy.

919. Dreifuss-Kattan, Esther. "Cancer and Creativity: Cancer Stories." *DAI* 51 (December 1990): 3127B.

A study of the autobiographical, fictional, and poetic accounts written by cancer patients. Their relation to loss, mourning, dying, and creativity has clinical implications.

920. Dunbar, George Luke. "The Cognitive Lexicon." *DAI* 50 (April 1990): 4794B.

Applies cognitive science to the mental lexicon, seeking to illustrate the flexibility of lexical meaning. Develops a space grammar model and relates it to linguistic phenomena.

921. Eddy, Linda W. "An Investigation of the Relationship of Abstract Thinking, Intuition, Tolerance for Ambiguity, and Isomorphism with Favorableness toward Counselor Use of Metaphor." *DAI* 51 (October 1990): 2045B.

Isomorphic metaphors that parallel clients' situations are most favorable in counseling. Suggests using metaphors carefully with intuitive, abstract-thinking clients.

922. Eisenberg, Eric M. "Jamming: Transcendence through Organizing." *ComR* 17 (April 1990): 139–164.

Describes characteristics of "jamming" experiences. Jamming allows people to feel part of a larger community without being obligated to reveal personal information.

923. Ellenhorn, Theodore J. "The Symbolic Transformations of Subjective Experience in Discourse." *DAI* 50 (January 1990): 3204B.

Explores the interplay between mental representations of experience and verbal processing through tasks of narrative, naming speed, and reasoning. Creates a model of referential processing.

924. Fitch-Hauser, Margaret, Deborah A. Barker, and Adele Hughes. "Receiver Apprehension and Listening Apprehension: A Linear or Curvilinear Relationship?" *SCJ* 56 (Fall 1990): 62–71.

Finds a significant linear relationship between receiver apprehension and listening apprehension.

925. Fletcher, Charles, and Susan T. Chrysler. "Surface Forms, Textbases, and Situation Models: Recognition Memory for Three Types of Textual Information." *DPr* 13 (April–June 1990): 175–190.

Experimental data argue for three levels of representation in memory of texts: a surface representation, an underlying propositional network, and a situational model.

926. Gesshel, Susan. "Metaphor, Cognitive Processing, and Psychotherapy: A Theoretical Perspective." *DAI* 51 (December 1990): 3130B.

Proposes a philosophical, experiential theory to integrate psychodynamic, or therapeutic, and cognitive approaches to metaphor.

927. Golding, Jonathan, Arthur Graesser, and Keith Mills. "What Makes a Good Answer to a Question? Testing a Psychological Model of Question Answering in the Context of Narrative Text." *DPr* 13 (July–September 1990): 305–325.

Subjects' judgments of the appropriateness of answers provided a test of QUEST, a model for question answering with mechanisms for searches and convergences of information.

928. Gopnik, Alison. "Knowing, Doing, and Talking: The Oxford Years." *HD* 33 (November–December 1990): 334–338.

Discusses Bruner's contributions to developmental psycholinguistics and describes the importance of relationships in language acquisition.

929. Graesser, Arthur, and Stanley Franklin. "QUEST: A Cognitive Model of Question Answering." *DPr* 13 (July–September 1990): 279–303.

QUEST specifies the data bases accessed to provide answers to questions. The model includes mechanisms for searches and convergences of information from different sources.

930. Graesser, Arthur, Richard Roberts, and Catherine Hackett-Renner. "Question Answering in the Context of Telephone Surveys, Business Interactions, and Interviews." *DPr* 13 (July–September 1990): 327–348.

Data from taped interviews provided a test of QUEST, a model for question answering.

931. Gregg, Noel, and Cheri Hoy. "Referencing: The Cohesive Use of Pronouns in the Written Narrative of College Underprepared Writers, Nondisabled Writers, and Writers with Learning Disabilities." *JLD* 23 (November 1990): 557–563.

Results show that students in each of the three groups studied could make effective use of pronoun referencing in written narratives.

932. Handel, Amos. "Formative Encounters in Early Adulthood: Mentoring Relationships for Mentees." *HD* 33 (July–October 1990): 289–303.

Explores the psychological nature and importance of mentoring relationships for mentees.

933. Hollander, Mark Boni. "The Unconscious Structured like a Language: A Study of the Paradigmatic/Syntactic Axes and Referential Activity of the Hysteroid and Obsessoid Subject." *DAI* 51 (December 1990): 3134B.

Empirically tests Lacan's suggested linguistic structure for the unconscious. Finds sex differences but little support for hypothesized relationships of personality, linguistic, and cognitive variables.

934. Ingram, Joyce Lavelle. "Metaphor in Psychotherapy Reconsidered: A Hermeneutic Approach." *DAI* 51 (September 1990): 1501B.

Determines that figurative language plays a significant role in sessions that attempt to identify the meanings of conflicts.

935. Jones, Janet Lee. "The Interactive Lexicon: Context-Dependent Access of Homonym Meanings across the Time Course of Activation." *DAI* 50 (May 1990): 5354B.

Using a semantic priming paradigm, finds that, in normal language comprehension, contextual information guides the selection of appropriate meaning without requiring all meanings to be considered.

936. Kellett, David A. J. "The Cognitive Benefits of Peer Tutoring and Peer Collaboration." *DAI* 50 (June 1990): 3897A.

Analyzes whether tutors develop cognitive benefits through tutoring or collaborating with students who have less information or poorer cognitive strategies than the tutors do.

937. Kelly, Renata K. "Toward a Theory of Metaphor as Cognitive Process and Linguistic Product." *DAI* 51 (July 1990): 153A.

Traces metaphor as a principle of transference that not only informs but also structures cognitive processes.

938. Keysar, Boaz. "Semantic and Pragmatic Factors in Metaphor Comprehension." *DAI* 50 (February 1990): 3732B.

Asserts that in a discourse analysis literal and metaphorical interpretations can be the product of similar inferences.

939. Kintsch, Eileen. "Macroprocesses and Microprocesses in the Development of Summarization Skill." *CI* 7 (Summer 1990): 161–195.

Results support an expected correlation among age group, representation of meaning, and the kinds of inferential processes on which the summaries were based.

940. Kyllonen, Patrick C., and Raymond E. Christal. "Reasoning Ability Is (Little More Than) Working-Memory Capacity?" *Intell* 14 (October–December 1990): 389–433.

Finds a "consistent and remarkably high correlation" between reasoning ability and working-memory capacity. General (verbal) knowledge and speed/efficiency processing are related to reading ability and working-memory capacity respectively.

941. Lauer, Thomas, and Eileen Peacock. "An Analysis of Comparison Questions in the Context of Auditing." *DPr* 13 (July–September 1990): 349–361.

Auditors can gauge the financial health of a company through comparison questions such as "How strong a market share do you have?"

942. Leader, Zachary. *Writer's Block*. Baltimore: The Johns Hopkins University Press, 1990. 272 pages

Looks at writer's block from psychoanalytical, historical, and poststructural perspectives in order to connect an internal condition with external factors. Seeks to know at what point externally imposed impediments—such as prohibitions of class, race, and gender—become internalized.

943. Loring, Annie. "Parsing Temporarily Ambiguous Verb Phrases." *DAI* 51 (September 1990): 1479B.

Examines timed continuous syntactic and lexical decision making and makes a case for the parser's flexibility.

944. McCardle, Peggy, and Bruce E. Wilson. "Hormonal Influences on Language Development in Physically Advanced Children." *BL* 38 (January–February 1990): 410–423.

Research supports a significant hormonal effect on language development.

945. McCutchen, Leighton Brooks. "The Social Language of Dialectics and Irony: Freud, Lacan, and Clinical Practice." *DAI* 51 (December 1990): 3140B.

Demonstrates how language structures can be understood as a "vocabulary of consciousness sustained by social field."

946. Meisel, Patsy Ann. "Identification of Themes in Communication-Related Critical Incidents in Newly Formed Stepfamilies." *DAI* 51 (October 1990): 1046A.

Investigates the common themes in family conflicts arising from the formation of new family units. Deals with the verbal responses.

947. Miller, Diana L. "Characterizing Mental Models in Narrative Comprehension." *DAI* 51 (August 1990): 1020B.

Studies how imaginal and nonimaginal components seem to comprise the mental model structure, drawing implications for story comprehension.

948. Miller, Lori Ann. "Who Knows How the Wind Blows: Cognitive Style in (and outside) the Classroom." *WE* 1 (Spring 1990): 44–49.

Reports on the author's conversations with three writing students, analyzed according to Myers-Briggs Type Indicator classifications.

949. Montague, Marjorie, Cleborne D. Maddux, and Mary I. Dereshiwsky. "Story Grammar and Comprehension and Production of Narrative Prose by Students with Learning Disabilities." *JLD* 23 (March 1990): 190–197.

Supports the hypothesis that students with learning disabilities have acquired a rudimentary but not fully developed schema for narrative prose.

950. Montaigne, John R. "The Derivation and Organization of Text Schemata: A Comparison of Hierarchical and Temporal Script Models." *DAI* 51 (October 1990): 2067B.

In narrative texts, finds hierarchical schematic effects evident in reading times but not in memory performance.

951. Morris, Mary, and Janice Leuenberger. "A Report of Cognitive, Academic, and Linguistic Profiles for College Students with and without Learning Disabilities." *JLD* 23 (June–July 1990): 355–360.

Results show significantly poorer language proficiency among students with similar levels of cognition who are experiencing academic difficulties.

952. Motley, Michael T. "Communication as Interaction: A Reply to Beach and Bavelas [*WJSC* 54 (Fall 1990)]." *WJSC* 54 (Fall 1990): 613–623.

Focuses on a consensus of perspectives about the complexities of communication phenomena.

953. Motley, Michael T. "On Whether One Can(not) Not Communicate: An Examination Via Traditional Postulates." *WJSC* 54 (Winter 1990): 1–20.

Concludes that each of four traditional postulates contradicts the axiom that affects general conceptualizations and specific claims about communication.

954. Mross, Ernest Frederick. "Macroprocessing in Expository Text Comprehension." *DAI* 50 (January 1990): 3195B.

Examines how people process topics or abstract the gist of expository prose. Marked topic sentences were better integrated into memory structures than unmarked sentences.

955. Neer, Michael R. "Reducing Situation Anxiety and Avoidance Behavior Associated with Classroom Apprehension." *SCJ* 56 (Fall 1990): 49–61.

Concludes that reducing state anxiety may depend more on reducing prior apprehension about classroom communication than on controlling contextual or situational factors.

956. Olson, David R. "Possible Minds: Reflections on Bruner's Recent Writings on Mind and Self." *HD* 33 (November–December 1990): 339–343.

Describes Bruner's constructivist views of self and calls for a similar view of the mind, thereby providing an alternative to the realism-idealism dichotomy.

957. Oosthuizen, Stanley. "Graphology as Predictor of Academic Achievement." *PMS* 71 (December 1990): 715–721.

　　The upper zone and waviness of lines of college students' handwriting were consistently related to their GPAs.

958. Payne, David A., Charles E. Goolsby, K. Evans, and Richard M. Barton. "Multivariate Analyses of Cognitive and Cognitive Style Variables Based on Hemisphere Specialization Theory Predictive of Success in a College Developmental Studies Program." *PMS* 71 (October 1990): 545–546.

　　Graduating high school students who did well in English tended to show a right-brained profile learning style on the Herrman Brain Dominance Profile.

959. Phillips, Ariel I. "Inner Voices, Inner Selves: A Study of Internal Conversation in Narrative." *DAI* 50 (February 1990): 3677B.

　　Analyzes interviews with 17 college students for instances of internal conversation. Noting gender differences in frequency and theme and cultural differences in tone and style, this study advocates integrating voice into research.

960. Price, Catherine Blanton. "The Influence of Textual Display in Printed Instruction on Attention and Performance." *DAI* 50 (June 1990): 3902A.

　　Examines how textual display in printed instructions influences learners' attention to the instructions and their performance of the instructional goal.

961. Ressler, Lawrence Emory. "The Effect of Compensation-Enhanced Social Work Direct Practice on Verbatim and Gist Recall among the Elderly." *DAI* 51 (September 1990): 1005A.

　　The verbal and visual presentation of information and compensation enhanced recall, supporting earlier research on geriatric memory.

962. Rothenberg, Albert. *Creativity and Madness: New Findings and Old Stereotypes*. Baltimore: The Johns Hopkins University Press, 1990. 200 pages

　　Overturns the myth of the troubled genius and argues that creative thinking generally occurs in a conscious, rational state of mind. Also explores the influence of upbringing and environment on creative artists.

963. Runco, Mark A., and Robert S. Albert, eds. *Theories of Creativity*. Sage Focus Editions, vol. 115. Newbury Park, Calif.: Sage, 1990. 280 pages

　　Eleven essays discuss empirical approaches to creativity. Encompasses a variety of psychological perspectives: behavioral, anthropological, cognitive, developmental, ecological, historiometric, psychometric, personological, and social.

964. Sides, Charles H. "Psychological Types and Teaching Writing." *WE* 1 (Spring 1990): 23–40.

　　Uses the Myers-Briggs Type Indicator to suggest more effective teaching strategies.

965. Singer, Murray. "Answering Questions about Discourse." *DPr* 13 (July–September 1990): 261–277.

　　Reviews recent work on the psychology of answering questions and focuses on responders' pragmatic strategies and memory searches.

966. Slattery, Patrick J. "Applying Intellectual Development Theory to Composition." *JBW* 9 (Fall 1990): 54–65.

　　Analyzes the "complex relationship between intellectual orientation and student writing" by drawing on current developmental research and a study of freshmen attempting "argumentative, multiple-source" essays.

967. Sternberg, Robert J., and John Kolligian, Jr., eds. *Competence Considered*. New Haven, Conn.: Yale University Press, 1990. 448 pages

　　Fifteen essays present recent research on competence and incompetence, perceived and real, from childhood through adulthood. Examines how these perceptions affect self-concept, goals, achievements, and academic performance.

968. Student, Menachem. "The Use of Metaphors in Studying Uncertainty in Entrepreneurs." *DAI* 50 (January 1990): 3220B.

Explores the reliability of analyzing metaphors quantitatively and qualitatively. Discusses the extent to which metaphors can enhance an understanding of the cognitive-affective relationship.

969. Stutman, Randall K., and Sara E. Newell. "Rehearsing for Confrontation." *Arg* 4 (May 1990): 185–198.

Results suggest that confronters maintain strategic and performance goals that guide both the decision to rehearse and the rehearsal process.

970. Turner, David H. "Linguistic Determinants of Performance on Formal Problems." *DAI* 51 (August 1990): 1023B.

Finds a matching bias involved in giving logically wrong answers to deductive reasoning problems. Comprehension may be based more in pragmatics than in grammatical features of sentences.

971. Vaughn, M. Lynn. "The Experience of Writing Poetry." *DAI* 51 (December 1990): 3116B.

A psychological study of the experience of writing poetry.

972. Walker, Jeffrey. "Of Brains and Rhetorics." *CE* 52 (March 1990): 301–322.

Argues that hemispheric theory and neurologists' new brain function paradigm are compatible with Aristotelian rhetorical theory. Discusses some tentative implications for writing instruction.

973. Wayne, John David A. "The Meaning of a Return to Freud in the French Critique of Logocentric Psychology." *DAI* 51 (July 1990): 446B.

Applies the structural linguistics of Saussure, adapted by Derrida and Lacan, to argue against psychologies that emphasize a conscious ego rather than a Freudian unconscious.

974. Welborn, Ralph Bearl. "Varying Knowledge Criteria and Technological Innovation: Explorations in Differing Epistemological Traditions." *DAI* 51 (October 1990): 1257A.

Discusses the relationship of technology to problem solving. Gives an analysis of epistemological technology.

975. Wilson, Steven R. "Development and Test of a Cognitive Rules Model of Interaction Goals." *ComM* 57 (June 1990): 81–103.

Suggests that people represent their knowledge about communication goals within an associative network model of memory that contains cognitive rules linking situational features and desired outcomes.

See also 7, 60, 65, 113, 125, 132, 179, 222, 242, 579, 591, 611, 627, 646, 654, 671, 686, 735, 757, 763, 989, 1365, 1457

2.10   EDUCATION

976. Applebee, Arthur N., Judith A. Langer, and Ina S. Mullis. *Crossroads in American Education: A Summary of Findings.* Princeton, N.J.: ETS, 1989. 56 pages

Analyzes data from students on the kinds of learning activities they have experienced in school. Concludes that "students are given limited opportunities to apply knowledge and procedures for new purposes."

977. Baack, Kristie L. "A Theory of the Language of Leaders." *DAI* 50 (March 1990): 2703A.

Creates a theory describing the rhetoric of leaders in educational environments.

978. Beyer, Landon E., and Michael W. Apple, eds. *The Curriculum: Problems, Politics, and Possibilities*. Frontiers in Education. Albany,

N.Y.: State University of New York Press, 1988. 368 pages

Seventeen essays define issues in curriculum studies.They explore the nature of the field, problems in planning curricula, criteria for including specific content areas, constraints imposed by the work place of teaching, the influence of technology, and curriculum evaluation.

979. Bleich, David. "Sexism in Academic Styles of Learning." *JAC* 10 (1990): 231–247.

A critique of sexist (aggressive) presumptions historically and currently operative in the sciences, social sciences, and humanities and in the hierarchical, competitive academic world.

980. Clower, John W. "Women's Contributions to the Theory of Language Pedagogy in the U.S.: The First Women Theorists." *DAI* 50 (June 1990): 3874A.

Proposes that the first American women to use the theory of language pedagogy were of the generation born in the last 15 years of the eighteenth century.

981. Gardner, Howard. "The Difficulties of School." *Daedalus* 119 (Spring 1990): 85–113.

Argues that problems in today's schools can be addressed by an individually configured approach to excellence.

982. Gellert, Claudius, Erich Leitner, and Jurgen Schramm, eds. *Research and Teaching at Universities: International and Comparative Perspectives*. European University Series. New York: Peter Lang, 1990. 192 pages

A collection of essays analyzing the historical origins, normative concepts, and theoretical implications of the changing relationship between research and teaching. Contributors are not indexed separately in this volume.

983. Giroux, Henry A. *Teachers as Intellectuals: Toward a Critical Pedagogy of Learning*. Westport, Conn.: Bergin & Garvey, 1989. 288 pages

Teachers must be seen as intellectuals who are capable of linking conception to practice, linking schooling to a democratic vision, and maintaining some control over the nature of their jobs. Students must also be treated as intellectuals by engaging them in a critical pedagogy so that they can better understand their own voices.

984. Gitlin, Andrew David. "Educative Research, Voice, and School Change." *HER* 60 (November 1990): 443–466.

Outlines theoretical assumptions behind educative research, a dialogical approach that challenges the alienating effects of traditional research methods. Describes the research value of personal and school histories.

985. Goodlad, John I., Roger Soder, and Kenneth A. Sirotnik, eds. *The Moral Dimensions of Teaching*. Jossey-Bass Education Series. San Francisco: Jossey-Bass, 1990. 375 pages

Ten essays "explore the critical moral questions that must be asked and answered before meaningful education reform can take place." Part One focuses on the nature and commitments of teaching as a profession; Part Two, on the moral mission of education and implications for the teaching profession.

986. Hawisher, Gail E., and Anna O. Soter, eds. *On Literacy and Its Teaching: Issues in English Education*. Literacy, Culture, and Learning: Theory and Practice. Albany, N.Y.: State University of New York Press, 1990. 352 pages

A collection of 15 essays that discuss professional issues of concern to English teachers and teacher educators. Four sections treat teaching as a profession, literature and writing, rhetoric and composition, and the learning of language.

987. Houghton, Robert Stuart. "A Chaotic Paradigm: An Alternative World View of the Foundations of Educational Inquiry." *DAI* 50 (May 1990): 3464A.

Applies Kuhn's theory of scientific revolutions to form alternative educational paradigms.

988. Lane, Mervin, ed. *Black Mountain College: Sprouted Seeds: An Anthology of Personal Accounts.* Knoxville, Tenn.: University of Tennessee Press, 1990. 352 pages

A collection of essays, poems, plays, and artwork that shows the effects of the Black Mountain experience on the contributors' conceptions of creativity, learning, and living over the past 50 years.

989. Miller, Robert J., Bill Snider, and Chet Rzonca. "Variables Related to the Decision of Young Adults with Learning Disabilities to Participate in Postsecondary Education." *JLD* 23 (June–July 1990): 349–354.

Results suggest that the more subjects are aware of and able to access community resources the more likely they are to attend a postsecondary institution.

990. National Center for Education Statistics. *The Condition of Education 1990.* Washington, D.C.: U.S. Government Printing Office, 1990. 453 pages

A two-volume statistical report on American education. Volume One covers elementary and secondary education; Volume Two, postsecondary education.

991. Nelson, Ron J., John M. Dodd, and Deborah J. Smith. "Faculty Willingness to Accommodate Students with Learning Disabilities: A Comparison among Academic Divisions." *JLD* 23 (March 1990): 185–189.

Questionnaire results show moderate differences among business, education, and arts and sciences faculty. Faculty comments indicate a willingness to accommodate but not at the expense of academic integrity.

992. Paringer, William Andrew. *John Dewey and the Paradox of Liberal Reform.* Albany, N.Y.: State University of New York Press, 1990. 215 pages

A critique of the American philosopher's concepts of science, nature, democracy, and experience, particularly as those concepts relate to educational practice.

993. Raines, Helon Howell. "Is There a Writing Program in This College? 236 Two-Year Schools Respond." *CCC* 41 (May 1990): 151–165.

Responses to this survey reveal some unique features of community college teaching and great diversity within that field.

994. Schaefer, William D. *Education without Compromise: From Chaos to Coherence in Higher Education.* Jossey-Bass Higher Education Series. San Francisco: Jossey-Bass, 1990. 175 pages

Argues that today's colleges and universities, in their attempt simultaneously to provide an academic education and train students for careers, have undermined the purpose and value of a traditional liberal arts education.

995. Weis, Lois, Philip G. Altbach, Gail P. Kelly, Hugh G. Petrie, and Sheila Slaughter, eds. *Crisis in Teaching: Perspectives on Current Reforms.* Frontiers in Education. Albany, N.Y.: State University of New York Press, 1989. 289 pages

A collection of 14 essays examines the "crisis in teaching." Explores the definition of *crisis,* the evidence for its existence, proposed reforms, and possible effects of reform proposals.

996. Young, Eva, and Mariwilda Padilla. "Mujeres Unidas en Accion: A Popular Education Process." *HER* 60 (February 1990): 1–18.

Describes the practices of a community agency helping low-income Massachusetts women to educate themselves. Offers a model for educational research.

See also 250, 299, 434, 484, 804, 958, 1048

2.11   JOURNALISM, PUBLISHING, TELEVISION, AND RADIO

997. Abdulrazak, Fawzi A. "The Kingdom of the Book: The History of Printing as an Agency of Change in Morocco between 1865 and 1912." *DAI* 51 (July 1990): 263A.

Argues that printing technology changed the manner in which Islamic tradition was transmitted and changed the power structure of the traditional Islamic leaders.

998. Amesley, Cassandra Elinor. " 'Star Trek' as a Cultural Text: Proprietary Audiences, Interpretive Grammars, and the Myth of the Relating Reader." *DAI* 51 (August 1990): 329A.

Explores the concept of interpretation through ethnographic research focused on "Star Trek" fans. Considers how interpretation can be "expanded, revised, negotiated, and transmitted."

999. Anderson, James A., ed. *Communication Yearbook 14*. Newbury Park, Calif.: Sage, 1990. 640 pages

Commentaries treat current research on audiences, the quality of mass media performance and public opinion, the implications of propaganda, organization studies, approaches to media, the pressure of public opinion, and media agenda setting, among other topics.

1000. Austin, Sydney B. "AIDS and Africa: U.S. Media and Racist Fantasy." *CCrit* 14 (Winter 1989–1990): 129–152.

Analyzes conventions of the AIDS story, including stock characters and recurring plots.

1001. Berry, Nicholas O. *Foreign Policy and the Press: An Analysis of The New York Times' Coverage of U. S. Foreign Policy*. New York: Greenwood Press, 1990. 164 pages

Examines the press' relationship with the foreign policy establishment through a content analysis of the *Times'* reports on foreign policy issues during the Kennedy, Johnson, Nixon, Carter, and Reagan administrations.

1002. Blankenship, Jenny. "A Look at the Media in Mainland China." *PC* 10 (Fall 1990): 23.

A former Radio Beijing journalist from the People's Republic of China discusses cultural differences between Chinese and American journalism.

1003. Bostian, Lloyd, and Barbara Hollander. "Technical Journal Editors and Writing Style." *JTWC* 20 (1990): 153–163.

Argues that most technical and scientific journals do not communicate efficiently because editors value scientific quality over stylistic clarity and have little training as editors.

1004. Brossman, Brent G., and Daniel G. Canary. "An Observational Analysis of Argument Structures: The Case of 'Nightline.' " *Arg* 4 (May 1990): 199–212.

An analysis of "Nightline" transcripts revealed more compound structural variations but fewer simple, convergent, and eroded argument structures than had been found in previous research.

1005. Brown, William J. "The Persuasive Appeal of Mediated Terrorism: The Case of the TWA Flight 847 Hijacking." *WJSC* 54 (Spring 1990): 219–236.

Suggests that narrative theory provides a valuable method for analyzing media coverage and its effects on distant audiences.

1006. Butler, Susan Lowell. "Keeping Score and Pushing for Change." *PC* 10 (Winter 1990): 10–11, 25.

Reports on a survey of women as reporters and newsmakers on television news. *Washington Post* columnist Judy Mann discusses women's treatment by the media.

1007. Carson, David L. "Editorial: The Jay R. Gould Twentieth Anniversary Volume." *JTWC* 20 (1990): 1–5.

Dedicates the twentieth volume of *JTWC* to the founding editor, Jay Reid Gould, and excerpts Professor Gould's first and final editorials.

1008. Carson, David L. "The Jay R. Gould Twentieth Anniversary Interview." *JTWC* 20 (1990): 7–8.

Surveys the career of Professor Jay Reid Gould, first and now retiring editor of *JTWC*.

1009. Chirco, Ann Patricia. "An Examination of Stepwise Regression Models of Adolescent Alcoholic and Marijuana Use with Special Attention to the Television Exposure/Teen Drinking Issue." *DAI* 51 (October 1990): 1034A.

Focuses on the role of television viewing in marijuana and alcohol use among teens.

1010. Cornfield, Michael Barker. "Presidential Copy: Feature Stories about President Harry S. Truman." *DAI* 50 (February 1990): 2630A.

Examines the interests of American political journalists in shaping the news into good stories.

1011. Crawford, Vallaurrie Lynn. "The Balimbing Press: Censorship and International Professional Ideology in Philippine Journalism." *DAI* 51 (August 1990): 624A.

Examines the interplay between the ideology of objective journalism and indigenous Philippine literary and cultural forms.

1012. Dickson, Sandra H. "Propaganada and the Press: The Treatment of the U.S.-Nicaraguan Conflict by the *Washington Post* and the *Washington Times*." *DAI* 50 (February 1990): 2284A.

Finds that themes of propaganda appeared in both papers but were portrayed differently, the press serving as a legitimator.

1013. "A Different Look at Television Ratings." *QRD* 16 (July 1990): 9.

Argues that television ratings raise more questions than they answer.

1014. Downing, John D. H. "U.S. Media Discourse on South Africa: The Development of a Situational Model." *D&S* 1 (July 1990): 39–60.

A discourse analysis of *Time* and *Newsweek* coverage of South Africa in 1948, 1960, and 1976 suggests that these media did not adequately inform the American public.

1015. Gunesekera, Manique. "Discourse Genres in English Newspapers of Singapore, South India, and Sri Lanka." *DAI* 50 (February 1990): 2472A.

Explains that lead stories and editorials constitute distinctive genres but that neither genre incorporates many examples of the new Englishes.

1016. Harris, Jeanette, and Joyce Kinkead. "An Interview with the Founding Editors of *The Writing Center Journal*." *WCJ* 11 (Fall–Winter 1990): 3–14.

An interview with Lil Brannon and Stephen North discusses the journal's inception and the institutional and research roles of writing centers over the last decade.

1017. Japp, Debra K. "Forging Bonds of Unity and Sympathy among Women: A Cultural-Rhetorical Analysis of the *Progressive Woman*, 1907–1914." *DAI* 51 (August 1990): 343A.

Examines how Josephine Conger-Kaneko's periodical helped Socialist women in the Midwest change women's societal roles.

1018. Kingston, Paul William, and Jonathan R. Cole. *The Wages of Writing: Per Word, Per Piece, or Perhaps*. New York: Columbia University Press, 1986. 209 pages

Provides information on authors' earnings, their time commitments, and their attitudes toward writing and other work that they do.

1019. "The Language of War." *QRD* 17 (October 1990): 11.

Reports on a 30-minute segment of a television series that deals with the language of war.

1020. "Legalized Lying." *QRD* 16 (July 1990): 8.

Explains the practice of specially preparing product packages for televison and magazine advertisements. Reprinted from *The Philadelphia Inquirer*, 25 May 1990.

1021. Luo, Catherine, and Mitsuo Nakamura. "An Afternoon with Jay R. Gould." *JTWC* 20 (1990): 9–17.

An interview with the first editor of *JTWC*. Describes the journal's origin, the beginnings of Rensselaer's graduate technical writing program, and Professor Gould's views on technical communication.

1022. Mayer, Michael E., William B. Gudykunst, Norman K. Perrill, and Bruce D. Merrill. "A Comparison of Competing Models of the News Diffusion Process." *WJSC* 54 (Winter 1990): 113–123.

Investigates the relative roles of interpersonal and mediated communication by analyzing the diffusion of information about the space shuttle Challenger explosion.

1023. Philo, Greg. *Seeing and Believing: The Influence of Television.* New York: Routledge, 1990. 244 pages

A study of how news coverage shapes public memory of events. British viewers were asked to write their own news programs about Britain's 1984 coal strike one year after it occurred.

1024. Polking, Kirk, Joan Bloss, and Colleen Cannon, eds. *Writing A to Z: The Terms, Procedures, and Facts of the Writing Business Defined, Explained, and Put within Reach.* Cincinnati: Writer's Digest Books, 1990. 545 pages

A slightly revised version of the compendium *Writer's Encyclopedia* (1983). Contains 1200 entries.

1025. "Project Censored." *QRD* 16 (July 1990): 6.

Explains the history and purpose of Project Censored and announces the top ten "censored" stories of 1989.

1026. Pufahl, Ingrid. "Informing the Public: A Comparison of Television News Discourse in the U.S. and the Federal Republic of Germany." *DAI* 50 (January 1990): 2039A.

Describes television news in terms of its structural properties, illustrating "different linguistic manifestations in German and U.S. news."

1027. Ramsey, Richard David. "The Life and Work of Jay R. Gould." *JTWC* 20 (1990): 19–24.

Describes the career of Jay R. Gould as "student, teacher, consultant, and author and editor, including services as the editor of *JTWC*."

1028. Rank, Hugh. "Bait and Switch, Loss Leaders, and Rain Checks: Surviving the Doublespeak of the Hard Sell." *QRD* 16 (July 1990): 9–10.

Analyzes bait-and-switch selling as examples of diversion and downplay. Argues that awareness is the best defense and explains how and where to file complaints.

1029. Rouzan, Laura V. "A Rhetorical Analysis of Editorials in *L'Union* and the *New Orleans Tribune*." *DAI* 51 (July 1990): 12A.

Examines the editorials of the first two black-owned newspapers in the U.S., discussing their content, arguments, Aristotelian appeals, and underlying philosophies.

1030. Rucinski, Dianne Marie. "Communication and Reciprocity: A Reconceptualization of Political Knowledge." *DAI* 50 (June 1990): 3782A.

Investigates the concept of political knowledge and how it has been used in studies of mass media.

1031. Rush, Laura M. "Covering a Rape." *PC* 10 (Fall 1990): 8–9, 19.

Discusses Nancy Ziegenmeyer's decision to have her name printed in Jane Schorer's articles for the *Des Moines Register* that covered Ziegenmeyer's rape and her attacker's trial.

1032. Sansom, Leslie. "Exploring New Territory on the Airwaves." *PC* 10 (Spring 1990): 13–14.

Describes the genesis and development of "51%," a half-hour weekly radio program devoted to issues affecting women.

1033. Sansom, Leslie. "A Long Way to Go." *PC* 10 (Summer 1990): 18–19.

A "Women in the Media" panel at an American University Forum concluded that much needs to be done to improve portrayals of women in the media.

1034. Sansom, Leslie. "Survey Shows Improvement." *PC* 10 (Summer 1990): 6–8.

Reports the results of a survey of male and female bylines, photos, and story sources on the front pages of 20 American newspapers during February 1990.

1035. Secrist, Patrice McDermott. "Politics and Scholarship: A Cultural Study of Feminist Academic Journals." *DAI* 51 (September 1990): 903A.

Examines the publishing practices of feminist academic journals, describing the construction, negotiation, and legitimation of new cultural knowledge.

1036. "Spending on Television Advertising." *QRD* 16 (July 1990): 9.

Names several companies and the amounts they have spent on television advertising, showing large increases over the last eight years.

1037. Stein, Heather L. "Behind Closed Doors—Usually." *PC* 10 (Fall 1990): 16–17, 19.

Documents Liz Randolph's successful civil suit against two disc jockeys and the management of Pittsburgh radio station WBZZ after two years of sexual harassment.

1038. Ward, R. J. "A Stylistic Analysis of Administrative English through a Qualitative and Quantitative Investigation of Government Information Leaflets." *DAI* 50 (April 1990): 3218A.

Although styles varied widely, the address to the reader can be classified either as personal or impersonal.

1039. White, Arden, and Barbara Klimowski. *Participation in the Journal of College Student Development as Author and Editorial Board Members: A Gender Study.* Alexandria, Va.: EDRS, 1988. ERIC ED 318 980. 6 pages

Studies the gender of authors and editorial board members for the *Journal of College Student Development* (formerly the *Journal of College Student Personnel*) from 1959 to 1988. Results show increased female participation.

1040. Wilhoit, G. Cleveland, and David H. Weaver. *Newsroom Guide to Polls and Surveys.* Bloomington, Ind.: Indiana University Press, 1990. 88 pages

An introduction to methods of research and the evaluation of data.

1041. Williams, David Edward. "Rhetoric of the Temperance Movement: A Study of Rhetorical Clusters and Representative Anecdotes in the *American Issue*." *DAI* 51 (December 1990): 1832A.

Discusses changes in rhetorical strategies in the temperance and prohibition movement between 1900 and 1933, focusing on the arguments presented by the Anti-Saloon League.

1042. Wilson, R. Jackson. *Figures of Speech: American Writers and the Literary Marketplace from Benjamin Franklin to Emily Dickinson.* Baltimore: The Johns Hopkins University Press, 1990. 312 pages

Examines how a literary audience whose interests were in commerce held idealistic notions about culture. This in turn affected how writers had to elaborate portraits of themselves as people for whom money and fame counted for nothing.

1043. Young, Brian M. *Television Advertising and Children.* New York: Oxford University Press, 1990. 360 pages

Uses data from the U.S. and Britain to examine the development of children's abilities to interpret and understand the goals of advertisements.

1044. Zeigler, Stephen McMillan. "The Editorial Rhetoric of Ralph McGill in the Civil Rights Era." *DAI* 51 (July 1990): 8A.

Affirms that the editor used his rhetorical skill to identify himself with Southern readers.

See also 28, 372, 453, 554, 568, 569, 579, 596, 648, 875, 1058

2.12   PHILOSOPHY

1045. Bineham, Jeffery L. "The Cartesian Anxiety in Epistemic Rhetoric: An Assessment of the Literature." *P&R* 23 (1990): 43–62.

Demonstrates differences among epistemic rhetorics and how they address Richard Bernstein's Cartesian anxiety, which assumes only objective foundationalism or relative skepticism.

1046. Canziani, Guido. "Some Aspects of Eloquence in Descartes' Works." *Arg* 4 (February 1990): 53–68.

Discusses the tensions in Descartes' work between his condemnation of the art of rhetoric and his concern about the persuasive power of pure intellectual evidence.

1047. Elliot, Norbert, and Paul Zelhart. "Hermeneutics and the Teaching of Technical Writing." *TWT* 17 (Spring 1990): 150–164.

Describes the usefulness of hermeneutic inquiry and its potential for technical writing teachers.

1048. Forster, Paul Dickinson. "Community, Consensus, and Progress: Problems in Prag-

matism from Peirce and Dewey to Putnam and Rorty." *DAI* 51 (October 1990): 1254A.

Deals with the central debates in modern pragmatism and describes the arguments involved.

1049. Gallo, Beverly Elaine. "Nietzsche's Self-Referential Paradox: Rhetoric, Style, and Interpretation." *DAI* 50 (February 1990): 2518A.

Nietzsche's nonassertive style creates an apparent paradox, but he offers alternative perspectives to challenge rather than to prove.

1050. Garns, Rudy Lee. "Really Knowing: An Essay on the Absolute Nature of Knowledge." *DAI* 50 (June 1990): 3979A.

Argues that knowledge is an absolute concept. The standards for knowing do not vary from context to context.

1051. Gasche, Rudolphe. "Some Reflections on the Notion of Hypotyposis in Kant." *Arg* 4 (February 1990): 85–100.

Examines Kant's use of the rhetorical concept "hypotyposis" to conceptualize and elaborate the philosophical problem of presentation.

1052. Hall, William Eiler. "Ethical Aspects of Kenneth Burke's *A Grammar of Motives, A Rhetoric of Motives,* and *The Rhetoric of Religion.*" *DAI* 51 (November 1990): 1442A.

Provides close textual readings, critical assessment, and comparative analyses with normative ethics.

1053. Hogan, Melinda Ann. "The Concept of Thought: Logical Form in the Account of Mental Representation." *DAI* 50 (June 1990): 3980A.

Explores how explaining the representational powers of belief can work with truth conditions determined by their logical forms.

1054. Howe, Leslie Alison. "Kierkegaard's Critique of Ethics." *DAI* 51 (October 1990): 1254A.

Studies the relationship between Kierkegaard's critique of ethics and his understanding of the self.

1055. Johnson, David Glenn. "Ethical Disbelief." *DAI* 51 (October 1990): 1255A.

A discussion of the epistemic implications of disbelief.

1056. Juneja, Bimaljeet. "Philosophical Disagreement." *DAI* 51 (November 1990): 1640A.

Disagreements over philosophical questions have inspired the development of analysis techniques and of descriptions of our knowledge of the world and language.

1057. Kidneigh, Barbara Jean. "The Potential Rhetorical Power of Myth: An Account Based on the Writings of Cassirer, Langer, and Burke." *DAI* 51 (December 1990): 1828A.

Identifies "mythic rhetoric potential" and demonstrates how mythic archetypal models "effect benevolent as well as malevolent consequences" in both individuals and cultures.

1058. Kostelnick, Charles. "Typographical Design, Modernist Aesthetics, and Professional Communication." *JBTC* 4 (January 1990): 5–24.

Traces modernist aesthetics—as developed from Bauhaus concepts of unity, economy, objectivity, and intuition—and its relation to text and information design.

1059. Kremer-Marietti, Angele. "Theory of Philosophy as a Science of the Symbolic." *Arg* 4 (August 1990): 363–373.

A metaphilosophical study linking Kant, Freud, and Lacan. The structure of "knowing" in philosophy is presented as a way of symbolizing.

1060. Marin, Louis. "Rhetorics of Truth, Justice, and Secrecy in Pascal's Text." *Arg* 4 (February 1990): 69–84.

Argues that Pascal attempted to erase himself as a subject of discourse in order to make truth and justice "speak" through his writing.

1061. Pickering, John, and Steve Attridge. "Viewpoints: Metaphor and Monsters—Children's Storytelling." *RTE* 24 (December 1990): 415–440.

Prefers Vichian to Cartesian perspectives on the integration of cognition and emotion.

1062. Plochmann, George Kimball. *Richard McKeon: A Study*. Chicago: University of Chicago Press, 1990. 276 pages

An examination and evaluation of McKeon's philosophical thought by a former student.

1063. Sini, Carlo. "Dialectic, Rhetoric, and Writing: The Problem of Method." *Arg* 4 (February 1990): 101–108.

While philosophy establishes truth by logical argument, the act of thinking is wider than the art of rhetoric, hence the crisis of the meaning of knowledge nowadays.

1064. Turbayne, Colin Murray. *Metaphors for the Mind: The Creative Mind and Origin*. Columbia, S.C.: University of South Carolina Press, 1990. 160 pages

Analyzes the significance of metaphor in human thought by exploring historical traditions of philosophy. Traces the influence Platonic metaphors have exerted on later philosophers such as Berkeley and Kant.

See also 57, 80, 126, 237, 253, 262, 294, 296, 301, 306, 308, 329, 818, 992, 1433

2.13   SCIENCE AND MEDICINE

1065. Barabas, Christine. *Technical Writing in a Corporate Culture: A Study of Nature of Information*. Writing Research Series, vol. 18. Norwood, N.J.: Ablex, 1990. 272 pages

Analyzes the relationships among writers' intentions, texts, and readers' expectations in technical writing produced within a research and development organization.

1066. Biklen, Douglas. "Communication Unbound: Autism and *Praxis*." *HER* 60 (August 1990): 291–314.

Illustrates the effectiveness of an "education-through-dialogue approach," showing how people labeled severely autistic can communicate in certain circumstances with certain facilitators. Challenges widely held assumptions.

1067. Bowen, Sheryl Perlmutter, and Paula Michal-Johnson. "A Rhetorical Perspective for HIV Education with Black Urban Adolescents." *ComR* 17 (December 1990): 848–866.

Using the rhetorical situation as the organizing schema, this essay examines the challenges in providing AIDS education to black urban adolescents.

1068. Condit, Celeste Michelle. "The Birth of Understanding: Chaste Science and the Harlot of the Arts." *ComM* 57 (December 1990): 323–327.

Views knowledge as discovered, produced, or reproduced. States that rhetoric and science have led each other away from their earlier ideals.

1069. Condit, Celeste Michelle. *Decoding Abortion Rhetoric: Communicating Social Change*. Champaign, Ill.: University of Illinois Press, 1990. 256 pages

Describes the ways in which the public interactions of various partisans molded legal and cultural consensus on abortion issues between 1960 and the mid-1980s.

1070. Connelly, Julia M. "The Whole Story." *L&M* 9 (1990): 150–161.

Uses fictional narratives of illness to argue that medical professionals must understand the complexities and totality of the illness narratives told by their patients.

1071. Cushman, Donald P. "A Window of Opportunity Argument." *ComM* 57 (December 1990): 328–332.

Discusses rhetorical inquiry—its nature, function, and scope—in light of whether science and rhetoric are compatible.

1072. Goldbort, Robert C. "Scientific Writing and the College Curriculum." *DAI* 50 (January 1990): 2041A.

Weighs two views regarding the origin of the plain style in scientific discourse. Argues that regarding scientific writing as "plain" is limited and misleading.

1073. Gould, Clinton A. "Beyond Disease: A Conceptual Analysis of the Language and Origins of the Meaning of AIDS in a Sociohistoric and Medical Context." *DAI* 51 (November 1990): 1537A.

Examines connections between language and the medical, cultural, sociohistoric, and epistemological contexts in which disease is identified and codified.

1074. Gragson, Gay, and Jack Selzer. "Fictionalizing the Readers of Scholarly Articles in Biology." *WC* 7 (January 1990): 25–58.

Uses reader-response criticism to contrast the very different "reader in the text" found in the opening pages of two articles on evolutionary biology.

1075. Harris, R. Allen. "Assent, Dissent, and Rhetoric in Science." *RSQ* 20 (Winter 1990): 13–37.

Sees knowledge making in science as pursuing two paths, dissent and assent, both of which regard truth and discourse as fundamentally inseparable.

1076. Holloway, Rachel Lynn. "America's Quest for Security and the Hydrogen Bomb Controversy." *DAI* 51 (December 1990): 1827A.

Analyzes the values and identifications in the rhetoric of Robert J. Oppenheimer and Edward Teller. Demonstrates why and how Teller's "terminology was reaffirmed."

1077. Holmquest, Anne. "The Rhetorical Strategy of Boundary-Work." *Arg* 4 (August 1990): 235–258.

Uses a case study of the Tarasoff Prece-
dent—the psychiatrist's "duty to warn"—
to demonstrate the central role of rhetoric
in demarcating science from nonscience.

1078. Hones, Sheila Anne. "Geography, Literature, and the Figurative Landscape." *DAI* 50
(January 1990): 2121A.

Develops a method for analyzing culturally
shared but unarticulated concepts about the
forms and meanings of the physical world.

1079. Journet, Debra. "Forms of Discourse and
the Science of the Mind: Luria, Sacks, and
the Role of Narrative in Neurological Case
Histories." *WC* 7 (April 1990): 171–199.

Examines conflicts between "logical,
quantitative exposition" and "narrative" as
respective manifestations of the physical
and human sciences in case histories by
Luria and Sacks.

1080. Lloyd, Carol V. *How Ideas Are Elaborated in One Topic across Three Biology Textbooks*. Bloomington, Ind.: ERIC/RCS, 1990.
ERIC ED 314 734. 29 pages

Examines three high school biology textbooks written for different audiences, noting differences in how ideas are elaborated.

1081. Maltz, Alesia. "The Role of Language in
the Discovery and Acceptance of Vitamins."
DAI 51 (September 1990): 981A.

Contrasts the languages of biochemists and
physicians, illustrating how differences de-
layed the acceptance of the vitamin defi-
ciency hypothesis in Great Britain.

1082. Maryman, Gary W. "Paradox and Psychotherapy." *DAI* 51 (July 1990): 436B.

Discusses how paradox may be implemented in therapy for prescribing and re-
straining symptoms.

1083. Merriam, Allen H. "Words and Numbers: Mathematical Dimensions of Rhetoric."
SCJ 55 (Summer 1990): 337–354.

Investigates how numbers function rhetorically in influencing persuasive appeals, the

structure of messages, and our use of language.

1084. Murdock, L. Phillip. "The Dynamics of
Collaboration: An Ethnographic Study of Scientific Writing." *DAI* 51 (September 1990):
833A.

Analyzes the influence of collaboration on
the research and writing of four physicists.

1085. Myers, Greg. *Writing Biology: Texts in
the Social Construction of Scientific Knowledge*. Madison, Wis.: University of Wisconsin Press, 1990. 320 pages

Argues that scientific "facts" emerge from
the processes of writing and revising, of
responding to criticisms and suggestions
from editors and referees, and of rewriting
scientific papers for a broader audience.

1086. Nelson, Marc S., Barbara L. Clayton,
and Roberto Moreno. "How Medical School
Faculty Regard Educational Research and
Make Pedagogical Decisions." *AM* 65 (February 1990): 122–126.

Faculty acknowledge the value of educational research in theory but rarely, if ever,
make use of it in reaching pedagogical decisions.

1087. Nolan, James Michael. "A Sociolinguistic Analysis of the Supervision of Female
Counselors." *DAI* 51 (September 1990):
1509B.

Investigates interactive discourse between
psychologist supervisors and counselor
trainees. Both parties were more satisfied
when supervisors spoke less and were less
active.

1088. Pieracci, E. Michael. "The Mythopoesis
of Psychotherapy: The Archetypal, Narrative,
and Mythic Themes in Stories about the Psychotherapy Experience." *DAI* 51 (August
1990): 998B.

Identifies archetypal themes of questing,
wisdom, nurturance, intimacy, acceptance, love, identity, and redemption in
stories about psychotherapy. They show

equal concern with achievement and relationship.

1089. Prelli, Lawrence J. "Rhetorical Logic and the Integration of Rhetoric and Science." *ComM* 57 (December 1990): 315–322.

A more integrative understanding of the relationship between rhetoric and logic in scientists' discourse is needed to show that science and rhetoric are robustly compatible.

1090. Pribble, Paula Tompkins. "Making an Ethical Commitment: A Rhetorical Case Study of Organizational Socialization." *ComQ* 38 (Summer 1990): 255–267.

A rhetorical-critical study of one organization's formal orientation to company objectives.

1091. Reeves, Carol. "The Characterization of a Medical Problem: An Analysis of the Writing on AIDS in Medical Science." *DAI* 50 (March 1990): 2875A.

Examines how AIDS is presented and validated in contemporary medical writing.

1092. Reeves, Carol. "Establishing a Phenomenon: The Rhetoric of Early Medical Reports on AIDS." *WC* 7 (July 1990): 393–416.

Examines and critiques the rhetorical goals of the first three medical reports on AIDS, which sought to establish and explain a mysterious new illness.

1093. Ribeiro, Branca M. "Coherence in Psychotic Discourse: Frame and Topic." *DAI* 50 (January 1990): 2039A.

Looks at how doctors and patients establish referential meaning, achieve or break down topic coherence, and convey larger messages and metamessages.

1094. Stewart, Susan. "The Rhetoric of Alcoholics Anonymous." *DAI* 51 (November 1990): 1443A.

Using Burke, examines AA's method as a transformation of motives, treating the meaning of alcoholism to the alcoholic rather than regarding the disease-as-entity.

1095. Waddell, Craig. "The Role of *Pathos* in the Decision-Making Process: A Study in the Rhetoric of Science Policy." *DAI* 50 (June 1990): 3931A.

Argues that the appropriateness of an emotional appeal depends on its inherent logical foundation, the rhetor's *ethos,* and the audience's character.

1096. Weinstein, Mark. "Towards an Account of Argumentation in Science." *Arg* 4 (August 1990): 269–298.

Proposes a complex model of scientific argumentation to account for its normativity and field dependence. Offers a framework for argument analysis that is domain-specific rather than abstract.

1097. Wolff, Janice M. "Bloody Deconstruction; or, The Semiotics of Surgery." *Reader* 24 (Fall 1990): 21–31.

An analysis of a surgical report suggests that writing is a putting off and a deferring, an absence as well as a presence.

1098. Wynne, Anna. "Rereading Written Data: On the Interpretability of Transcripts of Talk about Multiple Sclerosis." *DAI* 51 (December 1990): 2844B.

Analyzes interviews with multiple sclerosis patients as texts "whose value for research depends on their being different from either fiction or pure speculation."

See also 117, 267, 278, 309, 319, 345, 399, 427, 558, 572, 576, 607, 609, 797, 919, 944, 972, 1000, 1003

2.14   CROSS-DISCIPLINARY STUDIES

1099. Bacon-Smith, Camille M. "Enterprising Women: Television, Folklore, and Community." *DAI* 50 (January 1990): 2194A.

Studies the creation, use, and meaning to participants of art created in a group of science fiction fans.

1100. Bealle, John Rufus. "American Folklore Revival: A Study of an Old-Time Music and Dance Community." *DAI* 50 (January 1990): 2194A.

Studies a type of revival in which the folklore of another culture is engaged for the enhanced experience that it provides.

1101. Bloomer, Jennifer Allyn. "Towards an Architecture of Desire: The (S)Crypt of Joyce and Piranesi." *DAI* 50 (January 1990): 1827A.

Compares the geography of Piranesi's buildings to Joyce's *Finnegan's Wake* to explore "the area where architecture and writing slide into identity."

1102. Borillo, Mario. "A Logical Argumentation Model for Computer-Assisted Reasoning." *Arg* 4 (November 1990): 397–414.

A study of archaeologists' reasoning reveals the complexity and heterogenous nature of arguments used in building scientific knowledge. The article is translated by J.-P. van Noppen.

1103. Brown, Peggy Ann Chittenden. "The Visionary I: Translation, Photography, and the Art of Education." *DAI* 51 (December 1990): 2001A.

Proposes a translation-based model of communication that can serve as the basis of an interdisciplinary approach to the arts and humanities.

1104. Chadwick, Ryan. "Principles of Hypotaxis and Parataxis as Applied to Two Late Medieval Works: Salisbury Cathedral and the 'Missa Nobilis et Pulchra' by Walter Fry." *DAI* 50 (June 1990): 3771A.

Applies the principles of syntax to architectural analysis.

1105. Farnsworth, Rodney. "How the Other Half Sounds: An Historical Survey of Musical Rhetoric during the Baroque and After." *RSQ* 20 (Summer 1990): 207–224.

Surveys musical rhetoric of Baroque and Rococo theorists, arguing that it "functioned under the assumptions and principles of verbal rhetoric," the distinction between verbal and musical rhetoric being a recent development.

1106. Ghezzi, Ridie Wilson. "Ways of Speaking: An Ethnopoetic Analysis of Ojbwe Narratives." *DAI* 51 (November 1990): 1723A.

Examines narrative patterns in nine texts in order to clarify their transcription and revive their fundamental intentions.

1107. Hall, Stephanie Aileen. "'The Deaf Club Is like a Second Home': An Ethnography of Folklore Communication in American Sign Language." *DAI* 50 (January 1990): 2195A.

Considers methods the deaf use for passing on their language and values.

1108. Mansour, Yasser Mohammed. "The Language of Design: Conceptual Interpretations." *DAI* 51 (October 1990): 1025A.

Applies various theories of language to architectural discourse.

1109. Moreno, Maria Luisa. "Seventeenth- and Eighteenth-Century Descriptive Accounts on Mexican Architecture." *DAI* 50 (June 1990): 3774A.

Explores how written descriptions of dedication ceremonies for religious structures shape subsequent religious architectural design.

1110. Orban, Clara E. "Words and Images: The Semiotics of Futurism and Surrealism." *DAI* 51 (July 1990): 156A.

Assesses the connection or disjunction between word and image in the art works of Marinetti, Breton, Boccioni, and Magritte.

1111. Rhode, Deborah L., ed. *Theoretical Perspectives on Gender*. New Haven, Conn.: Yale University Press, 1990. 384 pages

Collects 21 essays in which leading scholars in history, philosophy, law, literary theory, biology, sociology, psychology, political science, and anthropology explore the difference gender makes.

1112. Riessman, Catherine Kohler. *Divorce Talk: Women and Men Make Sense of Per-*

sonal Relationships. New Brunswick, N.J.: Rutgers University Press, 1990. 276 pages

Analyzes how men and women who are undergoing divorces talk about their marriages. Shows how such narratives are used to persuade both the teller and listener that divorce is justified.

1113. Sheridan, Diana Brown. "Ecofeminist Strategies of Peacemaking." *DAI* 51 (November 1990): 1442A.

Discusses verbal and nonverbal rhetorical strategies of peacemaking that are drawn from a variety of human symbolic activities.

1114. Vidal, Mary Paula. "Watteau's Painted Conversations: Art, Literature, and Talk in Seventeenth- and Eighteenth-Century France." *DAI* 50 (February 1990): 2281A.

Suggests that Watteau uses visual representations of conversation to declare the independence of painting from the written word and to merge aesthetic and social codes.

1115. White, Cindy L. "Transformation and the Rhetorical Creation of Culture: A Meta-Analysis of the Evidence from Women's History." *DAI* 50 (June 1990): 3794A.

Studies the rhetorical potential of discourse to contribute to the creation of women's culture by examining central terms in women's history, rhetorical studies, and women's public address.

See also 171, 316, 357, 486, 630, 798

3

Teacher Education, Administration, and Social Roles

3.1 TEACHER EDUCATION

1116. Anderson, Richard C., and Bonnie B. Armbruster. *Some Maxims for Learning and Instruction.* CSR Technical Report, no. 491. Urbana, Ill.: CSR, 1990. ERIC ED 314 741. 15 pages

Offers nine maxims for use in teacher training programs.

1117. Anderson, Richard C., Bonnie B. Armbruster, and Mary Roe. "Improving the Education of Reading Teachers." *Daedalus* 119 (Spring 1990): 187–209.

Recommends the use of videotechnology to improve preservice teacher education.

1118. Batson, Lorie Goodman. "Defining Ourselves as Woman (in the Profession)." *Pre/Text* 10 (Spring-Summer 1989): 117–120.

Claims that women in the profession harbor conflicting loyalties, for they desire to be both in and of the profession but also radically to alter it.

1119. Bishop, Wendy. "Learning Our Own Ways to Situate Composition and Feminist Studies in the English Department." *JAC* 10 (1990): 339–355.

Speculates about the unwritten rules for how one plays being an English department member. Stresses the need for critical consciousness, neighborliness, mentoring, and the believing game for new teachers.

1120. Bishop, Wendy. *Something Old, Something New: College Writing Teachers and Classroom Change.* Studies in Writing and Rhetoric. Carbondale, Ill.: Southern Illinois University Press, 1990. ERIC ED 315 779. 190 pages

Bishop observed teachers enrolled in a doctoral seminar on teaching basic writing. She then collected case studies of five teachers in their college writing classrooms to investigate how their teaching practices changed and how their professional and personal histories influenced their ability to make those changes.

1121. Bixby, Mary Katherine. "Descriptive Inquiry into Preservice Journal Keeping for Teacher Educators." *DAI* 50 (January 1990): 1998A.

Describes how a teacher used individual and group journals as tools for inquiry in a 16-week preservice course dealing with methods of teaching reading.

1122. Bloom, Lynn Z. "Finding a Family, Finding a Voice: A Writing Teacher Teaches Writing Teachers." *JBW* 9 (Fall 1990): 3–14.

A first-person essay dramatizing a "paradigm shift" in the author's work with graduate students. Values "risk-taking" in forming a community of writers with unique voices.

1123. Broder, Peggy F. "Writing Center and Teacher Training." *WPA* 13 (Spring 1990): 37–45.

Sees the writing center as an effective training ground for prospective teachers for gaining insights into the reasons for students' difficulties with their writing processes.

1124. Burton, Larry Wayne. "The Writing Teacher's Role: From Cultural Literacy to Classroom Speech." *DAI* 50 (May 1990): 3503A.

Discusses the role of the writing teacher in resolving philosophical conflicts between the specialists and the literati.

1125. Callister, Thomas A., and Nicholas C. Burbules. "Computer Literacy Programs in Teacher Education: What Teachers Really Need to Learn." *CompEd* 14 (1990): 3–7.

Advocates breaking with the dominant type of introductory computer courses offered to preservice teachers. Suggests integrating technology into subject areas rather than learning it separately.

1126. Chorny, Merron, ed. *Teacher as Researcher*. Calgary, Alberta: The University of Calgary Language in the Classroom Project (distributed by NCTE), 1988. 475 pages

Seventeen essays written by graduate student teachers consider the role of talk, reading, and writing in their own learning about language and teaching. Discusses talking communities in which teachers "restored individuality to students and confirmed personal knowledge as a means to power and growth."

1127. Davis, Ruth. "Coping with the Paper Load." *CSSEDC Quarterly* 12 (February 1990): 5–6.

Describes a project that trains English education majors in holistic grading and simplified primary trait scoring to prepare them for the teacher's paper load.

1128. Digby, Opal Annette Dulaney. "The Efficacy of Self-Study to Improve Knowledge and Skill in Selected Preservice Language Arts Teachers." *DAI* 50 (May 1990): 3556A.

Suggests that self-instruction may be successful in mastering knowledge of grammar.

1129. Dill, David D., ed. *What Teachers Need to Know: The Knowledge, Skills, Values Essential to Good Teaching*. Jossey-Bass Higher Education Series. San Francisco: Jossey-Bass, 1990. 240 pages

Twelve essays in four sections discuss the knowledge essential to the craft of teaching, knowledge essential to teaching in a discipline, the moral dimension of teaching, and teaching reforms.

1130. Dreyer, Diane Y. "Teaching Quantitative Research Writing; or, How I Stopped Hating the Paper and Learned to Love the Process." *CSSEDC Quarterly* 12 (May 1990): 2–3.

Details a procedure for teaching quantitative research writing skills by outlining the process. Illustrates it with a mini-case study.

1131. Dunn, Richard J. "Teaching Assistance, Not Teaching Assistants." *BADE* 97 (Winter 1990): 47–50.

Recommends reasonable workloads and salaries, a clear progression of varied experience, greater integration between graduate study and teaching, and increased collaboration with the regular faculty.

1132. Dunstan, Angus, Judy Kirscht, John Reiff, Marjorie Roemer, and Nick Tingle. "Grounding Theory in Practice in the Composition Class." *JTW* 9 (Fall–Winter 1990): 159–174.

Five composition instructors reflect on videotapes of one another's classes. Perspectives include the political, teacherly, interdisciplinary, and epistemological.

1133. Dutton, Margaret Maloy. "An Investigation of the Relationship between Training in Cooperative Learning and Teacher Job Satisfaction." *DAI* 51 (November 1990): 1456A.

Gives special attention to collegiality and efficacy.

1134. Eads, Vivian Athens. "A Study of the Effects of Teacher Training in Writing on Students' Writing Abilities." *DAI* 50 (February 1990): 2459A.

Finds that students of teachers who attended writing workshops outperformed other students.

1135. Farber, Jerry. "Learning How to Teach: A Progress Report." *CE* 52 (February 1990): 135–141.

Discusses continuing problems with grading systems and with the relationship between teachers and students. Suggests that teachers must remain open to learning.

1136. Findley, Barbara D., and Paul W. Rea. "Interview with Maxine Hairston." *RR* 8 (Spring 1990): 310–320.

Hairston discusses the teaching of writing, paradigm shifts, orientations towards writing as process and product, retraining in English departments, helping students enjoy writing, and related issues.

1137. Freeman, David E., and Yvonne S. Freeman. "Using Case Studies to View Immigrant Students in New Ways." *CalE* 26 (May–June 1990): 8–9, 21–27.

Writing case studies helps teachers understand immigrant students and their strengths.

1138. Garko, Michael G. "Perspectives on and Conceptualizations of Compliance and Compliance Gaining." *ComQ* 38 (Spring 1990): 138–157.

Provides studies on teacher power in the classroom. Shows how teachers can adopt a power perspective without undercutting compliance gaining.

1139. Hagaman, John, ed. *Teacher-Researchers*. Lexington, Ky.: University of Kentucky English Department (distributed by NCTE), 1989. 100 pages

Collects 11 essays in which teacher-researchers present studies on several aspects of composition, including the uses of research journals and methods for training graduate teaching assistants to conduct research while teaching composition. Annotated bibliography. Originally published as *Kentucky English Bulletin* (Fall 1989).

1140. Hashimoto, Irvin Y. *Thirteen Weeks: A Guide to Teaching College Writing*. Portsmouth, N.H.: Boynton/Cook, 1990. 278 pages

Designed to introduce graduate students to the practical and theoretical issues involved in designing and implementing college writing courses. A book both about teaching and thinking about teaching, four sections cover plans and assumptions, assignments and evaluation, essentials, and style.

1141. Hollingsworth, Sandra. "Teachers as Researchers: Writing to Learn about Ourselves—and Others." *CSWQ* 12 (Fall 1990): 10–18.

Discusses alternative approaches to a class in teacher research.

1142. Hubbuch, Susan. "Confronting the Power in Empowering Students." *WI* 9 (Fall 1989–Winter 1990): 35–44.

Argues that teachers' relinquishing their authority is often a dangerous illusion because power is a reality of any social situation.

1143. Huber, Bettina J. "Incorporating Minorities into English Programs: The Challenge of the Nineties." *BADE* 95 (Spring 1990): 38–44.

Reviews statistics relating to minorities and argues for their increasing participation in undergraduate and graduate programs, thereby increasing the pool of potential faculty members.

1144. Jones, Martha Anne. "The Relationship between English Teachers' Attitudes toward Writing Instruction, Instructional Planning, and Classroom Behavior at the Prewriting Stage." *DAI* 50 (May 1990): 3504A.

Investigates the relationship between teachers' attitudes toward writing and their teaching.

1145. Kinkead, Joyce, and David F. Lancy. "Looking for Yourself: The Classroom Teacher as Researcher." *UEJ* 18 (1990): 4–13.

Offers a case study of case study research, including suggestions for beginning teacher research.

1146. Kirtz, Mary K. "Gypsy Scholarship and Stress: The Plight of Written Business Communication as an Academic Field." *BABC* 53 (March 1990): 37–39.

Discusses the stress experienced by business writing faculty in choosing research methodologies that will be acceptable to the departments in which they teach.

1147. Krest, Margie. "A Writer's Awakening." *JTW* 9 (Fall–Winter 1990): 187–193.

The author discusses her development as a writer with her own voice and as a teacher with her own reactions and questions for student writers.

1148. Kroll, Keith. "Building Communities: Joining the Community of Professional Writing Teachers." *TETYC* 17 (May 1990): 103–108.

Argues that community college teacher-researchers must develop a greater professional identity.

1149. Langham, Claire Koch. "Discourse Strategies and Classroom Learning: American and Foreign Teaching Assistants." *DAI* 50 (March 1990): 2857A.

Identifies several auxiliary classroom strategies.

1150. Lipa, Sally E., and Rebecca Harlin. "Assessment: Insights into Teachers' Beliefs and Practices about Process Writing." Paper presented at the Eastern Educational Research Association, Clearwater, Fla., February 1990. ERIC ED 320 161. 23 pages

Reports on a survey of 66 teachers intended to assess their understandings and beliefs about process writing. Results show that teachers use process writing to implement skills.

1151. Luce, Ronald Wilson. "The Naked Dance: Experiences on a Journey through Darkness: Exploring Writers' Self-Assessed Processes and the Implications for Teaching Writing." *DAI* 50 (February 1990): 2413A.

Suggests that teachers should study their own writing strategies to understand the differences between how they write and how writing is generally taught.

1152. Lyons, Nona. "Dilemmas of Knowing: Ethical and Epistemological Dimensions of Teachers' Work and Development." *HER* 60 (May 1990): 159–180.

Analyzes teachers' narratives, exploring ethical dilemmas teachers face. Examines student-teacher relations, offering an alternative perspective on current discussions about the role of teachers' knowledge.

1153. Magnotto, Joyce. "A Writing across the Curriculum Spin-Off: Writing for Pleasure and Profit." *CompC* 3 (April 1990): 8–9.

Presentations by professional writers helped other faculty members view themselves as writers.

1154. McKendy, Thomas F. "Canadian Letters to an American Cousin: A 20-Year Perspective on Teaching Writing." *CollT* 38 (Spring 1990): 52–55.

A Canadian reflects on teaching writing and literature in both Canada and the U.S.

1155. Nelson, Gayle L. "The Relationship between the Use of Personal Examples in Foreign Teaching Assistants' Lectures and Uncertainty Reduction, Student Attitude, Student Recall, and Ethnocentrism." *DAI* 50 (May 1990): 3414A.

Finds that self-disclosure by foreign teaching assistants reduces their uncertainty and increases their students' positive attitudes and abilities to recall information.

1156. Nist, Elizabeth A. "Colloquium: A Conversation about Excellence." *TETYC* 17 (February 1990): 30–33.

Staff development for part-time composition faculty includes a colloquium that participants are paid to attend.

1157. Owen, Frieda Misch. "Teaching as a Composing Process: How High School English Teachers Plan, Implement, and Reflect upon Learning Experiences Which Connect Reading and Writing." *DAI* 51 (August 1990): 438A.

Teachers who "carry away meaning from the text" rather than seeing reading as a transaction promote "once-is-enough" learning, assigning texts only once and impeding "transactional theories of language learning."

1158. Pagans, Jo Anne. *Exiles and Communities: Teaching in the Patriarchal Wilderness*. Albany, N.Y.: State University of New York Press, 1990. 165 pages

An autobiographical meditation on the profession of teaching that draws on methods of feminist psychoanalytical criticism.

1159. Power, Brenda Miller. "Research, Teaching, and All That Jazz: New Metaphors and Models for Working with Teachers." *EEd* 22 (October 1990): 179–191.

Describes how cases can be used to prepare writing teachers in the age of process instruction, cases that blend the roles of teacher, researcher, and student.

1160. Rawlings, Diane, O. J. Hammond, and John Gaughan. "Teachers or Scholars? A Better Balance: High School-University Collaboration." *JTW* 9 (Fall-Winter 1990): 239–246.

Selected teachers spent one year at Miami University teaching, studying theory, and doing research. They offer seven recommendations for balancing scholarship and teaching in high schools and universities.

1161. Reagan, Sally Barr. "Practicing What We Preach." *CEAF* 20 (1990): 16–18.

Teaching assistants should experience and observe collaborative learning.

1162. Richards, Jack C. *The Language Teaching Matrix*. Cambridge Language Teaching Library. Cambridge, England: Cambridge University Press, 1990. 185 pages

Sees effective second language teaching as resulting from interactions among students, teachers, curricula, methodology, and instructional materials. Eight chapters treat these elements, approaching teaching as a dynamic process.

1163. Richards, Jack C., and David Nunan, eds. *Second Language Teacher Education*. Cambridge Language Teaching Library. Cambridge, England: Cambridge University Press, 1990. 340 pages

Nineteen essays examine major issues and practices in educating second language teachers. "A source book for those designing programs and activities in classroom observation, supervision, teacher self-evaluation, teaching practice, and related components of either preservice or inservice teacher education programs."

1164. Robbins, Carol Ann. "College Freshman Composition Instructors: Qualifications, Attitudes, and Departmental Power." *DAI* 50 (May 1990): 3496A.

Compares the education, experience, and status of composition instructors with those who do not teach composition.

1165. Robinson, William S. "Teaching Composition Teachers How to Teach Writing." *CompC* 3 (December 1990): 4–6.

Describes the graduate composition program at San Francisco State University, including descriptions of specific courses.

1166. Rosen, Charlotte. "Reflections on Our Burnout." *BABC* 53 (March 1990): 39–40.

Discusses the reasons for stress among business communication faculty and suggests ways that faculty can cope with burnout.

1167. Sandel, Lenore. *"The Student's Right to Write" and "Composition Opinionnaire the Student's Right to Write": A Comparison of Responses across Decades.* Bloomington, Ind.: ERIC/RCS, 1989. ERIC ED 310 405. 43 pages

In the 20 years between surveys, changes have occurred in how teachers are trained and how they value their students' needs.

1168. Schuster, Jack H., and Daniel W. Wheeler, eds. *Enhancing Faculty Careers: Strategies for Development and Renewal.* Jossey-Bass Higher Education Series. San Francisco: Jossey-Bass, 1990. 340 pages

Offers 15 essays in four sections: faculty careers in a time of transition; programs and strategies for professional, personal, and organizational renewal; models of successful practice; and recommendations for institutional action.

1169. Schwartz, Mimi, ed. *Writer's Craft, Teacher's Art: Teaching What We Know.* Portsmouth, N.H.: Boynton/Cook, 1990. 192 pages

Seventeen writer-teachers describe connections between how they write and teach in essays that are both conversational and personal.

1170. Small, Robert C., Jr. "Traditional and Romantic Views of Teachers." *CSSEDC Quarterly* 12 (December 1990): 8–10.

Contrasts assumptions found in Lanier and Little's *Handbook of Research on Teaching* with those reflected in NCTE's *Guidelines for the Preparation of Teachers.*

1171. Smithee, Michael Bruce. "Factors Related to the Development and Implementation of a University-Wide Teaching Assistant Program." *DAI* 51 (October 1990): 1137A.

A modified case study of a program to prepare teaching assistants at Syracuse University. A major factor in its success is a concern for undergraduate students.

1172. Sosnoski, James J. "The Psycho-Politics of Error." *Pre/Text* 10 (Spring–Summer 1989): 33–52.

The heuristic value of heterodoxy may be the modern critic's and the modern university's solution to the "technocratic orthodoxy" that conflates "difference" with error.

1173. Stover, Lois. *A Conceptual Framework for Using Writing to Help Preservice Teachers Integrate the Knowledge Base.* Alexandria, Va.: EDRS, 1989. ERIC ED 317 527. 137 pages

Discusses writing across the curriculum as based on the premise that writing is a powerful tool for assisting learning. Includes detailed writing activities and discusses implications for research.

1174. Tebeaux, Elizabeth. "Technical Writing for English Majors: Discourse Education for the Information Age." *TETYC* 17 (October 1990): 197–208.

Presents an argument for including technical writing in the curriculum of English and English education majors.

1175. Weiser, Irwin. "Surveying New Teaching Assistants: Who They Are, What They

Know, and What They Want to Know." *WPA* 14 (Fall–Winter 1990): 63–71.

Discusses a questionnaire distributed to new teaching assistants before their orientation in an effort to make training responsive to their specific needs.

1176. Wennerstrom, Ann. *Techniques for Teachers: A Guide for Nonnative Speakers of English.* Ann Arbor, Mich.: University of Michigan Press, 1990. 240 pages

A videotape and workbook for international teaching assistants. The videotape depicts short segments of native speakers' classrooms and office conferences. The workbook includes exercises for analyzing the discourse of the video, discussion activities, and micro-teaching assignments.

1177. Zaharias, Jane A., and Kathleen T. Benghiat. "To Be, or Not to Be, a Second-Year Teacher." *CSSEDC Quarterly* 12 (October 1990): 2–5.

Reports on the most common problems faced by new English teachers. Suggests how department chairs might assist the neophyte.

See also 99, 915, 983, 986, 1193, 1203, 1210, 1233, 1249, 1258, 1274, 1598, 1603, 1612, 1720, 1812

3.2   ADMINISTRATION

1178. Ballard, Kim, and Linda Haynes. "New Pedagogical Grammar Resources." *WLN* 15 (December 1990): 15–16.

Reports the establishment of the Association of Teachers of Grammar. Describes *Syntax in the Schools,* its newsletter. Gives dates for the national conference.

1179. Brusich, Judy Marie. "Salient Factors in Career Development among Senior-Level Women Administrators in Higher Education in Georgia." *DAI* 51 (November 1990): 1454A.

Collects data on 14 women administrators and studies the influence of family and mentors, personal characteristics, and organized feminism on their careers.

1180. Burgan, Mary. "Academic Careers in the Nineties: Images and Realities." *BADE* 96 (Fall 1990): 19–24.

Identifies challenges facing English departments and argues that we can best meet them by crossing self-imposed disciplinary lines separating literature, composition, and creative writing.

1181. Ceccio, Joseph F. "Faculty Perceptions of Stress and Coping Strategies in the Teaching of Business and Professional Writing." *BABC* 53 (March 1990): 17–20.

Reports on a 1988 study of work-related stress among business and professional writing faculty.

1182. Collis, John. *Educational Malpractice: Liability of Educators, School Administrators, and School Officials.* Charlottesville, Va.: Michie, 1990. 702 pages

Includes a section on lawsuits at the college level in which, for example, students have accused institutions of failing to prepare them adequately for a career or of unlawfully canceling programs of study.

1183. Crain, Jeanie C. "A Response to Anne Cassebaum's 'A Comment on the Wyoming Resolution Opposing Unfair Salaries and Working Conditions for Post-Secondary Teachers of Writing' [*CE* 51 (October 1989)]." *CE* 52 (April 1990): 469–473.

Describes the differences between adjunct and full-time status as related to money, hours, responsibilities, respect, challenge, reward, freedom, political stance, cameraderie, legitimacy, and restored faith.

1184. Gage, John T. "The Uses of a Handbook for Teachers." *WPA* 13 (Spring 1990): 5–15.

Asserts the usefulness of a writing program handbook generated by the teachers themselves rather than by the director.

1185. Giles, Molly. "Untitled." *WE* 1 (Spring 1990): 80–94.

Presents a short story about a creative writing teacher's losing her job.

1186. Howard, Rebecca Moore, David J. Hess, and Margaret Flanders Darby. "Hiring across the Curriculum." *WPA* 13 (Spring 1990): 27–36.

Describes the interdisciplinary writing program faculty at Colgate University, regarding it as a model applicable to other programs.

1187. Mauch, James E., Jack W. Birch, and Jack Mathews. *The Emeritus Professor: Old Rank—New Meaning.* ASHE-ERIC Higher Education Reports. Washington, D.C.: George Washington University School of Education and Human Development, 1990. 88 pages

Suggests reevaluating emeritus rank as the compulsory retirement age is abolished. Argues that institutions should offer valued senior scholars a part-time "working emeritus rank" that would keep them active on campuses.

1188. Reynolds, John Frederick. "Motives, Metaphors, and Messages in Critical Receptions of Experimental Research: A Comment with Postscript." *JAC* 10 (1990): 110–116.

Argues that the dominant scholarly paradigm in composition journals is ignorant of and hostile to empirical research.

1189. Ronald, Ann. "Separate but (Sort of) Equal: Permanent Non-Tenure-Track Faculty Members in the Composition Program." *BADE* 95 (Spring 1990): 33–37.

Describes the University of Nevada at Reno's full-time permanent nontenured lectureships, proposing that the category be included in CCCC's statement of standards for the teaching of writing.

1190. Sergiovanni, Thomas. *Value-Added Leadership: How to Get Extraordinary Performance in Schools.* San Diego: Harcourt Brace Jovanovich, 1990. 192 pages

Explores effective school management and leadership principles drawn from studies in a broad range of settings.

1191. "Troubled Times for Tenure." *Time* (26 February 1990): 72.

Discusses challenges to the notion of tenure.

1192. Vogel, Mark. "Reviews of Recent Composition Textbooks." *Focuses* 3 (Fall 1990): 114–166.

Offers evaluative reviews of 20 selected textbooks for college writing classes.

1193. Weimer, Maryellen. *Improving College Teaching: Strategies for Developing Instructional Effectiveness.* Jossey-Bass Higher Education Series. San Francisco: Jossey-Bass, 1990. 240 pages

Outlines how administrators can create an environment that fosters teaching excellence. Presents case studies of improvement programs, explains how they can be tailored to the needs of particular institutions, and offers guidance for supporting professors as they work to improve their performance.

See also 200, 1131, 1164, 1168, 1177, 1213, 1230, 1245, 1365, 1659

3.3 SUPPORT SERVICES

1194. Allen, Nancy. "Developing an Effective Tutorial Style." *WLN* 15 (November 1990): 1–4.

An analysis of tutorials shows that brief interchanges in which the tutor "prompts with . . . fact-finding questions and pauses for responses" are effective.

1195. Ameter, Brenda, and Coralyn Dahl. "Coordination and Cooperation: A Writing Center Serves a Hearing-Impaired Student." *WLN* 14 (February 1990): 4–5.

An audiologist, an audiology graduate student, and a tutor trained in linguistics and

ESL devise strategies enabling a student to master word endings and tenses.

1196. Anderson, Jennifer. "Tutors' Column." *WLN* 14 (February 1990): 9.

Recounts feeling frustrated and incompetent while assisting students until a telephone caller asked for help with an epigraph or epitaph for a grave marker.

1197. Arkin, Marian. "A Tutoring Retrospective." *WLN* 14 (June 1990): 1–6, 15.

Traces developments, problems, and progress over 17 years. Cites better faculty development and tutor training as well as increased sensitivity to multicultural diversity.

1198. Bell, James Harrington. "Tutoring in a Writing Center." *DAI* 50 (March 1990): 2763A.

Describes the process and content of individual conferences conducted by peer tutors.

1199. Benson, Kirsten F. "Assessment and Development in Graduate Tutor Training." *Focuses* 3 (Spring 1990): 24–36.

Recommends assessing and training tutors on the basis of differences between their own abilities and those of beginning college writers with whom they will work.

1200. Berta, Renee. "Micro Style: Computer Modifications for Disabled Students." *WLN* 14 (May 1990): 6–7.

Identifies three groups—"the visually, orthopedically, and learning disabled"—and discusses their needs, recommending mechanical devices and physical modifications for computer labs.

1201. Bishop, Wendy. "Bringing Writers to the Center: Some Survey Results, Surmises, Suggestions." *WCJ* 10 (Spring–Summer 1990): 31–44.

Results suggest that efforts to promote writing center services should focus on writing instructors and on encouraging them to give students credit for visit opportunities.

1202. Brown, Alan. "Coping with Computers in the Writing Center." *WLN* 15 (December 1990): 13–15.

Concludes that the least effective computer programs offer drill and practice. Recommends programs that follow a tutorial approach and offers six guidelines for ordering programs.

1203. Brown, Lady Falls. "Stable Concept/Unstable Reality: Recreating the Writing Center." *WLN* 14 (April 1990): 6–8.

Recognizes that continual turnover in students, tutors, and faculty members necessitates developing strategies for ongoing tutor training and for advertising services.

1204. Chapman, David. "Evaluating the Writing Conference: A Comparison of Tutor and Student Responses." *WLN* 14 (January 1990): 4–8.

Describes an evaluation procedure. Most students rated conferences more successful than did tutors, who "frequently underrated, but virtually never overrated them."

1205. Chapman, David W. "What If We Stopped Writing Drafts and Started Drafting Writers." *WLN* 15 (September 1990): 4–5.

Creates a fantasy in which directors recruit as vigorously as major leagues recruit athletes people demonstrating superior intelligence, writing ability, and tutoring skills.

1206. Clark, Irene Lurkis. "Maintaining Chaos in the Writing Center: A Critical Perspective on Writing Center Dogma." *WCJ* 11 (Fall-Winter 1990): 81–93.

Critiques dogmas concerning "how students learn," how tutors should behave, how plagiarism is defined, and how useful software is.

1207. Davis, Kevin. "Responding to Writers: A Multivariate Approach to Peer Interaction." *WCJ* 10 (Spring–Summer 1990): 67–73.

Argues that tutors need flexibility to accommodate students' differing writing processes. Presents "a range of options available to writing conference participants."

1208. Devet, Bonnie, Erika Burroughs, Lydia Hopson, Donna Kenyon, Trisha Martin, Cheryl Sims, Hope Norment, Liz Young, Sylvia Gamboa, and Kathy Haney. "The Hurricane and the Writing Lab." *WLN* 14 (March 1990): 5–6.

Tutors discover the parameters of their roles as counselors when students write personal responses to the devastation of Hurricane Hugo.

1209. Dossin, Mary. "Expectations." *WLN* 14 (April 1990): 12.

To inform the expectations of students and faculty, the author publishes five points about the kinds of services the center does and does not offer.

1210. Dossin, Mary M. "Untrained Tutors." *WLN* 15 (December 1990): 11.

Untrained tutors look for grammatical and sentence errors, point out errors line by line, and talk too much. They become effective tutors through training.

1211. Doxey, Carolyn. "Tutors' Column." *WLN* 15 (December 1990): 9.

Having heard "war stories" about tutoring ESL students, the author expected problems. Instead, she found interesting, eager writers.

1212. Edmunds, Jane, Lorraine Lordi, Violet Dagdigian, and Leslie VanWagner. "Authority: Issues and Insights." *WLN* 15 (November 1990): 11–15.

Tutors play three roles—guide, counselor/listener, mentor/collaborator—while working with a student. Discusses changes in students' expectations and responsibilities.

1213. Elliot, M. A. "Writing Center Directors: Why Faculty Status Fits." *WLN* 14 (March 1990): 1–4.

Cites six reasons for giving directors faculty status. They know and practice composition theory, conduct research, train tutors, communicate with faculty, work with people, and have degrees.

1214. Elwart-Keys, Mary, and Marjorie Horton. "Collaborating in the Capture Lab: Computer Support for Group Writing." *BABC* 53 (June 1990): 38–44.

Describes a computer-supported conference room used by business teams and discusses how this laboratory might be used for collaborative writing.

1215. Fink, Darlynn. "Help! How Do I Tutor the International Student?" *WLN* 15 (September 1990): 14–16.

Responding to a questionnaire, 14 tutors cite problems ranging from language barriers and high student expectations to correcting surface errors. Suggests some solutions.

1216. Fischer, Fred. "The Effect of the Tutorial Writing Center on Underprepared Community College Students." *DAI* 50 (June 1990): 3833A.

Investigates the effects of individual diagnosis and subsequent assigned tutoring for academically underprepared writing students.

1217. Fox, Janna. "Interactional Differences in Writing Conferences between TAs and Students in the Writing Tutorial Service." *CALS* 6 (1989): 1–30.

Audiotaped initial tutorials with "mature," first-year, and ESL writers indicated that a tutoring style based on expectations about students' abilities limited the overall effectiveness of tutors working with ESL students.

1218. Galskis, Angelique. "Tutors' Column: The Painless Writing Sample." *WLN* 14 (March 1990): 9–10.

By asking students to complete "Writing makes me feel like . . . ," a tutor elicits writing samples that prompt discussions about students' writing problems.

1219. George, Diana, and Nancy Grimm. "Expanding Roles/Expanding Responsibilities: The Changing Nature of Writing Centers Today." *WCJ* 11 (Fall–Winter 1990): 59–66.

Applauds and critiques the expansion of writing centers. However, expansion can destroy the "strong human connection" fundamental to writing centers.

1220. Gills, Paula. "The Troubleshooter." *WLN* 14 (February 1990): 12–13.

Proposes nine approaches or strategies to assist learning-disabled students with their writing.

1221. Glenn, Coral Lou. "Tutors' Column: Mother Versus Tutor." *WLN* 14 (May 1990): 9.

A mother of eight describes her struggle "to set the parent . . . aside and allow students . . . to be responsible for their own papers."

1222. Hall, Marina. "Tutors' Column: Tutoring Teaches Tutors, Too." *WLN* 15 (September 1990): 9.

A tutor learns to use a handbook, masters strategies for generating and organizing ideas, becomes a critical reader, and seeks help from fellow tutors.

1223. Harris, Muriel. "What's Up and What's In: Trends and Traditions in Writing Centers." *WCJ* 11 (Fall–Winter 1990): 15–25.

A historical look at "defining characteristics" of writing centers.

1224. Harris, Vincent. "Tutors' Column: The Journey Continues." *WLN* 14 (June 1990): 9–10.

The author continues tutoring to combat ethnocentrism on campus and to fight the belief that students seeking help are "dumb."

1225. Haynes, Carole Ann Schaum. "A Study of Learning Centers in Southeastern Two-Year and Four-Year Public and Private Colleges and Universities." *DAI* 50 (May 1990): 3463A.

Discusses the types of services offered at learning centers and analyzes their levels of success.

1226. Hemmeter, Thomas. "The 'Smack of Difference': The Language of Writing Center Discourse." *WCJ* 11 (Fall–Winter 1990): 35–48.

Critiques definitions of writing centers that regard them in opposition to classrooms or integrated within institutions. Proposes new language to describe their part/whole relationship.

1227. Herek, Jennifer, and Mark Niquette. "Ethics in the Writing Lab: Tutoring under the Honor Code." *WLN* 14 (January 1990): 12–15.

Observing the code designed to assure that students' work is their own, tutors ask questions rather than offer interpretations, thus aiding students' intellectual development.

1228. Hobson, Eric H. "The Writer's Journal and the Artist's Sketchpad." *WLN* 15 (September 1990): 1–3, 7.

Realizes that composition terminology confuses many students. Suggests that tutors find parallels in the students' own disciplines to facilitate understanding the composing process.

1229. Holbrook, Jo Ann. "Tutors' Column." *WLN* 14 (January 1990): 9–10.

Describes an unsuccessful session with a shy, older, browbeaten woman who wanted advice about her poetry. Observes that tutors must be sensitive and supportive.

1230. Hollis, Karyn. "Hosting a Mini Peer Tutoring Conference: Easier Than You Might Think." *WLN* 14 (May 1990): 14–15.

Planning conferences involves creating the program schedule, finding funds, and arranging lodging and facilities.

1231. Hollis, Karyn. "Scheduler, Record Keeper, Teacher: The Computer in the Writing Program at Dickinson College." *WLN* 15 (September 1990): 11–13.

A computer provides current schedules for faculty members and tutors; quickly produces data; and calls up invention programs, spelling checkers, drill-and-practice exercises, and on-line editors.

1232. Hubbuch, Susan M. "The Writer's Stance: An Exploration of Context in Invention and Critical Thinking." *JAC* 10 (1990): 73–86.

Discusses a heuristic based on argument fields and schema theory to aid upper-level students suffering from "rhetorical vertigo" about their senior theses.

1233. Hutto, David. "Scenarios for Tutor Training." *WLN* 14 (February 1990): 1–3.

After reading and discussing scenarios, tutors learn different tutoring strategies, including offering fewer solutions and corrections and eliciting more talk.

1234. Hylton, Jaime. "Evaluating the Writing Lab: How Do We Know That We Are Helping?" *WLN* 15 (November 1990): 5–8.

Describes a method of evaluation. Lists five objectives, identifies the procedures, assigns responsibility, and develops questions necessary for achieving each objective.

1235. Kostelnick, Charles, Richard C. Freed, Thomas Kent, and Don Payne. "Centers for Applied Writing: A Conceptual Model." *TWT* 17 (Spring 1990): 136–149.

Defines a comprehensive center for applied writing and discusses the problems that the authors encountered in trying to start one.

1236. Kulkarni, Diane. "Tutors' Column: Writing to Discover." *WLN* 15 (November 1990): 9–10.

A tutor uses a poster-size cartoon containing 15 frames that demonstrate her composing process to describe the center's services.

1237. Leahy, Richard. "What the College Writing Center Is—and Isn't." *CollT* 38 (Spring 1990): 43–48.

Discusses ways to correct general faculty misconceptions and to focus on developing collaborative strategies for tutoring.

1238. Livesey, Matthew J. "Tutors' Column: Ours Is to Wonder Why." *WLN* 15 (October 1990): 9–11.

"Tutoring includes asking many, many questions. . . . The most important questions . . . are those . . . which students can ask themselves."

1239. Logan, Shirley W. "Facilitating Student and Teacher Empowerment in a Writing Computer Lab." Paper presented at the CCCC Convention, Chicago, March 1990. ERIC ED 318 020. 13 pages

Finds six positive effects among the interactions of students, tutors, and teachers in a computer writing lab.

1240. Lunsford, Andrea A. "Composing Ourselves: Politics, Commitment, and the Teaching of Writing." *CCC* 41 (February 1990): 71–82.

Argues that CCCC compose itself "historically and subjectively" in diverse voices, instead of defining itself or being composed by others.

1241. MacLennan, Tom. "Martin Buber and a Collaborative Learning *Ethos*." *WLN* 14 (February 1990): 6–8, 13.

In addition to discussing Buber's concepts of I-It/I-Thou and relation as reciprocity, this article cites works by Trimbur, Bruffee, Meyer, and others who relate tutoring to collaborative learning.

1242. McClure, Susan Harpham. "An Observational Study of the Behavior of First-Semester College Students as Tutors in a Writing Center." *DAI* 51 (September 1990): 771A.

Studies the efficacy and tutoring behaviors of four first-semester college students.

1243. Morris, Karen. "Closed Mouth, Open Ears: Listening in the Tutorial." *WLN* 15 (October 1990): 7–8, 14–15.

Describes types of active listening, suggesting four forms of feedback and nonverbal behaviors that increase student communication.

1244. Morrison, Margaret. "Peer Tutors as Postmodern Readers in a Writing Center." *FEN* 18 (Spring 1990): 12–15.

Part of the training of peer tutors should be to recognize their own projections and resistances as readers.

1245. Mullin, Joan A. "Empowering Ourselves: New Directions for the Nineties." *WLN* 14 (June 1990): 11–13.

One hundred directors responding to a questionnaire cited expanded services and increased responsibilities for campus-wide centers; however, they fear that success may diminish their time for teaching and tutoring.

1246. Nakayu, Lori Johnson. "Tutors' Column." *WLN* 14 (February 1990): 9–10.

Explains using computers to help students brainstorm, revise their work, and analyze its style.

1247. Nelson, Marie Ponsot. *At the Point of Need: Teaching Basic and ESL Writers*. Portsmouth, N.H.: Boynton/Cook, 1990. 228 pages

A detailed account of the experiences of teachers, tutors, and students in a university writing center over a five-year period. Shows the importance of addressing the needs of the whole writer.

1248. Neuleib, Janice, and Maurice Scharton. "Tutors and Computers: An Easy Alliance." *WCJ* 11 (Fall–Winter 1990): 49–58.

Illustrates the full-scale use of computers at Illinois State. Surveys 120 tutors on their professional and personal use of and attitudes toward computers.

1249. Neuleib, Janice, Maurice Scharton, Julia Visor, and Yvette Weber-Davis. "Using Videotapes to Train Tutors." *WLN* 14 (January 1990): 1–3, 8.

Discusses roleplaying and filming actual tutoring situations. Provides three sets of questions for evaluating tutoring methods.

1250. Nugent, Susan Monroe. "The Library Information Aide: Connecting Libraries, Writing Centers, and Classrooms." *WLN* 14 (March 1990): 13–15.

Explains training in research techniques for tutors assigned to targeted classes, the tutors' interactions with faculty members, and the program's benefits.

1251. Nugent, Susan Monroe. "One Woman's Ways of Knowing." *WCJ* 10 (Spring–Summer 1990): 17–29.

A study that follows one female writer through five stages of intellectual development. Describes implications for working with students and faculty in the writing center.

1252. Perdue, Virginia, and Deborah James. "Teaching in the Center." *WLN* 14 (June 1990): 7–8.

Argues that writing center tutorials that are student-centered, "informal, collaborative, and egalitarian" perform a significant teaching function important to writing programs.

1253. Polanski, Virginia. "Your Own In-House Writing Journal: A Source of Bricks for Building." Paper presented at the WPA Conference, Oxford, Ohio, July 1989. ERIC ED 309 452. 26 pages

Describes how to implement an in-house writing across the curriculum journal for students, faculty, and administrators.

1254. Posey, Evelyn. "Micro Style: Prewriting Options: Moving beyond the Word Processor." *WLN* 15 (October 1990): 12–13.

Cites four guidelines for choosing instructional software.

1255. Quinn, Helen, and Carole Flint. "The Technical Communications Resource Center and Writing Lab: Special Services for Basic, Technical, and Learning-Disabled Students." *WLN* 14 (May 1990): 10–14.

Describes procedures for computer training. Cites benefits to students, including students with learning disabilities, from working in a supportive environment.

1256. Ray, T. J. "I'll Show You My Fog Index If You'll Show Me Yours." *FEN* 19 (Fall 1990): 25–26.

A plea for less discussion of quantitative research at NCTE and CCCC conventions.

1257. Rodis, Karen. "Mending the Damaged Path: How to Avoid Conflict of Expectation When Setting Up a Writing Center." *WCJ* 10 (Spring-Summer 1990): 45–57.

Contrasts three writing centers, discussing how teachers, students, and tutors perceive their purposes and staff. Relates these perceptions to how the centers are structured.

1258. Rouse, Joy. "Tutor Recruitment and Training at Miami University." *WLN* 14 (April 1990): 1–3.

Explains the selection of tutors. Describes classroom training in listening, videotaping practice tutorials, and individual training with mentors and in workshop sessions.

1259. Rowan, Katherine. "Equipping Your Writing Center to Assist Journalistic Writers." *WLN* 15 (October 1990): 1–7.

Explains five ways tutors can assist journalistic writers. Recommends periodicals, books, guides, handouts, and software.

1260. Runciman, Lex. "Defining Ourselves: Do We Really Want to Use the Word *Tutor?*" *WCJ* 11 (Fall-Winter 1990): 27–34.

The terms *tutor* and *tutee* imply hierarchy and remediation, characteristics that seriously misconstrue writing center activity. Historical evidence explains these negative definitions.

1261. Rutland, Scheryl. "Scheryl's Collection of Bloopers." *WLN* 14 (May 1990): 8.

Lists 24 examples of student malapropisms and ambiguously worded sentences.

1262. Schuette, Lynn M. "Tutors' Column: Tutor? Why Should I?" *WLN* 14 (April 1990): 9–11.

Through tutoring, the author has learned humility, reflection, patience, accomplishment, pride, self-confidence, and compassion.

1263. Selfe, Cynthia. *Creating a Computer-Supported Writing Facility: A Blueprint for Action.* Advances in Computers and Composition Studies. Edited by Gail Hawisher. Houghton, Mich.: Computers and Composition, 1989. 153 pages

Focuses on planning, operating, and improving computer-supported writing laboratories and classrooms. Advocates using technology to facilitate collaboration, composing, research, and teaching.

1264. Sills, Caryl. "Developing Effective Pedagogy for Computer-Enhanced Writing Instruction." *CollM* 8 (November 1990): 329–333.

Examines "six advantages to teaching fundamentals of English to underprepared writers in a computer writing lab."

1265. Simson, Rennie. "Where's Professor Adjunct?" *WLN* 15 (November 1990): 7.

Describes a program involving advanced freshman composition students who undergo training, then attend class twice a week but tutor for a third hour in lieu of going to class.

1266. Smith, Jane Bowman. "A Tutorial Focusing on Concrete Details: Using Christenson's Levels of Generality." *WCJ* 10 (Spring–Summer 1990): 59–66.

Describes a tutoring session in which a student learns subordinate development, enabling him to add detail and shift his essay's purpose from informational to narrative.

1267. Smith, Louise Z. "Family Systems Theory and the Form of Conference Dialogue." *WCJ* 10 (Spring–Summer 1990): 3–16.

Analyzes idea units in conference dialogue as regulators of access and responsibility. Focuses on a student writing an essay for a literature course.

1268. Steward, Joyce S., and Mary K. Croft. "From Pens in the Leisure Lab." *WLN* 14 (May 1990): 15–16.

Retired writing center directors created *The Leisure Pen: A Book for Elderwriters,* which includes topics and strategies for writing autobiography, poetry, and fiction.

1269. Topel, Lissa. "Tutors' Column: Confessions of a Terrified Tutee." *WLN* 15 (December 1990): 9–10.

Explains the apprehension the author experienced when she first asked a tutor to read a paper. Now a tutor herself, she sympathizes with the students she helps.

1270. Waldo, Mark. "What Should the Relationship between the Writing Center and Writing Program Be?" *WCJ* 11 (Fall–Winter 1990): 73–80.

Centers should parallel the pedagogies and philosophies of their institutions' writing programs. Centers should not simply remediate or teach skills.

1271. Walker, Amy, and Gail Corso. "Tutoring Ties." *WLN* 14 (March 1990): 7–8, 11–12.

Presents a scenario involving three voices—the student's, the tutor's, and the tutor's inner voice—commenting on the transaction.

1272. Whitt, Margaret. "Writing Center Travels to Residence Halls." *WLN* 15 (November 1990): 15–16.

Describes the logistics of and funding for a "traveling writing center" in which tutors assist students in their dorms in the evenings.

1273. Word, Joan. "TSU Surveys Campus Writing/Learning Practices." *WLN* 14 (February 1990): 14–16.

A four-part survey reveals faculty apprehension about teaching writing, student support for writing-component courses, and a need for topic-specific workshops.

1274. Zander, Sherri. "Tutor Training: The Sharing of Perspectives within a Department." *WLN* 15 (December 1990): 12–13.

Describes an intensive two-day, collaborative training program attended by composition coordinators, faculty members, and tutors. Includes a discussion of policies, roleplaying, and computer training.

See also 6, 39, 1016, 1635, 1829

3.4   ROLE IN SOCIETY

1275. Armstrong, Paul B. "The English Coalition Conference and the English Major." *BADE* 96 (Fall 1990): 30–33.

Discusses five organizing goals for the English major: methodologies of interpretation, literary and cultural history, language and discourse, diversity of texts, and writing as inquiry.

1276. Barber, Phyllis Allran. "Making the English Coalition Report a Reality." *BADE* 96 (Fall 1990): 47–49.

Focuses on reform, supporting the Coalition's broad vision, citing evidence of critical needs, and calling for articulation and leadership.

1277. Cabot, C. Barry. "Going beyond the English Coalition Report." *BADE* 96 (Fall 1990): 38–41.

Finds that the report's breadth leads to superficiality. Questions its financial implications and argues that its implementation must fit local and specific needs.

1278. Clausen, Christopher. "Plantation Politics: The English Coalition and Its Report." *BADE* 96 (Fall 1990): 34–37.

Argues that the report is doctrinaire and vague, influenced by the beliefs of one group of compositionists characterized by "radically egalitarian" social views.

1279. Cox, Brian. "English Teaching: The Need for Reform." *EngT* 6 (January 1990): 20–28.

Proposed reforms affecting English teaching in England and Wales include extending the canon, assessing speaking and listening, and emphasizing the writing process.

1280. Denham, Robert D. "The English Coalition Conference: A Pocketful of Wye." *BADE* 96 (Fall 1990): 26–29.

Explains the nature and purpose of the English Coalition Conference and discusses the philosophical model of education that it developed.

1281. Elbow, Peter. *What Is English?* New York: MLA and NCTE, 1990. 271 pages

Elbow reflects on the 1987 English Coalition Conference, discussing theory, the canon, assessment, and teaching literature versus teaching writing. Teachers attending the Conference also express their views and experiences.

1282. Meriwether, Doris H. "The English Coalition Conference: 'Plain Living and High Thinking.' " *BADE* 96 (Fall 1990): 45–46.

Praises the collaborative efforts of the Coalition and argues for strengthening ties between higher education and the schools.

1283. Michaels, Lloyd. "Reclaiming the Realm of Pleasure: A Response to the English Coalition Report." *BADE* 96 (Fall 1990): 42–44.

Applauds the Coalition's strengthening connections among English teachers at all levels but criticizes the report for ignoring the role of pleasure in responding to literature.

1284. Mulhauser, Frederick. "Reviewing Bilingual Education Research for Congress." *Annals* 508 (March 1990): 107–118.

Describes Congress' reaction to a General Accounting Office's expert panel, whose mission was to interpret the validity of effectiveness claims made by proponents of bilingual education.

1285. "Reading, Writing, and Rhetoric." *Time* (12 February 1990): 54–55.

Reports on responses to President Bush's goals for educators.

1286. Secada, Walter G. "Research, Politics, and Bilingual Education." *Annals* 508 (March 1990): 81–106.

Narrates and analyzes the 1988 federal reauthorization fight over bilingual instruction, arguing that political motives lay behind the effort to increase all-English programs.

1287. Sheppard, R. Z. "Foul Weather for Fair Use." *Time* (30 April 1990): 86–87.

Discusses the impact of lawsuits concerning the "fair use" provision of copyright legislation.

1288. Speck, Bruce W., and Thomas J. Pabst. "A Cooperative Model for English Composition: Follow-Up Report." *IlEB* 77 (Winter 1990): 53–65.

Reports on a cooperative model that introduces high school students to the college climate through a composition course.

See also 495, 498, 508, 1320, 1323, 1836

4
Curriculum

4.1 GENERAL DISCUSSIONS

1289. Aber, John. "Confusing the Technical, the Practical, and the Emancipatory: A Habermasian Critique of Composition Pedagogy." Paper presented at the CCCC Convention, Seattle, March 1989. ERIC ED 311 438. 15 pages

Applies Habermas' sociological theory of knowledge and cognitive interests to composition instruction.

1290. Ashton-Jones, Evelyn, and Dene Kay Thomas. "Composition, Collaboration, and Women's Ways of Knowing: A Conversation with Mary Belenky." *JAC* 10 (1990): 275–292.

The coauthor of *Women's Ways of Knowing* discusses collaborative writing, divergent epistemologies and their pedagogical implications, and the relevance of doubting and believing games to gender.

1291. Autrey, Ken. "Connecting My Writer's Group and My Writing Class." Paper presented at the CCCC Convention, Chicago, March 1990. ERIC ED 320 152. 9 pages

Reports on the students' reactions when the teacher brought his own writing to class for a group critique, the value of which is viewing writing as a social act.

1292. Autrey, Ken. "What College Freshmen Say about Previous Writing Experience." Paper presented at the NCTE Convention, Baltimore, November 1989. ERIC ED 320 151. 10 pages

Examines how the writing performance and attitudes of college freshmen were influenced by middle and high school writing experiences.

1293. Bacig, Thomas D., Robert H. Evan, Donald W. Larmouth, and Kenneth C. Risdon. "Beyond Argumentation and Comparison/Contrast: Extending the Socrates CAI Design Principles to Classroom Teaching and the Production of Other Forms of Discourse." *CHum* 24 (February–April 1990): 15–41.

Finds that CAI students exhibited stronger critical reading and thinking, technical writing, collaboration, and argument skills than students in traditional classes.

1294. Bangert-Drowns, Robert. "Research on Word Processing and Writing Instruction." Paper presented at the AERA meeting, San Francisco, March 1989. ERIC ED 319 359. 6 pages

Analyzes 20 published studies using experimental and control groups to compare conventional writing instruction with instruction using word processing. Finds word processing beneficial.

1295. Bauer, Dale M. "The Other 'F' Word: The Feminist in the Classroom." *CE* 52 (April 1990): 385–396.

Argues that using feminist rhetoric combined with dialogics in the classroom can promote the persuasion and critical thinking that link English and rhetorical studies.

1296. Bayer, Ann Shea. *Collaborative-Apprenticeship Learning: Language and Thinking across the Curriculum, K–12.* Katonah, N.Y.: Richard C. Owen, 1990. 146 pages

Presents a theoretical base, after Vygotsky, for social learning. Gives strategies for changing the curriculum, planning within a specific content area, and communicating the results of evaluation. Includes case studies and sample lesson plans for a collaborative-apprenticeship classroom.

1297. Beidler, Peter G. "Introductory Voice." *ExEx* 35 (Spring 1990): 35–37.

Provides examples of voiceless and voice-filled papers as models for student writers.

1298. Bencich, Carole R. Beeghly. "Negotiated Meaning: The Dynamics of a Peer Writing Group." *DAI* 51 (August 1990): 437A.

A qualitative study of socially constructed meaning in writing groups. These groups encourage reading aloud, better writing, the discovery of voice, and self-assessment.

1299. Bishop, Wendy. "The 15-Sentence Portrait." *ExEx* 35 (Spring 1990): 5–8.

Provides directions for writing a descriptive paragraph about "individuals for whom they [student writers] feel powerful emotions."

1300. Bishop, Wendy. "'Traveling through the Dark': Teachers and Students Reading and Writing Together." *Reader* 24 (Fall 1990): 1–21.

Students and teachers must build an interpretive community within the classroom as a first bridge between disparate cultures. Doing so affirms writing and reading as interconnected, meaning-making, social activities.

1301. Bullock, Chris J. "Changing the Concept: Applying Feminist Perspectives to the Writing Class." *EQ* 22 (1990): 141–148.

Applies knowledge about the maleness and femaleness of language to the composition class.

1302. Calabrese, Marian Silverstein. "Technological Change and English Teaching: A Delphi Study of American and British English Educators' Views on the Future of Postsecondary Curriculum." *DAI* 50 (February 1990): 2367A.

A consensus of changes that educators expect centers on using computers, word processors, interactive software, and telecommunications.

1303. Cole, Robyn Rudolph. "The Effect of Writing Activities in Students' Preferred Learning Styles on Writing Achievement and Student Satisfaction." *DAI* 51 (December 1990): 1936A.

Analyzes the effects of pre-essay writing tasks on students' themes at a small liberal arts college.

1304. Collier, Mary Jane, and Robert Powell. "Ethnicity, Instructional Communication, and Classroom Systems." *ComQ* 38 (Fall 1990): 334–349.

Investigates how students' ethnic backgrounds relate to their views of instructional communication processes. Immediacy and effectiveness were strongly related throughout the course.

1305. Collins, James L., ed. *Vital Signs 2: Teaching and Learning Collaboratively.* Portsmouth, N.H.: Boynton/Cook, 1990. 160 pages

Fifteen essays detail how teachers help students work collaboratively to improve their reading and writing.

1306. Connor, James E. "Cutting Edge: Writing the Natural Way: Finding Your Own Voice." *JDEd* 13 (Spring 1990): 28–29.

Reviews Gabriele Rico's strategies for helping students learn to write.

1307. Couser, G. Thomas. "Seeing through Metaphor: Teaching Figurative Literacy." *RSQ* 20 (Spring 1990): 143–153.

Discusses problems in defining *metaphor* and suggests what an introductory college curriculum in metaphoric literacy ought to cover.

1308. Crafton, John Michael. "Marvelous Signals: The Usefulness of the In-Class Essay." Paper presented at the NCTE Spring Conference, Charleston, S.C., April 1989. ERIC ED 313 708. 15 pages

Provides a rationale for using the in-class essay in a process-centered writing classroom.

1309. Crafton, Lisa Plummer. "A Marriage of Heaven and Hell: A Successful Integration of Grammar and Writing." Paper presented at the NCTE Spring Conference, Charleston, S.C., April 1989. ERIC ED 312 654. 15 pages

Claims that grammar instruction can be integrated with process-oriented writing instruction. Recommends five strategies for teaching grammar.

1310. Darnell, Sara. "Descriptive Statements: From a Boring One-Liner to a Work of Art." *ExEx* 36 (Fall 1990): 3–4.

Describes an exercise in which students rewrite one-liners to photographs "taken from pictorial magazines such as *National Geographic.*"

1311. DeShaney, Rebecca Jacks. "The Best Prewriting Students Will Ever Eat." *ExEx* 35 (Spring 1990): 43–44.

Explains a five-step activity in which students examine, unwrap, eat, and write about a candy bar.

1312. Devine, Thomas G. *"Caveat Emptor:* The Writing Process Approach to College Writing." *JDEd* 14 (Fall 1990): 2–4.

Recommends that college teachers experiment with aspects of the process approach but continue to use many traditional instructional activities.

1313. DuBois, Barbara R. "Word Play." *ExEx* 35 (Spring 1990): 32–34.

Provides seven examples of class starters.

1314. Dyson, Anne Haas, ed. *Collaboration through Writing and Reading: Exploring Possibilities.* Urbana, Ill.: NCTE, 1989. 284 pages

Participants in a conference collaborated to produce essays that explore the history and possibilities for using writing, reading, and talking in the classroom. The collection studies the functions and interactions of writing, reading, and talking for individuals, alone and in group or community contexts.

1315. Easley, Rex Burton. "Common Ground: Fiction Writing and Composition." *DAI* 50 (February 1990): 2412A.

Similarities between writing processes suggest a pedagogy for composition based on fiction writing and interpretive reading.

1316. Ediger, Marlow. "Four Don'ts in the Teaching of Reading." *IlEB* 77 (Winter 1990): 66–70.

Delineates criteria for teaching reading effectively, recommending effective methods and discussing those that discourage meaningful interaction between teacher and learner.

1317. Eisenberg, Nora, ed. *Computers and College Writing: Selected College Profiles.* New York: City University of New York, 1989. ERIC ED 320 564. 282 pages

Contains profiles of computer-based writing programs at 49 colleges. These profiles offer advice on establishing programs and using computers in class.

1318. Forman, Janis. "Review: Rethinking Reading and Writing from the Perspective of Translation." *CE* 52 (October 1990): 676–682.

In reviewing two new books on translation, suggests that teachers of writing should reclaim translation as a valuable exercise in syntactic and rhetorical decision making.

1319. Fox, Thomas. *The Social Uses of Writing: Politics and Pedagogy.* Norwood, N.J.: Ablex, 1990. 140 pages

Critiques ethnography and draws on Friere to develop an interactive theory of composition pedagogy. Treats issues of gender, class, and race in teaching writing and argues that interpretation should replace evaluation.

1320. Gere, Anne Ruggles. "The Politics of Teaching Writing." *Focuses* 3 (Fall 1990): 89–98.

Considers power relationships at societal, institutional, and classroom levels. Finds that the meaning of "teaching writing" is too politicized for easy definition.

1321. Gibson, Wavie. "The Effects of Current-Traditional Instruction and New Rhetoric on the Holistic Quality and Audience Adaptation in College Freshmen's Writing." *DAI* 51 (July 1990): 68A.

Researches the writing of 100 first-semester college students, concluding that neither teaching procedure produces significant differences in the quality of the writing.

1322. Handa, Carolyn, ed. *Computers and Community: Teaching Composition in the Twenty-First Century.* Portsmouth, N.H.: Boynton/Cook, 1990. 276 pages

Nine essays focus on equipping the composition classroom, using hardware to create a sense of community through networking, conferencing on the computer, and understanding the social significance of using computers to teach students about their language.

1323. Handa, Carolyn, and Gretchen Flesher. "An Interview with Richard Lanham: Learning by Going Along." *WE* 2 (Fall 1990): 6–22.

Lanham traces the origins of his professional interests and discusses the interplay among electronic texts, the undergraduate curriculum, copyright law, and John Cage.

1324. Hannafin, Kathleen McDermott. "CBI Authoring Tools in Postsecondary Institutions: A Review and Critical Examination." *CompEd* 14 (1990): 197–204.

Reviews authoring developments, features, trends, issues, and next generation tools needed to create and promote effective authoring at the postsecondary level.

1325. Hara, Edward J. "A Description of Writing Curriculum in Four Classrooms." *DAI* 51 (November 1990): 1537A.

Discusses the influence on enacted writing activities of interactions between the teacher and the class and of varying definitions of *writing*.

1326. Hart, Francis Russell. *Beyond the Books: Reflections on Teaching and Learning.* Columbus, Ohio: Ohio State University Press, 1990. 198 pages

A personal reflection on teaching literature and critical thinking in introductory and general education courses.

1327. Hawisher, Gail E., and Cynthia L. Selfe, eds. *Critical Perspectives on Computers and Composition Instruction.* New York: Teachers College Press, 1989. 248 pages

Twelve essays discuss what we have learned about writers and computers during the past decade, how current political and practical concerns work against possible success for students and English departments, and how new perspectives on teaching with computers can enhance students' learning as well as extend the current knowledge base.

1328. Hill, Carolyn Erickson. *Writing from the Margins: Power and Pedagogy for Teachers of Composition.* New York: Oxford University Press, 1990. 292 pages

Drawing on feminist, cultural, and poststructuralist theory as well as work in the rhetorical tradition and composition studies, Hill offers methods of thinking that teachers can model for their students.

1329. Hill, Sharon Ann. "A Phenomenological Study of the Transfer of Training Experienced by Word-Processing Students in a Computer Literacy Class." *DAI* 51 (November 1990): 1486A.

Community college students were asked to complete assignments by using first a generic program and then Word Perfect.

1330. Holdstein, Deborah H., and Cynthia L. Selfe, eds. *Computers and Writing: Theory, Research, Practice.* New York: MLA, 1990. 150 pages

Ten essays discuss issues and problems associated with adopting computers in college English classrooms and departments. Explores ethical and political considerations as well as theoretical and critical contexts.

1331. Hostetler, Jerry C. "Authoring Tools Facilitate Lesson Development for Different Microcomputers." *CollM* 8 (August 1990): 225–230.

Argues that selecting a PILOT-based authoring language can help the author or developer design CAI.

1332. Hunter, Paul. "Synecdoche against Metonymy: Burke, Freire, and Writing Instruction." *FEN* 18 (Spring 1990): 2–6, 7–9.

Proposes using Burke's notion of "writing as mediation" and Freire's pedagogy of dialogue in the composition classroom.

1333. Hynds, Susan, and Donald L. Rubin, eds. *Perspectives on Talk and Learning.* Urbana, Ill.: NCTE, 1990. 305 pages

A "systematic discussion of talk and learning" in several kinds of composition classes, inspired by the recent recognition of a "culture of silence" created by political oppression. Eighteen essays study effective approaches for bringing students from oral-based cultural backgrounds into multicultural writing and reading communities.

1334. Jacobson, Jeanne M. "Writing a Conversation: Journals in the College Classroom." Paper presented at the NCTE Spring Conference, Charleston, S.C., April 1989. ERIC ED 311 462. 11 pages

Describes individual journals, class journals, and group journals.

1335. Janda, Mary Ann. "Collaboration in a Traditional Classroom Environment." *WC* 7 (July 1990): 291–315.

A detailed analysis of how traditional classroom discourse patterns undermined two teachers' efforts to introduce collaborative activities (in elementary classrooms).

1336. Jeske, Jeff. "Peer Response Groups: Answering the Critique." Paper presented at the CCCC Convention, Seattle, March 1989. ERIC ED 309 446. 23 pages

Presents a four-stage model for implementing peer-response groups and raising students' metacognitive awareness.

1337. Karloff, Kenneth. "Using Prereading Activities to Guide Students' Writing." *ExEx* 35 (Spring 1990): 3–4.

Suggests that students may gather and infer more information from texts by focusing on a brief passage before reading.

1338. Kaufer, David, and Cheryl Geisler. "Structuring Argumentation in a Social Constructivist Framework: A Pedagogy with

Computer Support." *Arg* 4 (November 1990): 379–396.

> Introduces a more complete characterization of socially constructed argumentation. Describes pedagogical strategies and reviews current and planned software that aids in reading and designing arguments.

1339. Kear, Lynn. "Attitudes toward Popular Film, Learning, and Education: A Survey of Undergraduate College Students." *DAI* 50 (May 1990): 3387A.

> Results of the study empirically suggest that using popular films in the classroom is an effective tool.

1340. Kearns, Michael. "Topical Knowledge and Revising." *JTW* 9 (Fall–Winter 1990): 195–207.

> During revision, acquiring new knowledge and having time increase macrostructure changes. Revisers learned that "a paper ought to grow in substance as the writer grows in knowledge."

1341. Kimball, John. "Implications of Theory for Collaborative Invention in College Composition." *DAI* 51 (December 1990): 1938A.

> Examines Plato's dialectic, Aristotle's art of persuasion, and Vygotsky's social constructivist epistemology as bases for collaborative invention among college writers.

1342. Kremers, Marshall. "Sharing Authority on a Synchronous Network: The Case for Riding the Beast." *CC* 7 (April 1990): 33–44.

> Describes two models for using real-time networking in writing classrooms.

1343. Kuhn, Elisabeth D. "Gender and Authority: Classroom Diplomacy in Frankfurt and Berkeley." *DAI* 51 (November 1990): 1597A.

> Finds that female professors in introductory class meetings are more likely to use "less authoritarian speech acts" than male professors.

1344. Landis, Kathleen. "The Knowledge of Composition." Paper presented at the CCCC

Convention, Chicago, March 1990. ERIC ED 319 048. 18 pages

> Argues that while writing instruction is often instruction in genres, it should also include ways to acquire knowledge.

1345. Lardner, Ted, and Michael McClure. "A Comment on 'Reinventing *Inventio*' [*CE* 51 (September 1989)]." *CE* 52 (October 1990): 686–687.

> Scolds Sloane for splitting rhetoric, "and specifically *inventio*, from the social and political context of rhetorical activities" and for teaching persuasive methods without values.

1346. Lavoie, Dan, and Ann Backus. "Students Write to Overcome Learning Blocks." *JCST* 19 (May 1990): 353–358.

> Correlates impediments to writing tasks with learning styles and offers particular writing strategies that remove these impediments.

1347. "Learning to Use Cooperative Learning." *CompC* 3 (February 1990): 2–3.

> Summarizes suggestions by Kate E. Sandberg about how to use cooperative learning in the writing classroom.

1348. Lewis, Janice. "A Study of Theoretical and Instructional Support for Integrated College Freshmen Reading and Writing Courses." *DAI* 50 (February 1990): 2412A.

> Suggests that language, study methods, and attitudes affect reading and that reading indirectly influences writing. Also studies teachers' commitments to combining these disciplines.

1349. Lewis, Magda. "Interrupting Patriarchy: Politics, Resistance, and Transformation in the Feminist Classroom." *HER* 60 (November 1990): 467–488.

> Analyzes students' resistance to feminist critiques of patriarchy. Identifies pedagogical strategies useful in subverting a gendered *status quo* of classroom interactions between men and women.

1350. Liechty, Anna L. *The Efficacy of Computer-Assisted Instruction in Teaching Composition*. South Bend, Ind.: Indiana University—South Bend, 1989. ERIC ED 314 023. 66 pages

Reviews 38 studies, recommending that computer use be combined with process instruction.

1351. Linden, Myra J., and Arthur Whimbey. *Why Johnny Can't Write: How to Improve Writing Skills*. Hillsdale, N.J.: Erlbaum, 1990. 136 pages

Presents two methods for teaching and improving writing skills—from spelling and grammar to logical organization. Also offers a rationale for rethinking the English classroom to make the educational system work more effectively.

1352. Major, James S., and Jean S. Filetti. "'Type'-Writing: Helping Students Write with the Myers-Briggs Type Indicator." *WLN* 15 (December 1990): 4–6.

Relates four basic personality types to different approaches to writing. Suggests strategies to assist each of the four types.

1353. Mark, Jorie Lester. "Twenty-Two Good Educational Practices." *AdLBEd* 13 (1989): 45–51.

Applicable to all levels and fields. Advocates process-type practices such as clear, measurable goals and individualized learning plans. Values techniques such as using small groups and peer tutoring.

1354. Marting, Janet. "Working Topics for Students' Papers." Paper presented at the College English Association, Buffalo, April 1990. ERIC ED 319 066. 9 pages

Reports on the success of using work as a theme in a writing class.

1355. Mayo, Wendall, Jr. "Teaching Composition and the Creative Writing Workshop." Paper presented at Challenge 1990: The Teaching of Undergraduate Writing, Columbus, Ohio, May 1990. ERIC ED 320 149. 9 pages

Reports on a study investigating students' awareness of the self, society, and authority in their writing and in writing workshops.

1356. McKinley, William, P. David Pearson, Rand J. Spiro, Kathleen Copeland, and Robert J. Tierney. *The Effects of Reading and Writing upon Thinking and Learning*. Urbana, Ill.: CSR, 1988. ERIC ED 310 353. 50 pages

By directing their own reading and writing engagements prior to composing a persuasive essay, several undergraduate students learned to write by creating a discourse community.

1357. Mohanty, Chandra Talpade. "On Race and Voice: Challenges for Liberal Education in the 1990s." *CCrit* 14 (Winter 1989–1990): 179–208.

Identifies some of the problems encountered when establishing a pedagogy that foregrounds issues of race and gender.

1358. Moran, Charles. "The Computer Writing Room: Authority and Control." *CC* 7 (April 1990): 61–69.

Argues that networked classrooms are in danger of becoming the new, lock-step grammar books and not centers for learning to write.

1359. Morenberg, Max. "Process/Schmocess: Why Not Combine a Sentence or Two?" Paper presented at the CCCC Convention, Chicago, March 1990. ERIC ED 319 040. 14 pages

Advocates using form-based sentence combining in writing instruction.

1360. Murabito, Stephen. "Writers and Societies of Writers: Reflections on In-Class Writing Time." *CEAF* 20 (1990): 15–16.

Argues that students should not be made to write in the presence of others.

1361. Murray, Donald M. "All Writing Is Autobiography." Paper presented at the CCCC Convention, Chicago, March 1990. ERIC ED 318 022. 15 pages

Argues that autobiography is essential to a writer's making meaning and may empower students in the composition class.

1362. Nagel, Stuart, and Lisa Bievenue. "Using Decision-Aiding Software for Teaching in All Fields of Knowledge." *CollM* 8 (August 1990): 171–182.

Analyzes software for use in CAI that can process a set of controversial issues in any discipline.

1363. Neuwirth, Christine M. *Intelligent Tutoring Systems: Exploring Issues in Learning and Teaching Writing*. Pittsburgh: Carnegie Mellon University Center for Educational Computing in English, 1988. ERIC ED 309 407. 43 pages

Describes a system of CAI for investigating the learning and teaching of writing.

1364. Nydahl, Joel. "Teaching Word Processors to Be CAI Programs." *CE* 52 (December 1990): 904–915.

Examines the CAI potential of several word processors as a possible method for increasing the adaptability of CAI in general.

1365. Palo, Susan. "An Interview with Mike Rose: 'Imagine a Writing Program.' " *WE* 1 (Spring 1990): 6–22.

Rose discusses the cognitive dimension of writing, the design of writing courses, effective teaching, and the role of writing programs within universities.

1366. Perdue, Virginia. "The Politics of Teaching Detail." *RR* 8 (Spring 1990): 280–288.

Analyzes using concrete language to capture a reader's attention while promoting change in a writer's sensory awareness and generating an understanding of broader social constructs.

1367. Piazza, Stephen, and Charles Suhor, comps. *Trends and Issues in English Instruction, 1990: Six Summaries of Informal Annual Discussions of Commissions of the National Council of Teachers of English*. Urbana, Ill.: NCTE, 1990. ERIC ED 315 793. 15 pages

The directors of six NCTE commissions summarize current trends and issues in English instruction.

1368. Quandahl, Ellen. "A Comment on 'Rhetoric and Ideology in the Writing Class' [*CE* 50 (September 1988)]." *CE* 52 (March 1990): 343–345.

Discusses Berlin's failure to analyze the connections between cognitive and social-epistemic rhetorics and suggests one way of doing so.

1369. Quinn, Kathleen A. "Directed Prewriting: The Key to Understanding Both Audience and Point of View." *ExEx* 35 (Spring 1990): 45–46.

Offers audiences and points of view for students to write for and from.

1370. Rabkin, Eric S., and Macklin Smith. *Teaching Writing That Works: A Group Approach to Practical English*. Ann Arbor, Mich.: University of Michigan Press, 1990. 224 pages

A guidebook for composition teachers that describes a curriculum and teaching techniques based on workshops using peer editing and evaluation and emphasizing the common aspects of written and spoken communication.

1371. Rankin, Elizabeth. "From Simple to Complex: Ideas of Order in Assignment Sequences." *JAC* 10 (1990): 126–135.

Surveys various meanings of going from "simple to complex" in writing tasks: hierarchical, developmental, formal, and cumulative primacy. "Assignment sequence is a necessary fiction."

1372. Rider, Janine. "Must Imitation Be the Mother of Invention?" *JTW* 9 (Fall-Winter 1990): 175–185.

Argues against David Bartholomae's notions about discourse. Advocates helping students find their own voices before adopting voices of the academy.

1373. Ritchie, Joy S. "Confronting the 'Essential' Problem: Reconnecting Feminist Theory and Pedagogy." *JAC* 10 (1990): 249–273.

An ethnography of a college course that integrates reading and writing from a feminist perspective, rejecting essentialist definitions of *woman*. Analyzes learning logs kept by participants.

1374. Robinson, Jay L. *Conversations on the Written Word: Essays on Language Literacy.* Portsmouth, N.H.: Boynton/Cook, 1990. 352 pages

Reflects upon a wide range of issues dealing with the current state of literacy education in schools and universities. Draws upon his experiences as a linguist, department chair, and director of a writing program and collaborates with three former students, now colleagues.

1375. Rosati, Annette C. "(Dis)Placement of Current-Traditional Rhetoric's Approach in a Composition Class." Paper presented at the Conference on Rhetoric and the Teaching of Writing, Indiana, Pa., July 1990. ERIC ED 321 271. 14 pages

Describes how some writing programs may mix process and product approaches illogically in a current-traditional paradigm.

1376. Sanzenbacher, Richard. "The Plural I; or, Generating Multiple Ways of Knowing." *ExEx* 36 (Fall 1990): 16–19.

Demonstrates that asking students to consider the categories of space, time, and cause/effect in relation to a cartoon can change their perceptions.

1377. Sardine, Janice. "Take a Byte of Technology: Integrate Computers into *Your* Classroom." *CalE* 26 (May June 1990): 10–11, 21.

Computer technology can be an effective addition to a writing class.

1378. Schneider, Melanie L. "Collaborative Learning: A Concept in Search of a Definition." *Issues* 3 (Fall–Winter 1990): 26–40.

Distinguishes among the "related concepts of collaborative learning, cooperative learning, and cooperative activities." Argues that understanding these distinctions will enable teachers to create classroom contexts that encourage learning.

1379. Schramm, Robert Maynard. "The Effects of Using Word-Processing Equipment in Writing Instruction: A Meta-Analysis." *DAI* 50 (February 1990): 2463A.

Finds that word processing has a positive effect on writing quality, essay length, and attitude but a negative effect on the quantity of revisions.

1380. Schwartz, Alex. "Professional Writers Don't Write like That, So Why Should You?" Paper presented at the CCCC Convention, Chicago, March 1990. ERIC ED 320 153. 14 pages

Reports on benefits to students in seeing professional writers work on several drafts and in hearing them talk about their writing.

1381. Sloan, Chris. "Propaganda in the Mass Media: The Poll Story." *ExEx* 36 (Fall 1990): 5–7.

This assignment requires students to strengthen their critical reading skills by writing lead sentences after analyzing statistical data.

1382. Sloane, Thomas. "Thomas Sloane Responds [to Lardner and McClure, *CE* 52 (October 1990)]." *CE* 52 (October 1990): 687–689.

Defends his article [*CE* 51 (September 1989)] with an example: a student, "a highly dogmatic believer in *laissez-faire* capitalism," finds himself arguing "directly contrary to his principles," thanks to pro/con training.

1383. Sperling, Melanie. "I Want to Talk to Each of You: Collaboration and the Teacher-Student Writing Conference." *RTE* 24 (October 1990): 279–321.

Quantitative and qualitative research indicates that student-teacher conferences constitute collaborative acts shaped by the rhetorical circumstances of the meeting.

1384. Stewig, John Warren. "Theory into Practice: The Contexts in Which Writing Is Taught." *EQ* 22 (1990): 79–88.

How successful writing programs are instituted depends on several contexts: the self, the classroom, the school, the district, the community, the state, and the nation.

1385. Strickland, James. "Computers and the Classroom: A Look at Changes in Pedagogy." Paper presented at the CCCC Convention, Seattle, March 1989. ERIC ED 315 791. 26 pages

Discusses how computers in the writing classroom change its activities, forcing a radical rethinking of spatial design.

1386. Stroble, Elizabeth. "Framing a Letter to Lincoln." *ExEx* 35 (Spring 1990): 22–24.

Describes an activity in which students write and read letters explaining modern inventions to Lincoln (a colleague in costume), who responds with questions.

1387. Strong, Bill. "Looking Back on Sentence Combining." *UEJ* 18 (1990): 34–36.

Describes Strong's personal introduction to transformational grammar and how he developed his approach to sentence combining.

1388. Svinicki, Marilla D., ed. *The Changing Face of College Teaching.* New Directions for Teaching and Learning, no. 42. San Francisco: Jossey-Bass, 1990. 135 pages

Discusses collaborative learning, writing across the curriculum, assessment, and strategies for instruction. Contributors are not indexed separately in this volume.

1389. Templeton, Robert John. "Writing as Private Displays of High School Seniors' Lived Experience in a Classroom." *DAI* 50 (March 1990): 2777A.

Analyzes influences on students' writing in a special course designed to foster critical reflection upon personal and educational experiences.

1390. Thompson, Diane. "Electronic Bulletin Boards: A Timeless Place for Collaborative Writing Projects." *CC* 7 (August 1990): 43–53.

Describes how bulletin boards can be used for writing collaboratively. Cumbersome projects and incompatible groups require teacher management for success.

1391. Thompson, Diane. "Network Capabilities and Academic Realities: Implementing Interactive Networking in a Community College Environment." *JCBI* 17 (Winter 1990): 17–22.

Despite the many writing-oriented activities made possible by local area networks, teachers and students underutilize these activities.

1392. Todd, Frankie. "Degrees of Freedom: A Study of Collaborative Learning in Higher Education." *DAI* 51 (September 1990): 760A.

Examines how the distribution of power in higher education affects learners' roles in the construction of knowledge.

1393. Vavra, Edward. "Vygotsky and Grammar Instruction." *CompC* 3 (February 1990): 4–6.

Vygotsky's theories can help determine when and how to teach grammar.

1394. Wiley, Mark. "Writing in the American Grain: Peter Elbow's and David Bartholomae's Emersonian Pedagogies of Empowerment." *WI* 9 (Fall 1989–Winter 1990): 57–66.

Considers how two composition theories are linked to the American tradition of individuality and resistance to authority, especially to Emersonian philosophies of power and language.

1395. Woods, Donald R. "Developing Students' Problem-Solving Skills." *JCST* 19 (December 1989–January 1990): 178–179.

Provides an overview of techniques for incorporating problem solving into the classroom.

1396. Zach, Cheryl. "Capturing Sights, Sounds, and Smells in Your Writing." *Writer* 103 (December 1990): 22–23, 41.

Outlines systems that students may use to maintain specificity in narrative descriptions.

1397. Zebroski, James. "New Perspectives on the Social in Composition: Lev Vygotsky's Theory of Process." *CompC* 3 (April 1990): 4–6.

Vygotsky's theories about thinking help to reconcile the social and individual views of composition.

1398. Zlotolow, Steve. "Development of an Instructional Strategy: Video Grammar and an Assimilative Process." *DAI* 50 (March 1990): 2779A.

Describes and tests a media-supported methodology for teaching grammar to college students.

See also 33, 34, 47, 100, 217, 227, 319, 467, 474, 483, 515, 678, 760, 859, 903, 964, 993, 1169, 1263, 1267

4.2   HIGHER EDUCATION

4.2.1 DEVELOPMENTAL WRITING

1399. Anderson, Edward. "Teaching Users of Diverse Dialects: Practical Approaches." *TETYC* 17 (October 1990): 172–177.

Practical approaches include comparing standard and nonstandard grammars; assigning mainstream authors to be read; asking students to write short papers, compose journals, and adopt roles. Grading should be nonthreatening.

1400. Anstendig, Linda, and Isabel Kimmel. "Basic Writers as Critical Thinkers." Paper presented at the CCCC Convention, Seattle, March 1989. ERIC ED 309 435. 22 pages

Describes a course that focuses on the theme of language and identity and that enables the cumulative development of thinking and composing.

1401. Burrows, Coralee Susan. "Basic Writing Students' Perceptions of Their Writing Problems and Their Strategies to Overcome Them." *DAI* 51 (September 1990): 724A.

Examines the perceptions of 23 community college basic writing students in order to describe and identify effective instructional practices.

1402. Cheatham, Judy Blankenship. "The Effects of Mode of Instruction on Basic Writing." *DAI* 50 (March 1990): 2765A.

Finds significant positive effects when the environmental method of teaching writing is used.

1403. Courage, Richard. "Basic Writing: End of a Frontier?" *JTW* 9 (Fall–Winter 1990): 247–260.

A review essay of *Errors and Expectations, Basic Writing,* and *A Sourcebook for Basic Writing Teachers* examines trends in basic writing instruction from 1977 to 1987.

1404. Cross, Geoffrey. "Left to Their Own Devices: Three Basic Writers Using Word Processing." *CC* 7 (April 1990): 47–58.

Concludes that basic writers need specific instruction and much coaching to use the potential of word processing in composition classes.

1405. Davis, Mary Beth Lindley. "Revisioning the Basic Writer as Seeker and Quester: A Preparatory Course Design." *TETYC* 17 (February 1990): 24–29.

Examines the quest motif as a metaphor for the process of remediation. Offers a course design based on stages of awareness, reality, and critical perspective.

1406. Di Matteo, Anthony. "Under Erasure: A Theory for Interactive Writing in Real Time." *CC* 7 (April 1990): 71–84.

Describes how speaking and writing move closer for students on a network, explores some of its demands, and points to new thinking about language and learning.

1407. DiPardo, Anne. "Narrative Discourse in the Basic Writing Class: Meeting the Challenge of Cultural Pluralism." *TETYC* 17 (February 1990): 45–53.

Discusses the necessity of valuing and negotiating differing narrative styles.

1408. Harris, Joseph. "Growth and Conflict in Basic Writing." Paper presented at the CCCC Convention, Chicago, March 1990. ERIC ED 319 056. 12 pages

Argues that basic writing courses should ignore the metaphors of growth and initiation and allow students to draw fully on their personal histories.

1409. Herrington, Anne J., and Marcia Curtis. "Basic Writing: Moving the Voices on the Margin to the Center." *HER* 60 (November 1990): 489–496.

Reports on the reconstruction of a basic writing course to give voice to minority students made academically and socially marginal within the university. Encourages students to reflect on the experience of marginalization.

1410. Herrmann, Daryl E., and Eleanor Beppler. "Motivating Students in Developmental Writing Programs." Paper presented at the Liberal Arts Network for Development Conference, East Lansing, Mich., February 1990. ERIC ED 318 529. 15 pages

Describes using reality therapy in developmental writing classes at Glen Oaks Community College. Reports positive attitudes towards writing.

1411. Hindman, Jane E. "The Effect of a Self-Cueing Treatment on Top-Level Goal-Setting Strategies and Attention to Task in Timed Writing Sessions." Paper presented at the Wyoming Conference, Laramie, June 1990. ERIC ED 321 289. 21 pages

A case study of a student with writing problems who is given cue cards containing directive statements. Finds little improvement.

1412. Hull, Glynda, and Mike Rose. *Rethinking Remediation: Toward a Social-Cognitive Understanding of Problematic Reading and Writing.* Berkeley, Calif.: CSW, 1989. ERIC ED 309 411. 19 pages

Provides a snapshot of the social and cognitive variables that define the underprepared writer in an inner-city community college.

1413. Kinsler, Kimberly. "Structured Peer Collaboration: Teaching Essay Revision to College Students Needing Writing Remediation." *CI* 7 (Autumn 1990): 303–321.

Collaboration increased audience awareness and the use of support statements. Exit essays, however, appeared to stress grammar and word choice abilities.

1414. McDoniel, Lawrence Joseph. "Modeling in the Basic Writing Class." *DAI* 50 (February 1990): 2413A.

Proposes modeling as a strategy for encouraging fluency and creativity, although the study fails to confirm the technique.

1415. Morrison, Constance. "A Literary, Whole Language College Reading Program." *JDEd* 14 (Winter 1990): 8–10, 12.

Explains an approach to teaching reading comprehension using verbal interaction and writing.

1416. Petrillo, Barbara. "The Process Approach Can Be a Source of Dilemmas for Writing Instructors." *Leaflet* 89 (Spring 1990): 38–46.

Addresses ethical problems that arise from teaching in a process-oriented writing program, problems particularly affecting student evaluation.

1417. Popken, Randall. "Some Sources of Writing Genre Interference in the Work of Basic Writers." Paper presented at the CCCC

Convention, Chicago, March 1990. ERIC ED 319 064. 17 pages

Reports on a study of 34 basic writers who confused journalistic writing with academic genres.

1418. Sawyer-Anderson, Athlyn. "Integrated Skills Curriculum for Second-Level Remedial Writing." *DAI* 50 (May 1990): 3470A.

Compares the achievement of students in a remedial writing class receiving integrated skills reinforcement and those taught by conventional methods.

1419. Sirc, Geoffrey, and Tom Reynolds. "The Face of Collaboration in the Networked Writing Classroom." *CC* 7 (April 1990): 53–70.

Instructors in basic writing classes should be sensitive to students' needs and personalities, for collaboration is not always on writing the text at hand.

1420. Suderman, James D. "The Computer as an Enabler of Writing." *CACJ* 5 (Summer 1990): 23–28.

When a class of developmental writing students wrote their essays on computers, they were able to locate more of their errors.

1421. Tebo-Messina, Margaret, and Doris B. Blough. "Penpals and Keypals: Networks for Student Writers." Paper presented at the NCTE Spring Conference, Charleston, S.C., April 1989. ERIC ED 321 257. 10 pages

Describes a program in which seventh graders and college students exchange papers.

1422. Trotter-Stewart, Ava Marie. "A Status Survey of Basic Writing Instruction in City University of New York Community Colleges." *DAI* 50 (March 1990): 2762A.

Examines relationships between traditional and process-oriented pedagogy used by teachers in community colleges.

1423. Trzyna, Thomas, and Margaret Batschelet. "The Ethical Complexity of Collaboration." *WE* 2 (Fall 1990): 23–33.

Collective assignments pose conflicts between the needs of individuals and groups that can be mediated by instruction in ethics and group processes.

1424. Varone, Sandra D'Amico, and Karen Nilson D'Agostino. "Beyond Software: Computers and the Composition Classroom." *CompC* 2 (January 1990): 4–6.

Describes an instructional approach to using computers in the basic writing classroom. Includes a classroom layout.

1425. Watson, Arden K. "Helping Developmental Students Overcome Communication Apprehension." *JDEd* 14 (September 1990): 10–17.

Suggests assessment techniques, alleviation strategies, and possible materials for overcoming communication apprehension.

1426. Word, Miriam F. *A Personalized Developmental Model for the Teaching of Communications I: A Practicum Report*. Fort Lauderdale, Fla.: Nova University, 1990. ERIC ED 316 271. 60 pages

Describes a program in which writing instruction was matched with individual students' learning styles as measured by the Myers-Briggs Type Indicator.

See also 24, 466, 1216, 1247, 1820, 1836

4.2.2 FRESHMAN COMPOSITION

1427. Aghbar, Ali-Asghar. "Selecting Reading Materials for a Writing Class." Paper presented at the English Association of the Pennsylvania State System of Higher Education, Carlisle, Pa., November 1987. ERIC ED 311 396. 10 pages

Argues that reading activities and materials should be used to the extent that they directly contribute to writing development.

1428. Albers, Randall K. "No More Lip Service: Voice Empowerment in a Story Workshop Composition Class." Paper presented at the NCTE Spring Conference, Charleston, S.C., April 1989. ERIC ED 311 440. 22 pages

Claims that the story workshop approach ensures that students will develop the power of their own voices.

1429. Anderson, Philip M. "In Defense of the Aesthetic: The Role of English Educators in Defining Culture and Fighting Censorship." Paper presented at the NCTE Spring Conference, Charleston, S.C., April 1989. ERIC ED 311 441. 20 pages

Providing literary experiences and aesthetic language experiences as well as promoting writing as dialogue in a social context make teaching a struggle.

1430. Bailey, Richard E. "A Case Method Approach to Academic Writing in Introductory Composition." *DAI* 51 (July 1990): 98A.

Argues that introductory composition not only should prepare for college writing but also should include actual subject-conditioned writing assignments drawn from mathematics, sciences, and literature.

1431. Bass, Barbara Kaplan. "Dialoguing over Time: A Method for Revision in Freshman Composition Classes." *ExEx* 36 (Fall 1990): 8–12.

Describes an activity to strengthen audience awareness.

1432. Bazerman, Charles. "Two Comments on 'A Common Ground: The Essay in Academe' [*CE* 51 (March 1989)]." *CE* 52 (March 1990): 329–330.

Bazerman defends his work by describing his intentions and by emphasizing the importance of personal voice in his and other writing across the curriculum textbooks.

1433. Beauvais, Paul Jude. "Sartre's Plea and the Purposes of Writing." *Pre/Text* 10 (Spring–Summer 1989): 11–31.

Sartre's marriage of existentialism with Marxism may serve as a guide to an anti-foundationalist curriculum for writing instruction.

1434. Belles, Sue, and Elizabeth Hoffman. "Two Comments on 'Recognizing the Learn-

ing-Disabled College Writer' [*CE* 51 (March 1989)]." *CE* 52 (March 1990): 338–340.

Supplements O'Hearn's article with details on the needs of learning-disabled students. Suggests how composition teachers might address these needs and gives sources of additional information.

1435. Bernhardt, Stephen A., Patricia G. Wojahn, and Penny R. Edwards. "Teaching College Composition with Computers: A Timed Observation Study." *WC* 7 (July 1990): 342–374.

Contrasts the behaviors of two teachers who each taught two sections of the same course, one using microcomputers half of the time and the other teaching a regular class.

1436. Brunner, Dianne D. "Strategies for Blending Public and Private Writing." *CompC* 3 (October 1990): 4–7.

Strategies include a dialectical notebook and revision options geared to specific assignments.

1437. Bump, Jerome. "Radical Changes in Class Discussion Using Networked Computers." *CHum* 24 (February–April 1990): 49–65.

The results of a student questionnaire favor class discussions conducted on a real-time networking program, despite some technological problems.

1438. Bundy, Marcia Seabury. "Sports Talk." *Leaflet* 89 (Fall 1990): 21–30.

Explores sports as a source of productive metaphors for student-teacher relationships and for learning writing.

1439. Burns, Jamie H. "Teaching Cohesion in College Composition Courses." *DAI* 51 (October 1990): 1217A.

Argues for teaching of concepts of cohesion that connect text, writer, reader, and context.

1440. Daane, Mary Constance. "A Study of the Understanding of Metaphor in Writing by

College Freshmen." *DAI* 51 (November 1990): 1536A.

> Examines the occurrence of "fresh" and "conventional" metaphors in a variety of discourse modes among developing writers.

1441. Davis, Wesley K. *The Effects of Christensen's Generative Rhetoric of a Sentence on the Right-Branched Free Modifiers of College Freshman Writing.* Bloomington, Ind.: ERIC/RCS, 1989. ERIC ED 313 706. 30 pages

> Describes an experimental study of first-year college students, finding significant effects on modification patterns.

1442. Draper, Virginia. "Writing Response Groups: From Power Trips to Empowerment." Paper presented at the CCCC Convention, Seattle, March 1989. ERIC ED 310 401. 13 pages

> Reports that freshman composition students shifted from engaging in power trips to participating in empowering conversations when discussing research papers in writing groups.

1443. Farmer, Frank. " 'A Language of One's Own': A Stylistic Pedagogy for the Dialogical Classroom." *FEN* 19 (Fall 1990): 16–17, 20–22.

> Presents exercise sequences for a writing classroom that is centered on "the relationship between knowledge and language."

1444. Fontaine, Sheryl L., John Peavoy, and Susan Hunter. "Unprivileged Voices in the Academy of the Privileged." *FEN* 19 (Fall 1990): 2–9.

> Presents three tactics for subverting the narrowly focused voices of privilege in schools where students are already empowered.

1445. Forrest, John, and Elisabeth Jackson. "Get Real: Empowering the Student through Oral History." *OralH* 18 (Spring 1990): 29–44.

> Oral histories vitalize student writing. This anthropological field methods course teaches the technique as tool by insisting on data students care about.

1446. George, E. Laurie. "Taking Women Professors Seriously: Female Authority in the Computerized Classroom." *CC* 7 (April 1990): 45–52.

> The author describes how she deals with male students who often write out their frustrations and "roles" on networked computers. Female teachers need to be both nurturing and authoritative.

1447. Greenway, William. "Imaginary Gardens with Real Toads: Nature Writing in the Curriculum." *TETYC* 17 (October 1990): 189–192.

> Students explore the relationships between nature essays and nature poetry in developing their own personal writing. The second part of the course generates a research paper based on a nature book.

1448. Guiher-Huff, Susan. "Involvement in a Current Problem as a Basis for Writing." *TETYC* 17 (October 1990): 187–188.

> Describes a course focusing on pollution awareness.

1449. Gylys, Beth. "Case Study: A Resistant Risk Taker." *TETYC* 17 (December 1990): 241–246.

> An exceptional student resists the workshop approach of a composition class, thereby teaching her teacher something about individual learning styles.

1450. Hocking, Joan. "Suggestions for Using the Microcomputer to Teach Revision." *CACJ* 4 (Spring 1990): 68–73.

> Offers seven exercises for teaching revision with computers. Describes four advantages of computer revision.

1451. Hollandsworth, Linda Padgett. "A Needs Assessment Model for College Writing Program Evaluation." *DAI* 51 (September 1990): 770A.

Analyzes the needs of 30 incoming first-year students who received low scores on holistically scored placement essay exams.

1452. Hovanec, Carol. "Internationalizing the Freshman English Curriculum." *FEN* 19 (Fall 1990): 22–25.

Presents a plan for using works by non-Western authors in a literature-based freshman composition course.

1453. Jennings, Edward M. "Paperless Writing Revisited." *CHum* 24 (February–April 1990): 43–48.

A followup study argues that writing classes conducted on a mainframe computer network alter student-teacher relationships. Endorses network pedagogy.

1454. Jewell, John. "English Composition on Cable TV: Results of One Experiment." *TETYC* 17 (May 1990): 127–132.

Instructors created their own television lectures. Students mailed assignments but came to campus to write their essays.

1455. Kelder, Richard. "Introducing Philosophy to the Composition Class." Paper presented at the State University of New York's Council on Writing, Brockport, N.Y., March 1986. ERIC ED 311 442. 19 pages

Discusses the benefits of engaging students in philosophical discussion in the composition class.

1456. Kelly, Erna, and Donna Raleigh. "Integrating Word-Processing Skills with Revision Skills." *CHum* 24 (February–April 1990): 5–13.

Describes two lab-classroom strategies for using word processing to improve students' structural revision skills.

1457. Landis, Kathleen. "The Knowledge of Composition." *FEN* 19 (Fall 1990): 9–13.

Considers the significance to the freshman writer of knowledge structures and topic knowledge. Applies a theory of cognitive development.

1458. Langley, David. "Composition Classroom Anthologies: Some Explanatory Thoughts and Suggestions for Further Research." Paper presented at the Conference on Rhetoric and the Teaching of Writing, Indiana, Pa., July 1990. ERIC ED 321 269. 13 pages

Analyzes 11 essay anthologies used for composition classes, finding three major problems in their approaches.

1459. Lotto, Edward. "Edward Lotto Responds [to Purves, *CE* 52 (September 1990)]." *CE* 52 (September 1990): 580–582.

Claims that, in fact, Lotto and Purves agree—differences between text and utterance are culturally evaluated—but Lotto refuses to dismiss them as unimportant.

1460. Mangan, Katherine S. "Battle Rages over Plan to Focus on Race and Gender in U. of Texas Course." *CHE* 37 (21 November 1990): A15.

Describes the controversy over the English Department's proposal to revise its required freshman writing course.

1461. Marting, Janet. "Toward a New Definition of Service Course." *CEAF* 20 (1990): 19–20.

The composition course should be meaning-based and not merely skills-based.

1462. McCleary, Bill. "Write It Down!" *CompC* 2 (January 1990): 7.

Argues for the importance of writing out assignments.

1463. McCleary, Bill. "You Can Write Model Essays for Students and Model the Writing Process While You're at It." *CompC* 3 (April 1990): 9–10.

This exercise helps students and teacher better understand the assignment and gives students models for academic writing.

1464. McLeod, Susan. "Cultural Literacy, Curricular Reform, and Freshman Composition." *RR* 8 (Spring 1990): 270–278.

Discusses Hirsch's notion of cultural literacy. Argues that the theory has far-reaching implications for the teaching of freshman composition.

1465. Miller, Richard. "From Opposition to Resistance: Popular Culture and the Composition Classroom." Paper presented at the CCCC Convention, Chicago, March 1990. ERIC ED 319 041. 12 pages

Argues that using popular culture in the composition classroom heightens the conflict between student and academic discourse, allowing it to become one of the subjects of study.

1466. Miller, Susan. "Two Comments on 'A Common Ground: The Essay in Academe' [*CE* 51 (March 1989)]." *CE* 52 (March 1990): 330–334.

Critiques Spellmeyer's essay by describing personal essays as constructed amid tensions rather than being reflections of discovered or created ideas.

1467. Mulcaire, Terry, and Frank Grady. "Composition and the Study of Popular Culture." Paper presented at the CCCC Convention, Chicago, March 1990. ERIC ED 318 029. 14 pages

Describes a freshman course at the University of California—Berkeley based on the assumption that skills in reading popular culture are related to composition skills.

1468. Ney, James W. *Teacher-Student Cooperative Learning in the Freshman Writing Course.* Bloomington, Ind.: ERIC/RCS, 1989. ERIC ED 312 659. 32 pages

Examines a teaching method that involves students in making presentations on readings and in grading their daily quizzes.

1469. Papoulis, Irene. " 'Personal Narrative,' 'Academic Writing,' and Feminist Theory: Reflections of a Freshman Composition Teacher." *FEN* 18 (Spring 1990): 9–12.

Argues that personal writing has value, that it is denigrated because of a false belief that

storytelling is less significant than abstract speaking.

1470. Purves, Alan C. "A Comment on 'Utterance and Text in Freshman English' [*CE* 51 (November 1989)]." *CE* 52 (September 1990): 579–580.

Takes Lotto to task for claiming that the thinking of a text is different from and superior to utterance, for confusing stylistic convention with intellectual quality.

1471. Ramage, John D., and John C. Bean. "Teaching Writing in Large Classes: Seven Years Later at Montana State University." *BADE* 97 (Winter 1990): 18–25.

Explores the issues and implications of a freshman English course enrolling 60 students per section and using collaborative learning with a cross-curricular focus.

1472. Raymond, Richard C. "Personal and Public Voices: Bridging the Gap from Comp 101 to Comp 102." *TETYC* 17 (December 1990): 273–282.

Offers sample heuristics and assignments for helping students move from personal to academic writing.

1473. Rode, Mary. "A Study concerning the Use of Microcomputers for Word Processing in College Freshman Composition at a Community College." *DAI* 51 (November 1990): 1488A.

Compares improvements in composing and proofreading between students who do and do not use word processors.

1474. Rosenthal, Rae. "Male and Female Discourse: A Bilingual Approach to English 101." *Focuses* 3 (Fall 1990): 99–113.

Discusses verbal gender differences and anticipates a syllabus and writing assignments that allow students to "discover the possibilities of the language of the 'other.' "

1475. Rowan, Katherine E. "Explaining the Difficult Ideas: Spotting, Tackling, and Rendering Them Sensible for Lay Readers." *EQ* 22 (1990): 55–63.

Defines "explanatory text" and presents a three-week composition unit for explaining difficult texts.

1476. Roy, Emil. "A Decision Support System for Improving First-Year Writing Courses." *CACJ* 4 (Spring 1990): 79–93.

Students' papers analyzed by *Rightwriter* text-analysis software were sent to *Lotus 1–2–3* spreadsheets, allowing the author to comment on and track writing improvement.

1477. Soven, Margot, and William M. Sullivan. "Demystifying the Academy: Can Exploratory Writing Help?" *FEN* 19 (Fall 1990): 13–16.

After discussing the nature of exploratory essays, the authors provide exploratory writing assignments.

1478. Spellmeyer, Kurt. "Kurt Spellmeyer Responds [to Bazerman and Miller, *CE* 52 (March 1990)]." *CE* 52 (March 1990): 334–338.

Identifies a contradiction in Bazerman's desire both to empower and warn students and suggests that Miller's emphasis denies agency to freshman writers.

1479. Tripp, Ellen. "Speak, Listen, Analyze, Respond: Problem-Solving Conferences." *TETYC* 17 (October 1990): 183–186.

Peer groups follow a six-step method and then write group reports.

1480. Watkins, Beverly T. "Issues of Racial and Social Diversity Are the Centerpiece of Revamped Freshman Writing Courses at U. of Mass." *CHE* 37 (19 December 1990): A13–A14.

Reports that the "decision to make diversity the centerpiece of freshman writing" has "not faced much opposition" from students or faculty.

1481. Willey, R. J. "Audience Awareness: Methods and Madness." *FEN* 18 (Spring 1990): 20–21, 23–25.

Suggests methods of teaching audience awareness that are more effective in freshman writing classes than stressing rhetorical perspectives.

1482. Yancey, Kathleen Blake. "Two Comments on 'Recognizing the Learning-Disabled College Writer' [*CE* 51 (March 1989)]." *CE* 52 (March 1990): 340–342.

Distinguishes between support services required by older and younger learning-disabled students. Identifies additional rhetorical problems some learning-disabled students confront.

See also 1140, 1288, 1322, 1665

4.2.3 ADVANCED COMPOSITION

1483. Adams, Katherine, and John L. Adams, eds. *Teaching Advanced Composition.* Portsmouth, N.H.: Boynton/Cook, 1990. 312 pages

Eighteen essays treat the differences between advanced and freshman composition and different ways of organizing an advanced composition course.

1484. Belcher, Diane. "Peer Versus Teacher Response in the Advanced Composition Class." *Issues* 2 (Spring–Summer 1990): 128–150.

Explores the problem of responding to discipline-specific writing in writing across the curriculum and ESP classes. Teacher and students' responding collaboratively "may help."

1485. Bloom, Lynn Z. "Why Don't We Write What We Teach? And Publish It?" *JAC* 10 (1990): 87–100.

Argues that advanced composition should teach literary nonfiction and that teachers should write and publish it as well. Helps define the genre.

1486. Juncker, Clara. "Beyond Mastery: Postmodern College Composition." *WE* 2 (Fall 1990): 69–79.

Analyzes classroom "experiments with feminine linguistic spaces [that] criss-crossed academic borders, existing simultaneously (and necessarily) within and without traditional institutional modes."

1487. Laditka, James N. "Semiology, Ideology, *Praxis:* Responsible Authority in the Composition Classroom." *JAC* 10 (1990): 357–373.

No classroom is ideologically neutral; classes attempting such neutrality support the prevailing ideology. Advises compositionists consciously to interrogate ideologies.

1488. Shumaker, Ronald C., Larry Dennis, and Lois Green. "Advanced Exposition: A Survey of Patterns and Problems." *JAC* 10 (1990): 136–144.

Summarizes questionnaire data from 124 schools. Finds little agreement about the form, content, or staffing of a general course in advanced composition.

1489. Vincent, Susan. "Motivating the Advanced Learner in Developing Writing Skills: A Project." *ELT* 44 (October 1990): 272–278.

Presents a class project for motivating advanced composition students by using actual audiences and purposes from the world outside the school.

4.2.4 BUSINESS COMMUNICATION

1490. Bacon, Terry R. "Collaboration in a Pressure Cooker." *BABC* 53 (June 1990): 4–8.

Discusses the purpose and effects of writing proposals in industry collaboratively. Includes a description of the storyboarding method of writing team projects.

1491. Beard, John D. "A Collaborative Simulation." *BABC* 53 (June 1990): 65–67.

Describes an introductory simulation intended to acquaint business communication students with strategies for effective group work.

1492. Beard, John D. "Principles of Business Communication: A Departure from Academic Writing." *WI* 9 (Spring-Summer 1990): 101–108.

Presents a reader-based approach to business writing in terms of four principles of business communication: building good will, outlining a course of action, stating the bottom line, and placing the most important point first.

1493. Bosley, Deborah S. "A National Study of the Uses of Collaborative Writing in Business Communication Courses among Members of the ABC." *DAI* 50 (March 1990): 2759A.

Findings indicate the need for heightened perceptions about collaborative writing and for more collaborative assignments.

1494. Burnett, Rebecca E. "Benefits of Collaborative Planning in the Business Communication Classroom." *BABC* 53 (June 1990): 9–17.

Discusses how business communication students can use collaborative planning in individual and group writing projects. Examples show students planning a coauthored document.

1495. Campbell, Kim Sydow. "Explanations in Negative Messages: More Insights from Speech-Act Theory." *JBC* 27 (Fall 1990): 357–375.

Contrary to textbook advice about negative messages, speech-act pragmatics support the use of explanations and offer five strategies for polite refusals.

1496. Carroll, Edna Ruth. "A Comparative Study of Achievement in College-Level Business Communication Using Lecture and Cooperative Learning Teaching Methods." *DAI* 50 (June 1990): 3832A.

Compares the effectiveness of primary lecture and cooperative learning methods for teaching business communication classes.

1497. Chan, Michele Marie. "Writing in a Small Business Management Course: Doing Business/Doing School." *DAI* 50 (February 1990): 2412A.

Maintains that students from the Chinese University of Hong Kong used writing to reason as business professionals, to work in groups, and to apply business knowledge.

1498. Cross, Mary. "Writing by Number: Teaching Students to Read the Balance Sheet." *BABC* 53 (December 1990): 21–24.

Discusses a method for teaching business writing students to read balance sheets. Describes a related short report assignment.

1499. Duin, Ann Hill. "Terms and Tools: A Theory- and Research-Based Approach to Collaborative Writing." *BABC* 53 (June 1990): 45–50.

Applies theory and research on collaboration to a professional writing course project. Computer technology supported students' work.

1500. Dyrud, Marilyn A. "One Teacher's Trash Is Another's Treasure." *BABC* 53 (December 1990): 30–33.

Describes a business communication assignment using direct mail to teach persuasive techniques.

1501. Easton, Annette, George Easton, Marie Flatley, and John Penrose. "Supporting Group Writing with Computer Software." *BABC* 53 (June 1990): 34–37.

Classifies writing tools for computer-supported collaborative work groups into two main categories, asynchronous and synchronous communication systems.

1502. Ewald, Helen Rothschild, and Virginia MacCallum. "Promoting Creative Tension within Collaborative Writing Groups." *BABC* 53 (June 1990): 23–26.

By describing business writing assignments, this article explains how assignment design can stimulate creative tension in collaborative writing groups.

1503. France, Alan W. "Teaching the Dialectics of 'Objective' Discourse: A Progressive Approach to Business and Professional Writing." *WI* 9 (Spring–Summer 1990): 79–86.

The syllabus highlights social conflict in business discourse and the role of language in creating "the reality of the objective world."

1504. Haar, Jerry, and Sharon Kossack. "Employee Benefit Packages: How Understandable Are They?" *JBC* 27 (Spring 1990): 185–200.

Researchers subjected 20 benefits packages from major companies to Fry readability and cloze tests. Documents tested at a much higher level than the presumed reading ability of employees.

1505. Hager, Peter J., and H. J. Scheiber. "Reading Smoke and Mirrors: The Rhetoric of Corporate Annual Reports." *JTWC* 20 (1990): 113–130.

Describes a process by which students are taught to analyze the rhetoric and ethics of corporate annual reports.

1506. Harcourt, Jules. "Developing Ethical Messages: A Unit of Instruction for the Basic Business Communication Course." *BABC* 53 (September 1990): 17–20.

Discusses incorporating a unit on ethics in the business communication course.

1507. Harcourt, Jules. "Teaching the Legal Aspects of Business Communication." *BABC* 53 (September 1990): 63–64.

Treats legal aspects of various types of business messages.

1508. Hiemstra, Kathleen M., Jacqueline J. Schmidt, and Roland L. Madison. "Certified Management Accountants: Perceptions of the Need for Communication Skills in Accounting." *BABC* 53 (December 1990): 5–9.

Surveys writing, speaking, and listening skills needed by certified management accountants.

1509. Hochhalter, Alyce. "My Favorite Assignment: Analyzing Annual Reports." *BABC* 53 (December 1990): 24–27.

Describes an assignment in organizational communication in which students analyze the audience, format, content, and organization of annual reports.

1510. Jacobi, Martin J. "Using the Enthymeme to Emphasize Ethics in Professional Writing Courses." *JBC* 27 (Summer 1990): 273–292.

Professional writing should be taught rhetorically. Assignments should be contextualized so that audience values can serve as a source of enthymematic moral premises.

1511. Johnson, Pamela R. "Employee Handbooks: An Integration of Technical Writing Concepts." *TWT* 17 (Winter 1990): 1–6.

Presents a writing assignment that integrates informative and persuasive writing.

1512. Johnson, Robert, and Mark Simpson. "Bridging the Problem-Solver Communication Gap: Toward an Art of Professional Case Design." *WI* 9 (Spring–Summer 1990): 109–120.

Reports on a "desktop case" used by Perdue's Writing Lab as a model for discussing the parameters and guidelines for improved case design for the classroom.

1513. Kirtz, Mary K., and Diana C. Reep. "A Survey of the Frequency, Types, and Importance of Writing Tasks in Four Career Areas." *BABC* 53 (December 1990): 3–4.

Analyzes a survey of writing in four fields.

1514. Kotler, Janet. "Educating for Citizenship: Teaching Public Issues." *BABC* 53 (December 1990): 55–58.

Sees value in discussing public issues in the business communication course.

1515. Leonard, Donald J., and Jeanette W. Gilsdorf. "Language in Change: Academics' and Executives' Perceptions of Usage Errors." *JBC* 27 (Spring 1990): 137–158.

Reports on 333 questionnaires from business executives and business communication specialists. Lexical "errors" were least distracting, and sentence errors such as run-ons were most distracting.

1516. Martin, Charles L., and Dorothy E. Ranson. "Spelling Skills of Business Students: An Empirical Investigation." *JBC* 27 (Fall 1990): 377–400.

Reports on a study of 439 college business students given a spelling test of both business and commonly used words. Overall scores were better than the high school baseline but ranged widely.

1517. Milliman, Ronald E., and Phillip J. Decker. "The Use of Post-Purchase Communication to Reduce Dissonance and Improve Direct Marketing Effectiveness." *JBC* 27 (Spring 1990): 159–170.

This study demonstrates the potentially positive effects of letters sent to mail-order customers after purchases. Reorder rates were higher and refund requests were lower.

1518. Morrow, Phillip R. "Varieties of Business English: A Linguistic Analysis of Written Texts." *DAI* 50 (January 1990): 2038A.

Investigates the nature, typologic classifications, users, and purposes of business English. Considers some pedagogical implications that follow from analyzing the structure of business English texts.

1519. Mulvihill, Peggy. "So That's Who You Are: An Exercise That Moves Students from 'I' to 'You' in Persuasive Writing." *BABC* 53 (September 1990): 57–59.

Describes a collaborative proposal assignment designed to teach business writing students the "you attitude."

1520. Neff, Alan. "A New Approach to Business Communication Education: Integrating Business Research Methods and Communication Skills." *JBTC* 4 (September 1990): 44–67.

Offers a theoretical justification, discusses premises and benefits, and describes the case-based course.

1521. Nelson, Sandra J., and Douglas C. Smith. "Maximizing Cohesion and Minimizing Conflict in Collaborative Writing Groups." *BABC* 53 (June 1990): 59–62.

Presents instructional strategies to assist collaborative writing groups in managing conflict.

1522. Noel, Rita Thomas, and Jay Wysocki. "How Do You Spell Relief? T-E-C-H-N-O-L-O-G-Y!" *BABC* 53 (March 1990): 25–28.

Discusses how environment and present skills can affect the degree of perceived stress of business writing faculty. Suggests how computer technology can assist teachers with these issues.

1523. Pomerenke, Paula J. "Using Annual Reports to Introduce Professional Writing Style." *BABC* 53 (December 1990): 25.

Describes a business writing assignment analyzing the style of corporate annual reports.

1524. Porter, James E. "Ideology and Collaboration in the Classroom and in the Corporation." *BABC* 53 (June 1990): 18–22.

Discusses the influence of ideology on collaborative writing in corporations and in students' business communication projects.

1525. Reinsch, N. L., Jr. "Ethics Research in Business Communication: The State of the Art." *JBC* 27 (Summer 1990): 251–272.

Surveys 30 years of ABC publications. Pedagogical papers agree that business communication is a moral subject, but they lack consensus on how to evaluate moral behavior.

1526. Renshaw, Debbie A. "My Favorite Assignment: In-Class Collaborative Cases." *BABC* 53 (June 1990): 63–65.

Describes using a series of four in-class cases with collaborative groups representing companies.

1527. Rogers, Priscilla S., and John M. Swales. "We the People? An Analysis of the Dana Corporation Policies Document." *JBC* 27 (Summer 1990): 293–313.

A close stylistic analysis of one company's code shows some "subtle rhetorical decisions that composers of ethical codes need to negotiate."

1528. Smith, Douglas C., and Sandra J. Nelson. "Stress in Business Communication: A Matter of Perception." *BABC* 53 (March 1990): 20–23.

Reports on a study comparing student perceptions of stress in business communication classes with faculty perceptions of their students' stress.

1529. Southard, Sherry G. "Interacting Successfully in Corporate Culture." *JBTC* 4 (September 1990): 79–90.

Presents lecture and exercise materials relevant to explaining corporate structures and protocol.

1530. Speck, Bruce W. "Writing Professional Codes of Ethics to Introduce Ethics in Business Writing." *BABC* 53 (September 1990): 21–26.

Describes a project in which business writing students write codes of ethics for their intended professions.

1531. Spencer, Barbara A., and Carol M. Lehman. "Analyzing Ethical Issues: Essential Ingredient in the Business Communication Course of the 1990s." *BABC* 53 (September 1990): 7–16.

Describes a technique for incorporating ethical analysis in the business communication course. Presents a case problem in ethics.

1532. Stratman, James F., and Thomas M. Duffy. "Conceptualizing Research on Written Management Communication." *MCQ* 3 (May 1990): 429–451.

Analyzes written management communication: at the core is readers' and writers' cognition, surrounded by the management task in its organizational, industrial, and cultural environments.

1533. Tebeaux, Elizabeth. "Toward an Understanding of Gender Differences in Written Business Communications: A Suggested Perspective for Future Research." *JBTC* 4 (January 1990): 25–43.

People-intensive work experience and business communication instruction apparently help writers develop androgynous language skills and eliminate gender-based characteristics.

1534. Tyler, Lisa. "Communicating about People with Disabilities: Does the Language We Use Make a Difference?" *BABC* 53 (September 1990): 65–67.

A survey examines readers' perceptions of language that uses a "people first" approach in discussing people with disabilities.

1535. Wells, Barron, and Nelda Spinks. " 'You Attitude' and 'Naturalness': Theory and Practice." *BABC* 53 (September 1990): 60–62.

Discusses the presentation of the "you attitude" and "naturalness" in business communication textbooks. Presents a survey of business correspondence concerning these concepts.

1536. Werner, Warren W. "A Comment on 'Do Good Grammar Skills Predict Success in a Business-Communication Course?' [*JBTC* 4 (September 1988)]." *JBTC* 4 (January 1990): 85–91.

Offers an alternative interpretation of the data, to which Waltman responds.

1537. Zhang, John Z. "Ranking of Indirectness in Professional Writing." *JTWC* 20 (1990): 291–305.

Offers principles by which technical writers can achieve a "desired degree of indirectness" and thereby be both clear and polite in their writing.

See also 5, 9, 32, 37, 74, 561, 581, 829, 1544, 1651, 1663, 1672

4.2.5 SCIENTIFIC AND TECHNICAL COMMUNICATION

1538. Allen, Jo. "The Case against Defining Technical Writing." *JBTC* 4 (September 1990): 68–77.

Apparently useful but in fact elusive, a definition of technical writing is inevitably obscure or arbitrary and should not be sought.

1539. Aylworth, Susan. "A Composition Teacher Becomes a Producer of Videos about Technical Writing." *CompC* 3 (April 1990): 6–7.

Classroom needs prompted the production of four videotapes.

1540. Christianson, Scott R., Julia M. Gergits, and James J. Schramer. "Students as Audience and Discourse Community in Technical Writing Courses." *WI* 9 (Spring–Summer 1990): 87–100.

Profiles three different types of technical writing students to illustrate how course definitions change according to the expectations and needs of specific student audiences.

1541. "A Conversation with a Pioneer of Technical Writing: Thomas E. Pearsall." *Issues* 3 (Fall–Winter 1990): 4–25.

Describes the founding of the Technical Communication Program at the University of Minnesota in 1969 and developments in the field of technical communication since the 1960s.

1542. Cox, Barbara G., Desmond A. Schatz, and L. H. S. VanMierop. "Scientific Writing Courses for Pediatric Fellows." *AM* 65 (October 1990): 652–653.

Describes a successful workshop covering grammar, syntax and style, the construction of scientific papers, and submission to scientific journals.

1543. Dell, Sherry A. "Promoting Equality of the Sexes through Technical Writing." *TC* 37 (August 1990): 248–251.

Opposes sexist language for all writing, then explains why gender-neutral words are especially preferable in technical writing.

1544. Dragga, Sam, and Gwendolyn Gong. *Editing: The Design of Rhetoric*. Technical Communications Series. Edited by Jay R. Gould. Amityville, N.Y.: Baywood, 1989. 231 pages

Familiarizes readers with the theoretical basis and practical applications of editing. Examines the rhetorical canons of invention, arrangement, style, and delivery in the context of corresponding objectives of editing: accuracy, clarity, propriety, and artistry.

1545. Dyrud, Marilyn, and Marshall Kremers. "The Paper Airplane Assignment Revisited." *Issues* 2 (Spring–Summer 1990): 161–175.

An assignment that requires students to write instructions for making a paper airplane helps them understand the demands of good technical writing.

1546. Eldridge, Elaine. "Teaching Technical Writing in Canada." *JTWC* 20 (1990): 177–187.

This survey finds that approximately half of the 35 responding institutions offered technical writing courses. Faculty attitudes toward such courses range from enthusiastic to disapproving.

1547. Feyerherm, Joel. "Application of Kenneth Burke's Theories to Teaching Technical Writing." *TWT* 17 (Winter 1990): 41–49.

Uses the pentad as the basis for analyzing writing tasks and their audiences in technical writing assignments.

1548. Hager, Peter J. "Mini-Internships: Work-World Technical Writing Experiences without Leaving Campus." *TWT* 17 (Spring 1990): 104–113.

Outlines procedures for creating an effective internship program for technical writing programs with limited administrative resources.

1549. Hall, Dean G., and Bonnie A. Nelson. "Sex-Based Language and the Technical Writing Teacher's Responsibility." *JBTC* 4 (January 1990): 69–79.

A survey of 82 Kansas State University female engineering graduates indicated that sexist language persists in the work place. Discusses the implications for professional ethics, textbook writing, and pedagogy.

1550. Hedges, Peter D., and W. J. Walley. "An Approach to the Integration of Communication Skills Development within an Undergraduate Civil Engineering Program." *JTWC* 20 (1990): 165–175.

Describes how the development of "written, oral, and decision-making skills" was integrated into a course in a British university.

1551. Killingsworth, M. Jimmie, and Preston Lynn Waller. "A Grammar of Person in Technical Writing." *TWT* 17 (Winter 1990): 26–40.

Provides a taxonomic grammar of technical writing genres, focusing on proposals, manuals, and reports.

1552. Krull, Robert, ed. *Word Processing for Technical Writers*. Technical Communications Series. Edited by Jay R. Gould. Amityville, N.Y.: Baywood, 1988. 172 pages

Eleven essays discuss implementing word processing, organizing to write, graphics, and electronic publishing.

1553. Lambert, Stephen M. "Humanizing Technical Communication: The Rhetorical Role of Metaphor in the Plain Style Tradition." *DAI* 51 (July 1990): 20A.

Examines the "shortcomings" of technical discourse and advocates a new understanding of metaphor as invention.

1554. McConathy, Terry Martin. "The Proposal in an Engineering Context: A Field Study of Document Development." *DAI* 50 (March 1990): 2885A.

Findings reveal disparities between textbook examples and real-life models.

1555. Messer, Vincent Christian. "Writing and Revising for Technical Professionals: A Comparison of Three Instructional Strategies." *DAI* 50 (January 1990): 1970A.

This study compared three methods for presenting a writing skills improvement workshop for technical professionals.

1556. Moore, Patrick. "Using Case Studies to Teach Courtesy Strategies." *TWT* 17 (Winter 1990): 8–25.

Defines "courtesy strategies" and shows how they can be taught effectively in a technical writing class through case studies.

1557. Parker, Anne. "Problem Solving Applied to Teaching Technical Writing." *TWT* 17 (Spring 1990): 95–103.

Describes a problem-solving approach to teaching technical communication to first-year rather than upper-level students.

1558. Pringle, Mary Beth. "Mythical Machines and the Teaching of Technical Writing." *TWT* 17 (Winter 1990): 69–75.

Outlines a method for organizing writing assignments that makes technical writing tasks relevant to students from a variety of academic majors.

1559. *Proceedings of the Thirty-Seventh International Technical Communication Conference.* San Diego: UNIVELT, 1990. 647 pages

A collection of papers was presented in Santa Clara, California, May 1990. Subjects include education, training, and professional development; management; research and technology; and visual communications. Contributors are not indexed separately in this volume.

1560. Raven, Mary Elizabeth. "New-Venture Techniques in a Communication Class." *TWT* 17 (Spring 1990): 124–130.

Describes writing and speaking assignments that prepare students for work in an entrepreneurial environment.

1561. Reynolds, John Frederick. "Desktop Publishing and Technical Writing: Problems and Strategies." *CACJ* 5 (Summer 1990): 18–22.

Discusses three strategies for integrating sophisticated desktop publishing into traditional technical writing courses.

1562. Samson, Donald C., Jr. "An Editing Project for Teaching Technical Editing." *TC* 37 (August 1990): 262–267.

Students solicit a technical manuscript and edit it for a specific target publication, conferring all along with the author.

1563. Samson, Donald C., Jr. "Technical Writing Situations in the Workplace." *TWT* 17 (Spring 1990): 114–118.

Describes an assignment that focuses on interpersonal or political challenges related to writing in a professional setting.

1564. Sims, Brenda R., and Donna DiMaggio. "Using Computerized Textual Analysis with Technical Writing Students: Is It Effective?" *TWT* 17 (Winter 1990): 61–68.

Determines that Writer's Workbench could be "an effective, but limited tool in teaching technical writing."

1565. Smith, Herb. "The Company Profile Case Study: A Multipurpose Assignment with an Industrial Slant." *TWT* 17 (Spring 1990): 119–123.

Describes a classroom assignment that generates student interest, has real-world dimensions, and teaches a variety of technical communication skills.

1566. Sullivan, Dale L. "Political-Ethical Implications of Defining Technical Communication as a Practice." *JAC* 10 (1990): 375–386.

Advocates seeing technical writing as *praxis,* not as a skill that supports the military-industrial complex. Students need both the skill and cultural criticism.

1567. Sullivan, Patricia. "Visual Markers for Navigating Instructional Texts." *JTWC* 20 (1990): 255–267.

Describes how students from different backgrounds use visual markers in instructional texts. Articulates theoretical issues and suggests pedagogical implications.

1568. Werner, Warren W. "The Work of Life: Teaching Technical Writing as a Subversive Activity." *WE* 1 (Spring 1990): 53–64.

Analyzes conflicts between conventions of a writing class and those of a corporate setting.

1569. Woodward, John B. "Numerical Analysis as Technical Communication." *TC* 37 (August 1990): 221–224.

Laying out mathematical notations that can be read easily requires careful document design.

See also 16, 192, 241, 527, 533, 561, 592, 829, 1021, 1072, 1174, 1529, 1715, 1719

4.2.6 WRITING IN LITERATURE COURSES

1570. Andrasick, Kathleen Dudden. *Opening Texts: Using Writing to Teach Literature.* Portsmouth, N.H.: Boynton/Cook, 1990. 224 pages

Provides a flexible model with concrete examples of how students can be helped to read with greater enthusiasm and to respond to what they read more critically. Based upon what we know about how readers and writers make meaning.

1571. Bishop, Wendy. "Poetry Parodies: Explorations and Limitations." *TETYC* 17 (February 1990): 40–44.

Writing parodies helps students engage literature.

1572. Bodmer, Paul. "The Reader's Notebook: A Tool for Thinking with Writing." Paper presented at the CCCC Convention, Chicago, March 1990. ERIC ED 318 014. 21 pages

Describes a technique in which students freewrite about a literary work before and after class discussions, with positive effects on students' understanding.

1573. Clark, Mark Andrew. "The Difficulty in Saying 'I': Identifying, Analyzing, and Cri-

tiquing Voices of Self, Difference, and Discourse in College Students' Reading and Writing about Literature." *DAI* 51 (November 1990): 1536A.

Examines reading and writing about literature as political acts of self, other, and institutions.

1574. Cohen, Saul. "Who Killed Homer Barron? A New Verdict for Emily Grierson." *ExEx* 36 (Fall 1990): 28–31.

Describes a mock trial in which students searched the text for evidence before role-playing the prosecution, defense, and jury.

1575. Collins, Jim. "Study Questions Writing-to-Learn." *CompC* 2 (January 1990): 8.

A tongue-in-cheek argument against using writing to teach literature.

1576. Davis, Jeffrey K. "Archetypal Puppets Spark Good Writing." *CollT* 38 (Spring 1990): 49–51.

Describes a project to increase students' understanding of archetypal narratives. Students conduct collaborative research, write scripts, construct puppets, and produce plays.

1577. Drew, Kitty. "Writing from the Inside Out: Write What You Know, Then Revise." *CalE* 26 (January–February 1990): 6–7.

Describes a revision exercise using examples from John Steinbeck.

1578. Foehr, Regina P. "Using the Simple to Teach the Complex: Teaching College Students to Interpret Complex Literature and to Write Literary Analysis Essays through Fairy Tales and Children's Stories." *DAI* 50 (March 1990): 2885A.

The experimental group exceeded the control group in the ability to "abstract" themes and in the overall writing quality of analytic essays. Neither group's reading comprehension improved.

1579. Hawkes, Peter. "Review through Parody." *ExEx* 35 (Spring 1990): 14–18.

Suggests that asking students to write parodies of works is an effective review for a comprehensive final examination in a literature survey.

1580. Helotes, Lynnette. "Responding to Literature Via the Essay of Persuasion." *ExEx* 35 (Spring 1990): 28–31.

Describes an activity in which students write responses to statements, then discuss them in class before rewriting papers.

1581. Hotchkiss, Chrisa L. "Teaching Literature Students Short Story Writing." *ExEx* 35 (Spring 1990): 38–42.

Provides a series of questions and guidelines to help students write their own short stories.

1582. Hull, Glynda, and Mike Rose. "'This Wooden Shack Place': The Logic of an Unconventional Reading." *CCC* 41 (October 1990): 287–298.

Analyzes a remedial student's interpretation of a poem and the instructor's difficulty in perceiving its unconventional logic.

1583. Johannessen, Larry R. "Teaching Strategies for Interpreting and Writing about Literature." Paper presented at the NCTE Convention, St. Louis, November 1988. ERIC ED 311 454. 23 pages

Describes a model for teaching character analysis that engages students in discussion and writing.

1584. Kinder, Rose Marie. "Teaching the Controversies: The Other within the Classroom." Paper presented at the CCCC Convention, Chicago, March 1990. ERIC ED 318 027. 19 pages

Argues that teachers in writing-about-literature courses should acknowledge opposition to their ideas, thus opening a classroom dialogue.

1585. Kliman, Bernice W. "Writing with and for Students." Paper presented at the MLA Convention, San Francisco, December 1988. ERIC ED 318 505. 9 pages

Describes a first-year course in literature and composition at Nassau Community College. Students were motivated by the instructor's participation in all writing exercises.

1586. Lampert, Kathleen W. "Cooperative Learning in the Literature Classroom." *ExEx* 36 (Fall 1990): 32–35.

Provides two sample assignments of structured activities in an honors classroom.

1587. McCormick, Frank. "Teaching Documentation in the Freshman Literature Course: Two Classroom Exercises." *ExEx* 36 (Fall 1990): 13–15.

Describes two exercises that demonstrate the "proper punctuation of quoted material and selection of apt phrases for quotation."

1588. McNeil, Lynda D. "Say It Again, Sam: Recursive Writing and Critical Thinking in the Literature Classroom." Paper presented at the CCCC Convention, Chicago, March 1990. ERIC ED 318 028. 17 pages

Describes the use of dialogue folders and cooperative learning groups to enact critical thinking and to broaden the scope of recursive writing.

1589. Parry, Sally E. "Becoming a Jezebel: Taking on Roles in Margaret Atwood's *The Handmaid's Tale*." *ExEx* 36 (Fall 1990): 26–27.

Student groups "justify their caste" in this exercise.

1590. Rea, Paul W. "Extra-Vagant Enough!: Teaching *Walden* as Rhetorical Exemplum." *JTW* 9 (Spring–Summer 1990): 99–113.

Teaches *Walden* by focusing on styles; *personae* and *ethos*; ethical appeals; and rational, imaginative, and emotional appeals to promote "critical thinking about rhetorical issues that matter."

1591. Riggen, Vicki. "Elizabethan England Comes to Life." *ExEx* 35 (Spring 1990): 25–27.

Reviews a videotape that a senior English class prepared for a hospitalized classmate.

1592. Sellers, Heather. "Writing Letters to Living Authors." *ExEx* 36 (Fall 1990): 22–25.

Includes three category headings—questions about craft, content, and process—from which students may develop questions.

1593. Spinner, Bettye Tyson. "A Study of Academic and Nonacademic Experiences That Promote and Sustain Adult Interest in the Reading and Writing of Poetry." *DAI* 51 (August 1990): 439A.

Finds that a good early language environment and a lack of imposed controls foster a continuing interest in poetry. Writing and sharing poetry in nonjudgmental settings encourage its writing.

1594. Weiner, Wendy F. "Composing Connections with Literature." *DAI* 50 (May 1990): 3506A.

Offers a prospectus for a literary text intended to help students understand literature through the use of the writing process.

See also 35, 624, 662, 702, 712, 1477

4.2.7 COMMUNICATION IN OTHER DISCIPLINES

1595. Agatucci, Cora. "Composing a Self in Student Autobiography." Paper presented at the CCCC Convention, Chicago, March 1990. ERIC ED 318 016. 19 pages

Describes an autobiography writing course for nontraditional community college students. The course had positive effects on students' writing and confidence.

1596. Barnhart, Kevin. "Teaching Journalists to Draw Makes Their Writing More Vivid." *JEd* 45 (Summer 1990): 69–72.

Argues that drawing should be a part of writing courses. Describes instructional objectives and activities that can be incorporated into a three-hour instructional module on drawing.

1597. Barrows, H. S. "Inquiry: The Pedagogical Importance of a Skill Central to Clinical Practice." *MEd* 24 (January 1990): 3–5.

Physicians need more structured instruction in and heuristics for inquiry used in research and diagnostics.

1598. Beadle, Mary E. "Evaluating Writing across the Curriculum: Struggles and Insights." Paper presented at the AERA meeting, San Francisco, March 1989. ERIC ED 316 562. 26 pages

Describes the program at Walsh College, including methods for training faculty to teach in the program.

1599. Beckman, Mary. "Writing across the Curriculum Pedagogy and Workplace Values." *Issues* 3 (Fall–Winter 1990): 80–97.

Because writing across the curriculum programs emphasize collaboration and process and because capitalism has historically stressed competition and product, students aware of these differences may do well in college and may also transform the work place.

1600. Birkerts, Sven. "The Reviewer's Craft." *Writer* 103 (May 1990): 15–17.

Provides advice for evaluating and discussing the writing of others to create a review that is a "conversation of culture."

1601. Bishop, Wendy. "Learning about Inspiration by Calling on the Muse." *ArEB* 32 (1990): 7–10.

Provides a lesson plan for writing muse poems or sketches that help students explore the sources of their own work.

1602. Bishop, Wendy. "On Being in the Same Boat: A History of Creative Writing and Composition Writing in American Universities." Paper presented at the annual meeting of the Associated Writing Programs, Denver, March 1990. ERIC ED 318 023. 17 pages

Compares theories underlying creative writing instruction and composition instruction in order to understand the difficulties facing creative writing teachers.

1603. Blau, Susan. "Writing across the Curriculum as a Subversive Activity." *TETYC* 17 (October 1990): 193–196.

Describes a program at Middlesex Community College that uses a common book selected by faculty members and extensive staff development.

1604. Bordage, Georges, and Madeleine Lemieux. "Which Medical Textbook to Read? Emphasizing Semantic Structures." *AM* 65 (September 1990): 523-524.

Discusses semantic structures for organizing complex materials in student textbooks. Suggests a labeling system (semantic, encyclopedic, taxonomic) for organizing textbooks.

1605. Bowser, Mary Chamberlin Seeley. "A Descriptive Analysis of the Intensive Workshops of the Young Writers Workshop at the University of Virginia." *DAI* 51 (August 1990): 393A.

A phenomenological study of six workshops. Describes seven instructional practices that author-teachers found most productive and that students valued most.

1606. Braine, George Stanley. "An Analysis of the Writing Tasks of Undergraduate Courses in the Natural Sciences and Engineering." *DAI* 50 (March 1990): 2764A.

Identifies and classifies the range of writing assignments required in the natural sciences and engineering.

1607. Carton, Kitty. "Collaborative Writing of Mathematics Problems." *MT* 83 (October 1990): 542–544.

Responds to the call for "opportunities for students to use mathematics as a tool for the communication of ideas."

1608. Castaldi, Teresa Marie. "Writing across the Curriculum: An Ethnographic Study of Nontraditional Students in an Undergraduate History Class." *DAI* 50 (March 1990): 2813A.

Life and work experiences influenced learning styles and information processing.

1609. Connolly, Paul, and Teresa Vilardi, eds. *Writing to Learn Mathematics and Science.* New York: Teachers College Press, 1989. 336 pages

Twenty-two essays explain how students from the elementary to the college level can use formal and informal writing to learn mathematics and science. In addition to suggesting classroom practices, the contributors also discuss problems and possibilities in using writing to learn.

1610. Cornell, Cynthia, and David J. Klooster. "Writing across the Curriculum: Transforming the Academy?" *WPA* 14 (Fall–Winter 1990): 7–16.

Addresses the complex nature of writing across the curriculum programs in the academy, where their aims are often threatened by conflicting agenda.

1611. Faltis, Christian. "Spanish for Native Speakers: Freirian and Vygotskian Perspectives." *FLA* 23 (April 1990): 117–126.

Proposes a curriculum focused on reading and writing critically about issues that concern learners. Language skills are tools for this critical reading and writing.

1612. Flanigan, Michael. "Writing across the Curriculum and Literacy at the University of Oklahoma: Constructing a Reality Takes More than Writing." Paper presented at the Midwest MLA, St. Louis, November 1988. ERIC ED 309 438. 8 pages

Discusses how a Ford Foundation grant improved undergraduate literacy through faculty development.

1613. Flanigan, Michael. "Writing across the Curriculum: Point of Departure to Full Literacy." Paper presented at the Midwest MLA, Minneapolis, November 1989. ERIC ED 313 717. 7 pages

Cites successful college programs and calls for more research on the value of writing to learn.

1614. Fontaine, Andre, and William A. Glavin, Jr. *The Art of Writing Nonfiction.* 2d ed. Syracuse, N.Y.: Syracuse University Press, 1990. 232 pages

Describes the process of interpretive journalism from researching and evaluating evidence to organizing and presenting the material.

1615. Freedman, Aviva, Julia Carey, and Antonina Miller. "Students' Stances: Dimensions Affecting Composing and Learning Processes." *CALS* 6 (1989): 84–106.

Nonintrusive observation of an undergraduate law course shows variation among learners in terms of possible "stances toward experience." Three significant stances and teaching interventions are described.

1616. Fulwiler, Toby. "The Friends and Enemies of Writing across the Curriculum." Paper presented at the CCCC Convention, Chicago, March 1990. ERIC ED 318 006. 7 pages

Discusses why opposition to writing across the curriculum occurs. Inertia in the academic system is one reason.

1617. Harmon, Gary P. "Personal Finance and Communication: A Natural Duo." *BABC* 53 (December 1990): 19–20.

Describes the use of oral and written assignments in a personal finance course.

1618. Hartman, Janet. "Integrating Writing Activities in Computer Science Assignments." *CACJ* 5 (Summer 1990): 1–7.

Suggests three ways of modifying assignments in a computer science class to increase the amount of writing involved.

1619. Henschen, Beth M., and Edward I. Sidlow. "Collaborative Writing." *CollT* 38 (Winter 1990): 29–32.

Describes political science students' writing for grant-funded cash prizes. Teams from paired universities wrote and exchanged papers on different sides of contemporary political issues.

1620. Hresan, Sally L. "Toward the Integration of the Process Writing Technique with the Teaching of Journalism News Writing." *DAI* 51 (December 1990): 1812A.

Finds that journalism students can successfully integrate process-centered writing exercises with traditional, product-oriented pedagogy.

1621. Hurwitz, Marsha. "Student-Authored Manuals as Semester Projects." *MT* 83 (December 1990): 701–703.

Writing about mathematics in words rather than in symbols committed to memory helps students analyze a formula before applying it.

1622. Klein, Ilona. "Teaching in a Liberal Arts College: How Foreign Language Courses Contribute to Writing across the Curriculum Programs." *MLJ* 74 (Spring 1990): 28–35.

Argues that writing and foreign language programs should collaborate in teaching basic English grammatical structures and nomenclature.

1623. Laufer, Batia. "Ease and Difficulty in Vocabulary Learning: Some Teaching Implications." *FLA* 23 (April 1990): 147–155.

Discusses six components of word knowledge and factors that can interfere with learning words in a second language.

1624. Lutcavage, Charles. "The Advanced German Course: A Multidimensional Approach." *FLA* 23 (May 1990): 185–194.

Describes the writing component of the course, which emphasizes the challenges of writing in a foreign language.

1625. Morris, Ardith Ann. "Collective Creation Practices." *DAI* 50 (February 1990): 2306A.

Examines collective creation as a process for generating scripts and bringing scripted material to performance.

1626. Nelson, Jack A. "Are We Failing to Educate Reporters Who Can Write?" *JEd* 45 (Winter 1990): 20–25.

Identifies five aspects of writing quality and gives examples of how these characteristics improve writing, narration, dialogue, characterization, and interpretation.

1627. Nelson, Jennie. "This Was an Easy Assignment: Examining How Students Interpret Academic Writing Tasks." *RTE* 24 (December 1990): 362–393.

Three case studies reveal the variety of influences (beyond teachers' expectations) in the everyday writing contexts of college freshmen.

1628. Norris, Joe. "Some Authorities as Co-Authors in a Collective Creation Production." *DAI* 50 (May 1990): 3416A.

A participant-observation study that explores the concept of coauthorship in a high school classroom in which students collaboratively write a play.

1629. Peek, Lucia E., and George S. Peek. "Using Practitioner Articles to Develop Computer, Writing, and Critical Thinking Skills: Examples from the Accounting Curriculum." *BABC* 53 (December 1990): 17–19.

Describes a writing assignment in an accounting course that uses articles about computer applications in accounting.

1630. Procter, Kenneth. "Writing in Art History: An Instrument for Teaching Course Content." *Issues* 2 (Spring–Summer 1990): 117–127.

An art history teacher describes his use of writing to teach the "language, conceptual framework, and intellectual skills of the discipline." Describes three writing assignments.

1631. Ramsland, Katherine. "Writing Biographies: The Problems and the Process." *Writer* 103 (October 1990): 13–15.

Advises adopting a different writing process when writing about others. Cautions against using the omniscient voice.

1632. Reese, Diane, and Paula Zielonka. "Writing to Comprehend in the Content Area." Paper presented at the Florida Reading

Association meeting, Fort Lauderdale, October 1989. ERIC ED 315 767. 12 pages

Argues that students can use writing to comprehend content-area texts in various ways based on the objectives for a particular assignment.

1633. Regan-Smith, Martha G., and Donald A. West. "Teaching Critical Thinking in the Context of Substance Abuse in a Psychiatry Clerkship." *AM* 65 (February 1990): 89.

Describes a psychiatry clerkship, the written scripts participants provide, and the improvements seen in the oral, writing, and cognitive skills of the participants.

1634. Robards, Brooks. "The Basic Media Writing Course." Paper presented at the SCA meeting, San Francisco, November 1989. ERIC ED 313 710. 10 pages

Describes a media writing course for college students.

1635. Schaffer, J. L., Marcia Z. Wile, and R. C. Griggs. "Students Teaching Students: A Medical School Peer Tutorial Programme." *MEd* 24 (July 1990): 336–343.

An open peer tutorial program provided statistically significant improvement for men and women on examination scores.

1636. Schofer, Peter. "Literature and Communicative Competence: A Springboard for the Development of Critical Thinking and Aesthetic Appreciation of Literature in the Land of Language." *FLA* 23 (September 1990): 325–334.

Advocates integrating literature into foreign language instruction and gives several reasons why. Literature encompasses several levels of social discourse and need not be "saved" for more advanced study.

1637. Schroeder, Gertrude. *Writing across the Curriculum Program.* Washington, D.C.: American Association of State Colleges and Universities, 1989. ERIC ED 321 652. 24 pages

Reports on research and planning for Troy State University's writing across the curriculum program.

1638. Sheldon, Stephen H., and Peter A. Noronha. "Using Classic Mystery Stories in Teaching." *AM* 65 (April 1990): 234–235.

Describes using excerpts from Sherlock Holmes' tales with solutions written by students to teach reading, study skills, and critical thinking.

1639. Sherman, Lawrence. "A Cooperative Pedagogical Strategy for Teaching Developmental Theories through Writing: Dyadic Confrontations." Paper presented at the International Convention on Cooperative Learning, Baltimore, July 1990. ERIC ED 321 721. 36 pages

Describes using writing as an instructional strategy to integrate issues deriving from human development theories in psychology.

1640. Smith, William Edward. "News Writing Students Prefer Computer Simulations." *JEd* 45 (Summer 1990): 38–44.

Reports on a study designed to determine how effective computer simulations would be in preparing journalists. The computer simulation was superior in interest, amount learned, and amount and usefulness of feedback.

1641. Snell, Luke M. "Teaching Memo and Letter Writing Techniques in the Classroom." *EnEd* 80 (May–June 1990): 481–483.

"Explains techniques used in a sophomore construction materials course that requires students to write memos and letters in a 'real life' environment."

1642. Spear, Shelley, Lori Liff, Alan Hunt, and John Jarvis. "Multicultural Literacy: A Context for Composition." *TETYC* 17 (December 1990): 247–252.

Describes an interdisciplinary English 101/ World Civilizations course.

1643. Sprengelmeyer, Robert John. "Students' Written Art Criticism as Measured by a Content Analysis Instrument." *DAI* 50 (March 1990): 2684A.

Examines the language used by college students when writing about their perceptions of paintings.

1644. Stanislawski, David A. "Writing Assignments? But This Is a Chemistry Class, Not English." *JCE* 67 (July 1990): 575–576.

Describes writing assignments used in a first-year chemistry class. Summarizes students' generally favorable reactions to writing in science classes.

1645. Stout, David E., Donald E. Wygal, and Katharine T. Hoff. "Writing across the Disciplines: Applications to the Accounting Classroom." *BABC* 53 (December 1990): 10–16.

Discusses the need for writing instruction in accounting courses and presents techniques for introducing writing in this discipline.

1646. Strauss, Michael, and Toby Fulwiler. "Writing to Learn in Large Lecture Classes." *JCST* 19 (December 1989–January 1990): 158–163.

Describes three techniques—visualizing internal thought, chemistry logs, and lab workshops—as well as offering caveats and advice for such classes.

1647. Swanson, Larry, and Hamid M. R. Aboutorabi. "The Technical Memorandum: An Effective Way of Developing Technical Writing Skills." *EnEd* 80 (Spring 1990): 479–480.

Discusses the use of a technical memo to improve technical writing skills in tradiational engineering courses.

1648. Vanderbilt, Heidi. "Journal Keeping for Fiction Writers." *Writer* 103 (February 1990): 15–20.

Suggests reasons for keeping daily journals and presents methods for writing effective entries that can be helpful years hence.

1649. Walker, Lou Ann. "How to Write a Profile." *Writer* 103 (February 1990): 21–23.

Offers suggestions for translating material into interesting profiles that capture a subject on paper.

1650. Watkins, Beverly T. "More and More Professors in Many Academic Disciplines Routinely Require Students to Do Extensive Writing." *CHE* 36 (18 July 1990): A13–A14, A16.

Traces the writing across the curriculum movement and describes programs established at several universities.

1651. Worsham, Fabian Clements. "Common Ground: The Development of Practical Business Communication and Human Relations Skills in the Creative Writing Workshop." *Issues* 3 (Fall–Winter 1990): 68–79.

Creative writing courses can teach students in business and technical fields practical skills in small-group dynamics and in oral and written communications.

1652. Youngberg, Susan Alrone Troug. "The Effect of Writing Assignments on Student Achievement in a College-Level Elementary Algebra Class." *DAI* 50 (March 1990): 2819A.

Findings reveal that writing assignments improved achievement and that students' attitudes toward such assignments were neutral.

See also 117, 333, 432, 450, 1070, 1186, 1232, 1253, 1259, 1273, 1432, 1477, 1478, 1542, 1544, 1703, 1812, 1831, 1835, 1840

4.3   ADULT AND GRADUATE EDUCATION

1653. Ackerman, John Martin. "Reading and Writing in the Academy: A Comparison of Two Disciplines." *DAI* 51 (August 1990): 464A.

Compares 40 essays by graduate students in two disciplines. Confirms the "interrelat-edness of [reading] comprehension and composing processes" and suggests that reading and writing rhetorically is required for success.

1654. Arlington County Public Schools. *Perspectives on Organizing a Work Place Literacy Program.* Arlington, Va.: Arlington County Public Schools, 1989. ERIC ED 313 927. 58 pages

Provides suggestions for implementing and evaluating a work place literacy program.

1655. Artiss, Phyllis Katherine. "Whose Voices? Case Studies of Two Students Writing Their Way through University." *DAI* 51 (August 1990): 422A.

Analyzes the academic multidisciplinary writing of male and female M.A. students, examining the "voices" of each.

1656. Bogert, Judith, and David Butt. "Opportunities Lost, Challenges Met: Understanding and Applying Group Dynamics in Writing Projects." *BABC* 53 (June 1990): 51–58.

Describes the use of instrumented forms to improve group process in an M.B.A. communication course. Forms are included in the article's appendix.

1657. Brandt, Rose. *Manual for Volunteer Literacy Site Managers.* Philadelphia: Center for Literacy, 1985. ERIC ED 313 549. 50 pages

Offers a manual for leaders of voluntary literacy organizations. Provides forms and discusses such duties as recruiting tutors and arranging publicity.

1658. Casanave, Christine R. Pearson. "The Role of Writing in Socializing Graduate Students into an Academic Discipline in the Social Sciences." *DAI* 51 (September 1990): 804A.

This 18-month ethnographic study assesses the socialization through writing of first-year doctoral students in sociology.

1659. Charrer, Ivan, and Shirley Fox. *Improving Work Place Literacy through Community Collaboration: Leader's Guide and Work-*

book. Washington, D.C.: Academy for Educational Development, 1989. ERIC ED 313 538. 159 pages

Provides a leader's guide and workbook for a workshop to improve literacy in the work place.

1660. Chynoweth, Judith K. *Enhancing Literacy for Jobs and Productivity.* Washington, D.C.: Council of State Policy and Planning Agencies, 1989. ERIC ED 313 583. 122 pages

Describes work place literacy programs in nine states.

1661. Davis, Peggy. "Caution: Human Beings Here! Handle with Care! Confidence Builders for Adult Learners." *AdLBEd* 13 (1989): 1–6.

Recommends certain writing assignments as one tool for making students feel important.

1662. Denny, Verna Haskins, Janice Lee Albert, and Joan Manes. *Focus on Adult Literacy: Expectations, Experiences, and Needs of New York City's Adult Literacy Students.* New York: Literacy Assistance Center, 1989. ERIC ED 314 589. 88 pages

Surveys the backgrounds and needs of students enrolled in 70 adult literacy classes in 1988 and 1989.

1663. Dougherty, Mary Ellen. "Be of Words a Little More Careful: Teaching the Corporate Learner." *CollT* 38 (Spring 1990): 56–58.

Describes seminars offered for businesses in the Baltimore area. Stresses flexibility in designing instruction and gives examples of revising texts.

1664. Forman, Janis. "Leadership Dynamics of Computer-Supported Writing Groups." *CC* 7 (April 1990): 35–46.

Reports on research from the UCLA Graduate School of Management about how student groups select software. Gives insights into ways of assessing the technological contributions to collaboration.

1665. Greenwood, Claudia M. "'It's Scary at First': Reentry Women in College Composi-

tion Classes." *TETYC* 17 (May 1990): 133–142.

Twelve reentering women report their fears, difficulties, and successes in a freshman composition course. Instructors must understand adult students' needs and create an atmosphere of trust.

1666. Hansen, Abby, and Elizabeth Armstrong. "Of Doctors and Documents: Report on a Faculty Writing Program at a Health Maintenance Organization." *Issues* 2 (Spring–Summer 1990): 150–160.

Describes a program established at the Harvard Community Health Plan Teaching Center to increase faculty publications.

1667. Pates, Andrew, and Maggie Evan. "Writing Workshops: An Experience from British Adult Literacy." *JR* 34 (December 1990): 244–248.

Describes the writing workshop as it developed in the British adult literacy movement. Identifies the sequence of stages through which a workshop moves.

1668. Patterson, Martha. *Work Place Literacy: A Review of the Literature.* Fredericton, Canada: Fredericton, New Brunswick, Department of Advanced Education and Training, 1989. ERIC ED 314 142. 22 pages

Review article noting the increased support for work place literacy programs.

1669. Ruzich, Constance M. "Investing in Writing: A Study of Negotiated Meanings of Writing in Two Graduate Business Classes." *DAI* 51 (July 1990): 99A.

Examines the creation of meaning in a discourse community and the roles of writing models, audience awareness, response, and purpose in the writing process.

1670. Soifer, Rena, Barbara Crumrine, Blair Simmons, Deborah Young, Emo Honzaki, and Martha Irwin. *The Complete Theory-to-Practice Handbook of Adult Literacy.* Language and Literacy Series. New York: Teachers College Press, 1990. 232 pages

Offers guidelines for curriculum design teaching and approaches for adult education programs in community education, business, and industry.

1671. Stahl, Norman A. *The Development of Graduate Level Emphases for Adult Reading-Literacy Instruction and Post-Secondary Reading-Learning Instruction.* DeKalb, Ill.: Northern Illinois University College of Education, 1989. ERIC ED 314 729. 47 pages

Offers recommendations for doctoral and masters programs in adult reading and literacy.

1672. Terkelson, Care. "The Effects of a Communication Skill Training Program upon Interpersonal Communication in a Fortune 500 Company." *DAI* 51 (November 1990): 1482A.

Examines the effects of a training program on employees and on managers' perceptions of employees.

1673. Wilcoxon, Cynthia Wilson. "Reentry Shock as a Variable in the Academic Performance of Adult Students in Higher Education." *DAI* 51 (November 1990): 1511A.

Focuses on the possibility of a predictable pattern.

See also 1, 41, 475, 996, 1122, 1165, 1268, 1684, 1726, 1729, 1733

4.4   ENGLISH AS A SECOND LANGUAGE

1674. Alexander, Louis. "Fads and Fashions in English Language Teaching." *EngT* 6 (January 1990): 35–56.

Describes the development of the organized syllabus in teaching ESL.

1675. Ali, Hisham A. "A Process-Based Approach to Teaching Written English to First-Year University Students in Lebanon: An Exploratory Study." *DAI* 50 (April 1990): 3170A.

Results of a controlled study using 52 students show that the writing performance of the experimental (process) group was significantly better than that of the control (product) group.

1676. Arena, Louis A., ed. *Language Proficiency: Defining, Teaching, and Testing.* New York: Plenum, 1990. 180 pages

Collects 19 essays on teaching, testing, and defining second language proficiency.

1677. Badger, Richard. "Referential Cohesion in Law Cases." Paper presented at the International Association of Teachers of English as a Foreign Language, Coventry, England, April 1989. ERIC ED 312 886. 9 pages

Analyzes cohesive references in a newspaper report of a law case, with the intention of helping ESL students read such texts.

1678. Belcher, Diane D. *Is There an Audience in the Advanced EAP Composition Class?* Alexandria, Va.: EDRS, 1989. ERIC ED 316 028. 35 pages

Argues that students in English for academic purposes classes should act as peer reviewers for papers in the content areas of their disciplines.

1679. Benesch, Sarah, ed. *ESL in America: Myths and Possibilities.* Portsmouth, N.H.: Boynton/Cook, 1990. 176 pages

Nine essays review the social, economic, and political context of second language and bilingual education. Organized into three sections: myths, educational policy, and possibilities.

1680. Bowman, Brenda, Grace Burkart, and Barbara Robson. *Teaching English as a Foreign or Second Language.* Washington, D.C.: Center for Applied Linguistics, 1989. ERIC ED 313 902. 236 pages

Provides a guide for Peace Corps volunteers, covering primary grades through college and the work place.

1681. Brock, Mark N. *The Computer as Writing Tutor: Is There a Place in the Process for*

Computer-Based Text Analysis? Alexandria, Va.: EDRS, 1988. ERIC ED 318 429. 55 pages

Studies two approaches to CAI by comparing two students receiving product-oriented feedback with two students receiving process-oriented feedback. Product-oriented feedback resulted in shorter drafts with fewer meaningful revisions.

1682. Chastain, Kenneth. "Characteristics of Graded and Ungraded Compositions." *MLJ* 74 (Spring 1990): 10–14.

Examines how L2 learners' expectation of a grade influences paper length, sentence length and type, number and type of errors, and content and organization.

1683. Costello, Jacqueline. "Promoting Literacy through Literature: Reading and Writing in ESL Composition." *JBW* 9 (Spring 1990): 20–30.

Argues that "as reading comprehension improves, so does mastery of grammar, rhetoric, and Western culture." Recommends coursework in reading and writing narratives.

1684. D'Annunzio, Anthony. "A Nondirective Combinatory Model in an Adult ESL Program." *JR* 34 (November 1990): 198.

Describes how adult ESL students can be taught by pedagogically unsophisticated bilinguals. The tutors used the language experience approach and individualized reading.

1685. De Pourbaix, Renata, and Lynne Young. "Can Students Learn What to Expect in Academia? An Interview." *CALS* 6 (1989): 31–39.

Describes an ESL course in which students researched a non-ESL course to discover what linguistic and academic skills are expected of students taking the course.

1686. Diab, Turki Ahmad Ali. "The Role of Dictionaries in ESP, with Particular Reference to Student Nurses at the University of Jordan." *DAI* 50 (April 1990): 3215A.

An empirical study of dictionary use by 415 student nurses argues for an ESP approach to lexicography. Describes an ESP dictionary and the integration of dictionaries into the curriculum.

1687. Dolly, Martha R. "Adult ESL Students' Management of Dialogue Journal Conversation." *TESOLQ* 24 (Summer 1990): 317–321.

Using conversational analysis, describes the interaction between 12 nonnative speakers (students) and one native speaker (teacher) writing dialogue journals. Classifies interaction types.

1688. Dolly, Martha R. *Conversation Management in the Dialogue Journals of Adult ESL Students.* Washington, D.C.: ERIC/FLL, 1989. ERIC ED 311 711. 39 pages

Reports on a study of patterns of giving and soliciting in the dialogue journals of 12 ESL students and their native English-speaking conversational partners.

1689. Dreyer, Diana. "Diversity in the Writing Workshop: Interaction, Acquisition, and Integration." Paper presented at the CCCC Convention, Chicago, March 1990. ERIC ED 318 021. 14 pages

Describes a workshop approach to writing, following Gere and Abbott, that emphasizes discussion in a mixed class of native and nonnative speakers of English.

1690. Edelsky, Carole, and Sarah Hudelson. *Contextual Complexities: Written Classroom Policies for Bilingual Education.* CSW Occasional Paper, no. 10. Berkeley, Calif.: CSW, 1989. ERIC ED 314 943. 21 pages

Argues the importance of local autonomy for bilingual literacy programs.

1691. Erbaugh, Mary S. "Taking Advantage of China's Literary Tradition in Teaching Chinese Students." *MLJ* 74 (Spring 1990): 15–27.

Explains how Chinese beliefs about writing and literary genres influence students' responses to language teaching assignments.

Describes successful assignments that acknowledge those beliefs.

1692. Farrell, Alan. "Oral Patterns and Written Composition." Paper presented at the Conference on the Teaching of Foreign Languages and Literatures, Youngstown, Ohio, October 1988. ERIC ED 318 216. 36 pages

Describes several exercises to help ESL students distinguish acceptable oral and written patterns.

1693. Fukushima, Norikazu Jun. "A Study of Japanese Communication: Compliment-Rejection Production and Second Language Instruction." *DAI* 51 (November 1990): 1493A.

Examines linguistic characteristics of Japanese politeness. Offers pedagogical applications for curriculum design, cross-cultural communication, and language teaching.

1694. Gee, Roger W. "Recognition of a Problem/Solution Text Structure by Low- and High-Proficiency ESL Community College Students." *DAI* 51 (November 1990): 1559A.

Investigates the use of a high-level reading strategy—the recognition of a text's logical structure—among ESL students.

1695. Goldstein, Lynn M., and Susan M. Conrad. "Student Input and Negotiation of Meaning in ESL Writing Conferences." *TESOLQ* 24 (Autumn 1990): 443–460.

Collects data from three advanced ESL writers (Vietnamese, Iranian, Philippine) and concludes that students' negotiating meaning in conferences leads to successful revising.

1696. Gondwe, Loveness. "Factors in the Design of an English Language Syllabus for Engineering Students at the Malawi Polytechnic." *DAI* 50 (April 1990): 3171A.

Reviews research on language acquisition, motivation, and attitudes. Discusses the design and implementation of the syllabus.

1697. Graber-Wilson, Geraldine Louise. "The Extent of the Relationship between Reading and Writing Achievement among International Students Enrolled in a University Freshman Composition Course." *DAI* 50 (February 1990): 2351A.

A study of timed writing samples and reading tests finds a strong, positive relationship between reading and writing skills, especially for low-level readers.

1698. Haas, Teri, and Trudy Smoke. "Talking to Learn: Conversation Workshops for ESL Students." *JDEd* 14 (Winter 1990): 14–16, 18.

Successfully uses conversation to help ESL students improve both oral and written language competence.

1699. Hall, Chris. "Managing the Complexity of Revising across Languages." *TESOLQ* 24 (Spring 1990): 43–60.

Examines similarities and differences of L1 and L2 revising of four advanced ESL writers speaking Polish, French, Norwegian, and Chinese. Focuses on argumentation.

1700. Hamdallah, Rami W. "Syntactic Errors in Written English: Study of Errors Made by Arab Students of English." *DAI* 50 (March 1990): 2814A.

Identifies, catalogues, and explains common syntactic errors found in the target group's writing.

1701. Hirsch, Linda. "Are Principles of Writing across the Curriculum Applicable to ESL Students in Content Courses? Research Findings." Paper presented at the NCTE Convention, Baltimore, November 1989. ERIC ED 319 264. 20 pages

Reports on two studies in which adult, advanced, and post-ESL students participated in tutorials using writing and talking as learning aids.

1702. Howard, Tharon, and Dave Dedo. "Cultural Criticism and ESL Composition." Paper presented at the NCTE Convention, Baltimore, November 1989. ERIC ED 317 062. 8 pages

Argues that ESL composition teachers should act not as guardians of "correct" English but as cultural or ideological critics.

1703. Howe, P. M. "The Problem of the Problem Question in English for Academic Legal Purposes." *ESP* 9 (1990): 215–236.

Examines 20 scripts by law students and teachers as to their schema within the macrostructure of the legal problem question.

1704. Kroll, Barbara. "The Rhetoric/Syntax Split: Designing a Curriculum for ESL Students." *JBW* 9 (Spring 1990): 40–55.

Advocates evaluating and placing students "based on a separate consideration of their rhetorical and syntactic skills." Analyzes sample essays and describes an ideal curriculum.

1705. Lebauer, Roni. *A Collaborative Computer-Assisted Reading and Writing Project: Dynamic Stories*. Alexandria, Va.: EDRS, 1990. ERIC ED 321 546. 18 pages

Describes a technique of having ESL students write dynamic stories to improve their lexical and grammatical skills.

1706. Lin, Chun Chung. "The Structures of English and Chinese Narratives Written by College Students in Taiwan." *DAI* 50 (January 1990): 2036A.

Quantitative and qualitative studies reveal that Chinese and English narratives consist of a setting and an episode system. English narratives contain fewer episodes, however.

1707. Liou, Hsien-Chin. "The Impact of Formal Instruction on Second Language Grammatical Accuracy." *DAI* 50 (May 1990): 3504A.

Suggests that formal instruction and communicative language teaching should be included in programs designed to teach oral and written skills in a second language.

1708. Lynch, Anthony J. "Grading Foreign Language Listening Comprehension Materi-

als: The Use of Naturally Modified Interaction." *DAI* 50 (April 1990): 3171A.

Reports on an experiment that explores the possibility of recording spoken texts in which "natural grading" might occur.

1709. Macero, Jeanette D., Barbara J. Agor, and Nancy Tumposky, eds. *Realizing the Dream: Selected Conference Proceedings of the Annual Meeting of the New York State TESOL*. New York: New York State TESOL, 1989. ERIC ED 314 949. 132 pages

Collects 12 papers presented at a conference on the contributions of new immigrants to North America. Conference proceedings are available as ERIC ED 314 949 but are abstracted as ERIC ED 314 950 to 314 960.

1710. Master, Peter. "Teaching the English Articles as a Binary System." *TESOLQ* 24 (Autumn 1990): 461–478.

Describes English articles as classifed (*a* and 0) and identified (*the*). Suggests that this simplified system makes articles more teachable in ESL classes.

1711. Mattar, Hameed Ebrahim. "A Cross-Sectional Error Analysis Study of the Common Writing Errors Made by Adult Arabic-Speaking EFL Learners in Bahrain." *DAI* 50 (April 1990): 3171A.

Presents data on the most common writing errors of adult EFL learners in Bahrain.

1712. Min, Chan K. "The Effects of Assignments in ESL/EFL Compositions." *DAI* 50 (February 1990): 2473A.

Concludes that Korean students prefer to write on subjective topics and perform better when provided with little information.

1713. Mitchell, Candace J. "Ideology and Practice: The Acquisition of Academic Literacy in a University ESL Writing Class." *DAI* 51 (August 1990): 495A.

Argues that success in a writing class is related to previous experience in academic contexts and to experience with oral and written academic discourse.

1714. Nunan, David. *Designing Tasks for the Communicative Classroom.* Cambridge Language Teaching Library. Cambridge, England: Cambridge University Press, 1989. 211 pages

Regards curriculum planning as integrating both syllabus design and methodology. Presents learning tasks for second language instruction appropriate to a variety of instructional settings and age groups.

1715. Parkhurst, Christine. "The Composition Process of Science Writers." *ESP* 9 (1990): 169–179.

Compares a process-oriented composition class with the scientific writing process, discussing the writing processes of native and nonnative English proficient scientific workers.

1716. Perkins, Kyle, and Sheila R. Brutten. "Writing: A Holistic or Atomistic Entity?" *JBW* 9 (Spring 1990): 75–84.

Presents empirical analyses of essays by 110 undergraduate international students. Recommends emphasizing "function, meaning, and purpose" in writing instruction.

1717. Peyton, Joy Kreeft, and Jana Staton. *Dialogue Journals in the Multilingual Classroom: Building Language Fluency and Writing Skills through Writing Interaction.* Writing Research Series. Edited by Marcia Farr. Norwood, N.J.: Ablex, 1990.

Describes how dialogue journal writing can be implemented in the multilingual classroom. Gives advice for starting and maintaining the practice, exploiting its benefits, and avoiding the pitfalls.

1718. Peyton, Joy Kreeft, Jana Staton, Gina Richardson, and Walt Wolfram. "The Influence of Writing Task on ESL Students' Written Production." *RTE* 24 (May 1990): 142–171.

Determined that the quantity and maturity of students' writing in dialogue journals was equivalent to assigned writing on all

measures. Sometimes journal writing showed more complex linguistic expression.

1719. Rainey, Kenneth T. "Teaching Technical Writing to Nonnative Speakers." *TWT* 17 (Spring 1990): 131–135.

Outlines instructional principles and pedagogical approaches that technical writing instructors should use with nonnative speakers.

1720. Roen, Duane H., and Donna M. Johnson, eds. *Richness in Writing: Empowering ESL Students.* New York: Longman, 1989. 306 pages

Eighteen essays by experts in composition as well as ESL and bilingual education define the contexts in which ESL students engage in composing, address rhetorical concerns for second language students, and focus on cultural issues in the writing of ESL students.

1721. Sasser, Linda, and Carole Cromwell. "Testimony: Writing Cooperatively." Paper presented at the California Association of Teachers of English to Speakers of Other Languages, Los Angeles, November 1987. ERIC ED 317 046. 20 pages

Describes a lesson plan and materials for reading and cooperative writing based on the story "Testimony."

1722. Sato, Taeko. "Revising Strategies in Japanese Students' Writing in English as a Foreign Language." *DAI* 51 (December 1990): 2005A.

High- and low-rated essays, holistically scored, differed depending on the number of "successful" revisions rather than the number of total revisions.

1723. Seidhofer, Barbara. "Summary Judgments: Perspectives on Reading and Writing." Paper presented at the International Association of Teachers of English as a Foreign Language, Dublin, March 1990. ERIC ED 321 571. 19 pages

Reports on the role of summarization in deriving writing from reading. Focuses on two kinds of summaries, abbreviated versions and brief accounts.

1724. Stevick, Earl W. "Research on What? Some Terminology." *MLJ* 74 (Summer 1990): 143–153.

Points out ambiguities in terms from research on second language acquisition to urge more precise use of language.

1725. Sun, Michelle C. "Code Switching and Writing in a Second Language: A Study of Chinese Students Writing in English." *DAI* 50 (February 1990): 2475A.

Suggests "that ESL students should not be discouraged from thinking in their native language" while drafting, since code switching aids the holistic exploration of ideas.

1726. Terdy, Dennis, and Laura Bercovitz. *Home English Literacy for Parents: An ESL Family Curriculum*. Washington, D.C.: Office of Bilingual Education and Minority Languages Affairs, 1989. ERIC ED 313 926. 127 pages

Offers a literacy curriculum encouraging parental involvement.

1727. Tracy, Glenn Edward. "The Effect of Sentence-Combining Practice on Syntactic Maturity and Writing Quality in ESL Students in Freshman Composition." *DAI* 50 (March 1990): 2777A.

Findings suggest a need for extensive rather than occasional practice to elicit maximum improvement.

1728. Wardell, David. "Writing: The Development of Coherent Rhetorical Forms in Advanced Learners of a Second Language." Paper presented at the Communication Association of Japan, Tokyo, June 1990. ERIC ED 321 558. 20 pages

Describes a program for advanced ESL students in Japan that attends to rhetorical patterns in developing students' writing skills.

1729. Weinstein-Shr, Gail. *From Problem Solving to Celebration: Discovering and Creating Meanings through Literacy*. Washington, D.C.: ERIC/FLL, 1989. ERIC ED 313 916. 35 pages

Offers a case study of one teacher and three adult literacy students from the Hmong community in Philadelphia.

1730. White, Ron. *Laying It on the Line*. Alexandria, Va.: EDRS, 1990. ERIC ED 319 233. 35 pages

Reports on using a process-oriented writing curriculum with Japanese students.

1731. Winfield, Marie Yolette. *Fundamentally Speaking: A Focus on English as a Second Language*. Alexandria, Va.: EDRS, 1989. ERIC ED 320 393. 13 pages

Argues that techniques to teach spoken and written English must be reevaluated for cultural sensitivity.

1732. Wyatt-Brown, Anne. "Life after Graduate School: Skill Development for International Scholarship." Paper presented at the TESOL meeting, San Francisco, March 1990. ERIC ED 319 241. 20 pages

Describes a course on research and technical writing for ESL students planning to publish in English language journals and at English language conferences.

1733. Xu, Ming. "Assessment of International Graduate Students' Perceived Language Needs, Proficiency, and Academic Performance." *DAI* 51 (November 1990): 1538A.

Examines the extent to which language proficiency is regarded as important for academic success in a variety of disciplines.

1734. Yuen, Steve Chi-Yin. *Computer-Assisted Instruction: A Handbook for ESL Teachers*. Alexandria, Va.: EDRS, 1989. ERIC ED 317 044. 76 pages

This handbook, developed at the University of Southern Mississippi, guides teachers to computer materials for ESL students working on the Apple IIe.

1735. Zamel, Vivian. "Through Students' Eyes: The Experiences of Three ESL Writers." *JBW* 9 (Fall 1990): 83–98.

Emphasizes that, "because they play a central role in the writing classroom, students' beliefs, expectations, and perspectives need to be explored," particularly through teacher-generated research.

See also 10, 11, 21, 38, 40, 97, 466, 495, 508, 796, 808, 884, 896, 1211, 1215, 1247, 1284, 1286, 1484, 1623, 1738, 1757, 1775, 1808

4.5 RESEARCH AND STUDY SKILLS

1736. Bernath, Mary G. "Real Research for Real Readers." *CSSEDC Quarterly* 12 (May 1990): 3–6.

Uses the *New Yorker* as a textbook and model to teach research writing. Describes assignments modeled on the magazine's format and content.

1737. Bigger, Margaret G. "The Library: A Researcher's Best Friend." *Writer* 103 (November 1990): 30–31.

Offers advice for using a library's various services for in-depth research.

1738. Brenner, Catherine A. *Teaching the Research Paper to ESL Students in American Colleges and Universities*. Washington, D.C.: ERIC/FLL, 1989. ERIC ED 311 714. 82 pages

Examines challenges faced by ESL students in learning to write research papers. Describes a classroom procedure for teaching the steps in developing a research paper.

1739. Connors, Patricia. "The Research Paper: What Students Have to Say." *TETYC* 17 (October 1990): 180–182.

Students have the greatest problems with managing their time, but they also express concern about choosing topics, managing

sources, and controlling the writing process.

1740. Fick, Virginia Gunn. "A History-Based Research Paper Course." *TETYC* 17 (February 1990): 34–35.

Students examine the 1930s in America.

1741. Friend, Christy M. "Research on Essay Exams: Using Inquiry to Enhance Students' Learning and Performance." Paper presented at the CCCC Convention, Chicago, March 1990. ERIC ED 318 025. 11 pages

Compared with a standard textbook unit on writing essay examinations, an inquiry unit focusing on individual writing skills produced superior results.

1742. Hult, Christine. "Expanded Roles of Computers in Writing Research Papers and Reports." *TETYC* 17 (May 1990): 114–119.

Computers help in finding and handling information and in the writing process.

1743. Kantz, Margaret. *Shirley and the Battle of Agincourt: Why Is It So Hard for Students to Write Persuasive Researched Analyses?* CSW Occasional Paper, no. 14. Berkeley, Calif.: CSW, 1989. ERIC ED 312 669. 39 pages

Argues that reading rhetorically can lead to the discovery of original ideas about source materials.

1744. Koehler, Boyd, and Kathryn Swanson. "Basic Writers and the Library: A Plan for Providing Meaningful Bibliographic Instruction." *JBW* 9 (Spring 1990): 56–74.

Report on a three-year study of instructional methods emphasizing "immediacy, relevance, and individualization."

1745. Malinowski, Patricia. "The Research Paper: From Personal to Academic Writing." *TETYC* 17 (December 1990): 265–266.

Research papers are based on students' career interests.

1746. Malinowski, Patricia. "Using Personal Writing to Introduce Research Skills." *ExEx* 36 (Fall 1990): 36–37.

Describes the Job Interest Project, which draws upon personnel from the career center, the library, and various professions.

1747. Murphy, Richard. "Anorexia: The Cheating Disorder." *CE* 52 (December 1990): 898–903.

A personal essay about plagiarism incorporating anecdotes from the author's teaching experience.

1748. Simpson, Michele L., and Sherrie L. Nist. "Textbook Annotation: An Effective and Efficient Study Strategy for College Students." *JR* 34 (October 1990): 122–129.

A description of the authors' annotation research with 60 undergraduate students and practical suggestions emanating from it. Provides examples of annotating.

1749. Stone, Nancy R. "Ideas in Practice: Developing Critical Thinkers: Content and Process." *JDEd* 13 (Spring 1990): 20–22, 26.

A successful revision of a study skills course includes unified content and instruction in strategies for critical thinking, reading, and writing.

1750. Strode, Susan Louise. "Reevaluation of the Effects of Annotation Training on Summary Writing and Comprehension of College Students." *DAI* 50 (April 1990): 3196A.

A study of 144 students concludes that training improves the succinctness of summaries but does not contribute to improved reading comprehension.

1751. Wade, Suzanne E., Woodrow Trathen, and Gregory Schraw. "An Analysis of Spontaneous Study Strategies." *RRQ* 25 (Spring 1990): 147–166.

An analysis of college students reveals six types of study strategies.

See also 741, 1130, 1227, 1250

4.6   OTHER

1752. Bristow, Diane, Harry Murphy, Gail Pickering, and Marshall Raskind. "Technology Reaching Out to Special Education Students." *MM* 26 (May–June 1990): 38–40.

Describes advancements in computer-assisted technology that allow visually impaired, severely communicatively impaired, hearing-impaired, and physically challenged students to produce and comprehend written texts.

1753. Faieta, Jean Lane Crockett. "A Comparison of Two Instructional Techniques: Sentence Writing Versus Tutorial in Teaching College Students Identified as Learning Disabled." *DAI* 50 (March 1990): 2859A.

Finds sentence writing to be the more viable method of teaching writing skills.

1754. Hunter, Paul. "Learning Disabilities: New Doubts, New Inquiries." *CE* 52 (January 1990): 92–97.

Reviews three books and discusses their implications for teachers of composition and basic writing.

1755. Smith, Charles Arthur. "The Effects of Handwriting Versus Word Processing on Learning-Disabled Students' Written Compositions." *DAI* 50 (February 1990): 2378A.

Finds that the word processor helped learning-disabled students only in terms of spelling and fluency. Proficiency in keyboarding seems to have been a factor.

1756. Stewart, Donald C. "What Is an English Major? Some Afterthoughts." *RR* 9 (Fall 1990): 128–131.

Argues that English departments should require undergraduate English majors to take courses in the history of rhetoric and in rhetorical theory.

See also 991, 1066, 1195, 1220, 1255, 1434, 1482

5

Testing, Measurement, and Evaluation

5.1 EVALUATION OF STUDENTS

1757. Adjakey, Komi M. "Second Language Speakers as Translators: Implications for Linguistic Theory and Second Language Acquisition." *DAI* 50 (March 1990): 2877A.

Finds that language proficiency assessment in tests is heavily influenced by the evaluator's ideolect and ideology and by knowledge of the subject matter and discourse.

1758. Alexander, John, and Roxanne Cullen. *The Writing of Ferris State University Students: A View across the Curriculum.* Big Rapids, Mich.: Ferris State University, 1990. ERIC ED 319 342. 199 pages

Evaluates growth in writing as gauged by selected variables pertaining to graduating seniors. Results show a correlation between sex and GPA and writing performance.

1759. Applebee, Arthur N., Judith A. Langer, Lynn B. Jenkins, Ina V. S. Mullis, and Mary A. Foertsch. *Learning to Write in Our Na-tion's Schools: Instruction and Achievement in 1988 at Grades 4, 8, and 12.* Princeton, N.J.: NAEP and ETS, 1990.

Reports on a 1988 assessment of writing ability among 20,000 students performing persuasive, narrative, and informative writing tasks.

1760. Applebee, Arthur N., Judith A. Langer, Ina V. S. Mullis, and Lynn B. Jenkins. *The Writing Report Card, 1984–88: Findings from the Nation's Report Card.* Princeton, N.J.: NAEP and ETS, 1990. 110 pages

Reports on two national assessments of writing proficiency conducted during the school years ending in 1984 and 1988 among 18,000 students in grades four, eight, and eleven.

1761. Aubrecht, Gordon J., II. "Is There a Connection between Testing and Teaching?" *JCST* 20 (December 1990): 152–157.

Teachers should use a "map" reflecting a course's goals and philosophies to write examinations. Patterns of errors on tests show weaknesses in teachers' exam-writing skills.

1762. Auten, Janet Gebhart. "The Text in the Margin: A Theoretical Analysis of Teacher Commentary on Student Writing." *DAI* 50 (May 1990): 3503A.

Discusses the limited benefit of marginal comments on students' writing and suggests ways these comments can be altered so that they will be more helpful.

1763. Barbour, Dennis H. "Collaborative Writing in the Business Writing Classroom: An Ethical Dilemma for the Teacher." *BABC* 53 (September 1990): 33–35.

Discusses ethical problems associated with grading collaborative writing assignments in business writing courses.

1764. Bear, Donald R., Pat Truex, and Diane Barone. "In Search of Meaningful Diagnosis: Spelling-by-Stage Assessment of Literacy Proficiency." *AdLBEd* 13 (1989): 165–185.

A spelling inventory causes less anxiety, diagnoses reading ability more effectively, and guides instruction more supportively than does assessment by word recognition in isolation.

1765. Bender, Carol Francine. "A Study of Teacher and Peer Comments in the Revision Process of College Writers." *DAI* 51 (August 1990): 437A.

Investigates theoretical and pedagogical implications of instructor's comments. Suggests that students use three-way written dialogues among writer, peer-editor, and teacher.

1766. Bizzaro, Patrick. "Evaluating Student Poetry Writing: A Primary-Trait Scoring Model." *TETYC* 17 (February 1990): 54–61.

Grading is based on the student's revisions according to traits derived from the individual poem.

1767. Breland, Hunter, and Eldon Lytle. "Computer-Assisted Writing Skill Assessment Using WordMAP." Paper presented at

the joint meeting of the AERA and National Council on Measurement in Education, Boston, April 1990. ERIC ED 317 586. 19 pages

WordMAP is used to predict scores on several standardized tests.

1768. Carver, Ronald P. "Rescaling the Degrees of Reading Power Test to Provide Valid Scores for Selecting Materials at the Instructional Level." *JRB* 22 (1990): 1–18.

The Degrees of Reading Power test has been rescaled to provide new scores and grade equivalents that appear more valid for selecting materials.

1769. Caudrey, Tim. "The Validity of Timed Essay Tests in the Assessment of Writing Skills." *ELT* 44 (April 1990): 122–131.

Compares scores from timed and untimed essays by adolescent students, finding little difference in the results.

1770. Clark, Beverly Lyon, and Roger D. Clark. "On Placing and Misplacing Students: Some Thoughts on Exemption." *WPA* 13 (Spring 1990): 17–26.

Raises questions about exemption procedures for composition students and calls for more attention to the effect of these practices on students.

1771. Coffin-Prince, Lynne. "To Err Is Human—To Grade, Demonic." *CalE* 26 (March–April 1990): 6–7, 26.

Suggests strategies for grading student writing.

1772. Cumming, Alister. "Expertise in Evaluating Second Language Compositions." *LT* 7 (June 1990): 21–51.

Verbal reports of 13 ESL teachers who rated compositions revealed 28 common decision-making behaviors, which differed for novice and expert raters.

1773. Davis, Todd M., Robert A. Kaiser, Jerry N. Bonne, and Jane McGuire. "Caution in Testing." *JDEd* 13 (Spring 1990): 2–4.

Discusses a Tennessee study of variations in performance according to ability, age, sex, race, and institution on a timed reading placement test.

1774. Dinitz, Sue, and Jean Kiedaisch. "Persuasion from an 18-Year-Old's Perspective: Perry and Piaget." *JTW* 9 (Fall–Winter 1990): 209–221.

Teachers must consider cognitive developmental limits when evaluating students. If peers are the real audience responding to drafts, students may seriously consider the audience's needs.

1775. Dissayanake, Asoka S., Basil A. Ali, and Usha Nayar. "English Proficiency in Multiple-Choice Questions." *AM* 65 (February 1990): 101.

If multiple-choice questions are constructed using clear, simple English, proficiency in ESL is not a major determinant of the pattern of answer changes on tests.

1776. Dohrer, Gary Ray. "How Undergraduate Students Respond during Revision to Teachers' Written Comments: A Case Study." *DAI* 50 (March 1990): 2814A.

Describes and analyzes the revision processes of seven college students.

1777. Edwards, Renee. "Sensitivity to Feedback and the Development of Self." *ComQ* 38 (Spring 1990): 101–111.

Two investigations suggest that sensitivity to feedback mediates the ways in which students process self-relevant feedback.

1778. Flanigan, Michael. "Establishing Criteria for Judgment: Writers Construct Methodologies for Truth." Paper presented at the South Central MLA, New Orleans, October 1989. ERIC ED 314 758. 12 pages

Suggests ways to teach criteria for writing effective definition essays, offering a sample assignment.

1779. Gilson, Joan T. *The Written English Proficiency Test at UMKC: An Intelligent Answer to an Unintelligent Question.* Bloomington, Ind.: ERIC/RCS, 1989. ERIC ED 309 430. 32 pages

Describes the University of Missouri at Kansas City's use of a large-scale test of writing to assess performance and progress in the English writing curriculum.

1780. Goddard, M. Lee. "Avoiding Teacher Burnout in Evaluating Business Communication Assignments." *BABC* 53 (March 1990): 23–25.

Suggests 17 strategies enabling faculty to deal with the work load stress of evaluating business communication assignments.

1781. Goulden, Nancy. "A Comparison of Reliability and Validity of Holistic and Analytic Methods of Scoring Classroom Speeches." *DAI* 51 (November 1990): 1441A.

Applies composition scoring methods to the scoring of 12 videotaped classroom speeches.

1782. Goulden, Nancy. "Theoretical and Empirical Comparisons of Holistic and Analytic Scoring of Written and Spoken Discourse." Paper presented at the SCA meeting, San Francisco, November 1989. ERIC ED 315 799. 27 pages

Analytic and holistic methods of rating written products can be adapted to evaluate oral products and performances.

1783. Hebert, Kathleen. "A Description of the Interrelationships of Qualitative Scores, Quantitative Counts and Averages, and Student Demographic Characteristics Associated with the Assessment of College Freshmen Placement Essays." *DAI* 50 (February 1990): 2369A.

Finds differences between male and female and minority and nonminority writers. Concludes that current methods only allow for a partial assessment of writing.

1784. Herzer, Scott, and Carolyn Kremers. " 'Experiments' with Anonymous Partner Evaluation." *ExEx* 35 (Spring 1990): 9–13.

Reviews a case study of two instructors' classes that served as an audience for each other's writing.

1785. Hock, Dennis J. "A Correlational Study of Computer-Measured Traits and Holistic Assessment Ratings of First-Year College Students' Essays." *DAI* 51 (November 1990): 1596A.

Uses Grammatik III to measure stylistic variables, arguing that computers are capable of reliably predicting the holistic quality ratings trained human evaluators give to essays.

1786. Huot, Brian. "The Literature of Direct Writing Assessment: Major Concerns and Prevailing Trends." *RER* 60 (Spring 1990): 237–263.

Reviews past concerns and suggests future directions.

1787. Huot, Brian. "Reliability, Validity, and Holistic Scoring: What We Know and What We Need to Know." *CCC* 41 (May 1990): 201–213.

Discusses the "state of holistic writing evaluation, inflated position of reliability, and neglected status of validity" in order to establish "theoretic soundness" for holistic scoring.

1788. Hyland, Ken. "Providing Productive Feedback." *ELT* 44 (October 1990): 279–285.

Presents a rationale and process for using minimal marking and taped comments as interactive feedback for students.

1789. Hyslop, Nancy. *Evaluating Student Writing: Methods and Measurement*. Bloomington, Ind.: ERIC/RCS, 1990. ERIC ED 315 785. 4 pages

Offers an overview of current research in the ERIC data base on evaluating student writing.

1790. Johnson, De S., and Patricia Deduck. *General Studies Advancement Examinations in Writing and Mathematics*. Washington, D.C.: American Association of State Colleges and Universities, 1990. ERIC ED 316 145. 12 pages

Reports on efforts at Southwest Texas State University to develop an examination program testing writing skills.

1791. Keh, Claudia L. "Feedback in the Writing Process: A Model and Methods for Implementation." *ELT* 44 (October 1990): 294–304.

Presents a model for giving successful feedback within the process approach. Uses a system of peer reading, conferences, and comments.

1792. Kepner, Christine Goring. "A Study of the Relationship between Types of Teacher-Administered Written Feedback and the Development of Writing Proficiency in Intermediate College Level Students of Spanish." *DAI* 51 (August 1990): 438A.

In students' journals, instructors' comments produced no significant change in surface-level errors, but content-related comments produced a greater use of "higher-level propositions."

1793. Kosmoski, Georgia Jean. "Relationship between Cultural Literacy and Academic Achievement." *DAI* 50 (March 1990): 2771A.

Findings indicate a significant correlation between cultural literacy and academic performance.

1794. Langer, Judith A., Arthur N. Applebee, Mary A. Foertsch, and Ina V. S. Mullis. *Learning to Read in Our Nation's Schools: Instruction and Achievement in 1988 at Grades 4, 8, and 12*. Princeton, N.J.: NAEP and ETS, 1990. 116 pages

Reports on a 1988 assessment of reading achievement among 13,000 students attending public and private schools.

1795. Leslie, Connie, and Pat Wingert. "Not as Easy as A, B, or C." *Newsweek* (8 January 1990): 56–58.

Discusses the need for better tests to assess learning and especially thinking skills.

1796. Linn, Jeffrey Benjamin. "The Development of a Reliable and Valid Scale to Measure

Writing Attitudes." *DAI* 51 (September 1990): 771A.

Studies 239 freshman composition and pre-service education students, employing the Writing Attitude Scale and other instruments to measure writing attitudes.

1797. Mabrito, Mark. "Writing Apprehension and Computer-Mediated Peer Response Groups: A Case Study of Four High- and Four Low-Apprehensive Writers Communicating Face-to-Face Versus Electronic Mail." *DAI* 50 (April 1990): 3171A.

Findings suggest that peer-response groups using electronic mail create the initial response experience for high-apprehensive writers.

1798. Miller, Hildy. "Kaleidoscope of Values: Composition Instructors, Noncomposition Faculty, and Students Respond to Academic Writing." *JTW* 9 (Spring-Summer 1990): 31–43.

Compares and contrasts patterns of response by composition faculty, noncomposition faculty, and students who rated an essay by using university criteria. Concludes that definitions of academic writing must be broadened.

1799. Millward, Jody. "Placement and Pedagogy: UC Santa Barbara's Preparatory Program." *JBW* 9 (Fall 1990): 99–113.

The University of California at Santa Barbara has attempted "to make testing fairer and to turn placement into pedagogy" through a collaborative project with 10 high schools.

1800. Morante, Edward A. "Selecting Tests and Placing Students." *JDEd* 13 (Winter 1989): 2–4, 6.

Challenges the right-to-fail philosophy. Offers suggestions for selecting tests, making placement decisions, and developing administrative guidelines for creating an institutional placement process.

1801. Nettles, Michael T., ed. *The Effect of Assessment on Minority Student Participation.* New Directions for Institutional Re-

search, no. 65. San Francisco: Jossey-Bass, 1990. 110 pages

Discusses academic assessment policies and current concerns about minority student access and achievement in higher education. Topics include how assessment affects access to teacher education programs and what impact Florida's College Academic Skills Test has had on minority students.

1802. New, Clara Ann Connor. "Factors Influencing the Academic Achievement of Black and White Freshmen at the University of Wisconsin—Milwaukee." *DAI* 50 (June 1990): 3864A.

Determines whether age, sex, race, geographical region, and selected academic measures from high school and college appropriately predict freshman grades.

1803. Oostdam, R. J. "Empirical Research on the Identification of Singular, Multiple, and Subordinate Argumentation." *Arg* 4 (May 1990): 223–234.

Argues that it is possible to construct subtests to measure secondary school students' abilities to identify singular, multiple, and subordinate argument structures.

1804. Raimes, Ann. "The TOEFL Test of Written English: Causes for Concern." *TESOLQ* 24 (Autumn 1990): 427–442.

Reviews the development of the Test of Written English and presents seven concerns and recommendations for ESL instructors. Especially critical of topic types on the test.

1805. Rankin, Libby. "An Anatomy of Awkwardness." *JTW* 9 (Spring–Summer 1990): 45–57.

People's use and perception of AWK are influenced by their experience with language, the reader-writer relationship, time constraints, context, the writing assignment, and their knowledge of the subject.

1806. Read, John. "Providing Relevant Content in an EAP Writing Test." *ESP* 9 (1990): 109–121.

Compares three types of writing tasks used to evaluate university students, finding that guided and experience-based writing tasks are the best qualifiers of written academic ability.

1807. Scharton, Maurice A. "Writing Assessment as Values Clarification." *JDEd* 13 (Winter 1989): 8–10, 12.

Supports the validity of writing assessment programs and practices. Offers strategies for developing assignments and scoring guides and for conducting scoring sessions.

1808. Silva, Tony. "A Review of Research in the Evaluation of ESL Writing." Paper presented at the CCCC Convention, Seattle, March 1989. ERIC ED 309 643. 16 pages

Discusses issues in ESL writing assessment, including the use of various instruments, indirect measures, correlational results, and other language testing matters.

1809. Sloan, Gary. "Frequency of Errors in Essays by College Freshmen and by Professional Writers." *CCC* 41 (October 1990): 299–308.

Both groups showed similar frequencies of errors. The most common errors among professional writers were triteness, verbiage, and structural ambiguity; among freshmen errors, spelling and word choice.

1810. Smit, David. "Evaluating a Portfolio System." *WPA* 14 (Fall–Winter 1990): 51–62.

Presents evaluative procedures adopted by the writing program at Kansas State University as contributing to the study of portfolio systems.

1811. Stoffel, Judy. "Comic Quizzes: Focusing on Dull Materials with Less Pain." *ExEx* 35 (Spring 1990): 19–21.

Provides samples of comic multiple-choice items.

1812. Strenski, Ellen, ed. *Possibilities: Scenarios and Scripts to Help Teaching Assistants Respond to Student Writing in All Disciplines.* Los Angeles: UCLA, 1986. ERIC ED 315 768. 45 pages

Suggests questions and comments that teaching assistants and nonwriting specialists can use in responding to students who need help with their writing assignments.

1813. Sworder, Steven. *A Review of the English Composition Assessment of Saddle College Students through the Matriculation Program.* Mission Viejo, Calif.: Saddleback Community College, 1990. ERIC ED 316 291. 21 pages

Describes a placement program at Saddleback College that uses the College English Placement Test.

1814. Taylor, Denny. *Teaching without Testing.* Urbana, Ill.: NCTE, 1990. 82 pages

Argues that current methods of assessing students' writing simplify our understanding of students' complex experiences and capabilities in language and literacy. Instead, we should stress the same holistic integration of language skills that we work towards in teaching composition. Originally published as a special issue of *English Education.*

1815. Tedick, Diane J. "ESL Writing Assessment: Subject-Matter Knowledge and Its Impact on Performance." *ESP* 9 (1990): 123–143.

Focuses on topic choice as a variable when assessing writing ability, recommending field-specific topics over general topics.

1816. Thompson, Roger M. "Writing-Proficiency Tests and Remediation: Some Cultural Differences." *TESOLQ* 24 (Spring 1990): 99–102.

Collected in Florida, data suggest that Southeast Asians were least prepared in writing, Latin Americans were least prepared academically, and Middle Easterners were least likely to take remedial courses.

1817. Thrush, Emily. "Cooperative and Collaborative Education: Implications for Research on Computer Use in Language Instruction." *CACJ* 4 (Winter 1990): 41–54.

Argues that grades for students using cooperative and collaborative learning with computers should be based on how much was learned by the *others* in their group.

1818. Vatalaro, Paul. "Putting Students in Charge of Peer Review." *JTW* 9 (Spring–Summer 1990): 21–29.

Describes procedures developed, used, and modified by students for responding to the work of their peers. Explains how the teacher set conditions for students' success with peer feedback.

1819. Wagner, Mary Ann Blakely. "Creator or Creation? Evaluating Creative Writing." *CalE* 26 (March–April 1990): 10–11, 26–27.

Suggests that evaluations of creative writing can be based on the demands of genre, the mastery of technique, and revision.

1820. Wambach, Catherine, and Thomas Brothen. "An Alternative to the Prediction-Placement Model." *JDEd* 13 (Spring 1990): 14–15, 24–26.

Argues that the best place for assessing students' academic skills and delivering appropriate interventions is in the content classroom.

1821. Welch, Catherine. *Differential Performance on a Direct Measure of Writing Skills for Black and White College Freshmen.* ACT Research Report Series, 89–8. Iowa City: American College Testing Program, 1989. ERIC ED 320 955. 21 pages

Compares 998 black and 3727 white examinees' responses to two essay prompts. Results show that black students' responses received lower scores than the responses of whites.

1822. Wherritt, Irene, and T. Anne Cleary. "A National Survey of Spanish Language Testing for Placement or Outcome Assessment at B.A.-Granting Institutions in the U.S." *FLA* 23 (April 1990): 157–165.

Reports on a survey of 126 schools. Only six percent include writing samples in their tests, but others indicate plans to include them.

1823. Wiener, Harvey S. "Evaluating Assessment Programs in Basic Skills." *JDEd* 13 (Winter 1989): 24–26.

Questions basic skills testing and assessment practices. Introduces the College Assessment Program Evaluation process, which encourages local rather than standardized national control of assessment.

1824. Wilson, Mary Elizabeth. "Validity of Placements in Transfer Writing Courses in an Innovative Community College." *DAI* 50 (May 1990): 3498A.

Analyzes students' test performances and grades in writing to find out whether placement affects students' success in transfer writing courses.

1825. Wolcott, Willa Joan Buckley. "Perspectives on Holistic Scoring: The Impact of Monitoring on Writing Evaluation." *DAI* 51 (November 1990): 1499A.

Examines reliability and validity, arguing that trained readers respond to similar rhetorical and mechanical elements in scoring.

1826. Wood, Nancy V. "Reading Tests and Reading Assessment." *JDEd* 13 (Winter 1989): 14–16, 18.

Discusses strengths and weaknesses of five standardized and seven informal methods for testing reading. Considers testing criteria and their relationship to curricula. Extensive bibliography.

1827. Zak, Frances. "Exclusively Positive Responses to Student Writing." *JBW* 9 (Fall 1990): 40–53.

Compares the results of using exclusively positive comments and regular comments in a nongraded basic writing course. Concludes that students may benefit more from less directive responses.

1828. Zorn, Jeff. "How Numbers Numb: 1.325 Case Studies." *CalE* 26 (March–April 1990): 8, 26.

Argues that evaluating writing numerically gives only the appearance of objectivity.

See also 82, 154, 781, 801, 960, 1127, 1135, 1676, 1682, 1700, 1704, 1837

5.2 EVALUATION OF TEACHERS

1829. Devet, Bonnie. "A Method for Observing and Evaluating Writing Lab Tutorials." *WCJ* 10 (Spring–Summer 1990): 75–83.

Describes an adaptation of Flanders' Interaction Analysis Categories for use in observing and evaluating tutorials. Outlines what observers should look for in 10 different categories.

1830. Johnson, Samuel R. "Male and Female College Students' Perceptions of Source Credibility of Microenvironmental Faculty-Office Settings." *DAI* 50 (April 1990): 3105A.

Examines the impact of gender and clutter on students' perceptions of an instructor's credibility.

See also 1146, 1204, 1249, 1838

5.3 EVALUATION OF PROGRAMS

1831. Dvorak, Jack. "College Students Evaluate Their Scholastic Journalism Courses." *JEd* 45 (Spring 1990): 36–45.

College students rated English, journalism, and elective classes in six competency areas: writing, editing, sources, critical thinking, language use, and affective domain. Journalism ranked highest.

1832. Gale, Irene. "Conflicting Paradigms: Theoretical and Administrative Tensions in Writing Program Administration." *WPA* 14 (Fall–Winter 1990): 41–50.

Considers the theoretical inconsistencies of the writing program of one large state university and suggests possible resolutions to such paradigmatic conflicts.

1833. McCleary, Bill. "Missouri College Writing Teachers Cooperating on Statewide Self-Study." *CompC* 3 (October 1990): 1–2.

Reports on a survey of writing in Missouri community colleges and four-year schools.

1834. McGee, Diane, and Christine Starnes. *Evaluation as Empowerment: Holistic Evalu-*

ation across the Curriculum. Sainte Anne de Bellevue, Canada: John Abbott College, 1988. ERIC ED 319 425. 74 pages

Reports on a study to establish the reliability and validity of holistic evaluations used to assess learning in content courses.

1835. McMullen, Judith Q., and J. Douglas Wellman. "Writing Programs outside the English Department: An Assessment of a Five-Year Program." *WPA* 14 (Fall–Winter 1990): 17–25.

Describes, evaluates, and considers the future of a Writing Improvement Program begun at Virginia Polytechnic Institute and State University.

1836. Meeker, Linda Hanson. "Pragmatic Politics: Using Assessment Tools to (Re)Shape a Curriculum." *JBW* 9 (Spring 1990): 3–19.

Describes assessment practices at Ball State University, which instituted changes "to create a positive public and legislative perception" of basic writing courses.

1837. Olds, Barbara M. "Does a Writing Program Make a Difference? A 10-Year Comparison of Faculty Attitudes about Writing." *WPA* 14 (Fall–Winter 1990): 27–40.

The results of two faculty attitude surveys conducted 10 years apart at the Colorado School of Mines reveal that the writing program made a difference.

1838. Pickett, Nell Ann. "Teaching Technical Communication in Two-Year Colleges: The Courses and the Teachers." *TWT* 17 (Winter 1990): 76–85.

Presents statistical results of a survey of 87 two-year colleges and concludes that these teachers are more informed and better prepared than their predecessors.

1839. Stone, Gerald. "Measurement of Excellence in Newspaper Writing Courses." *JEd* 45 (Winter 1990): 4–19.

The objective of this study was to identify characteristics that differentiate nationally recognized writing programs from those not attaining such notoriety.

1840. Webb, Tracy Anne. "Student and Faculty Response to Writing to Learn at the College Level." *DAI* 51 (November 1990): 1538A.

Examines students' responses to writing to learn curricula and how teachers' attitudes toward and implementation of writing to learn influence those responses.

1841. White, Edward M. "Language and Reality in Writing Assessment." *CCC* 41 (May 1990): 187–200.

Contrasts perceptions about and applications of writing assessment in the writing community and in the measurement community.

See also 1234

5.4   OTHER

1842. Bergeron, Bryan P. "Program Instrumentation: A Technique for Evaluating Educational Software." *CollM* 8 (Spring 1990): 34–46.

Discusses using program instrumentation, an evaluation technique based on automatic computer monitoring, to test the effectiveness of prototypes during educational software development.

1843. Bers, Trudy R., and Kerry E. Smith. "Assessing Assessment Programs: The Theory and Practice of Examining Reliability and Validity of a Writing Placement Test." *CCR* 18 (Winter 1990): 17–27.

Presents a model for analyzing the reliability and validity of an English placement test. Explores the implications of the model.

1844. Boldt, Robert F. "Latent Structure Analysis of the Test of English as a Foreign Language." *LT* 6 (December 1989): 123–142.

Reports on a large-scale statistical study. A single factor accounted for test scores across all TOEFL subtests and all national groups.

1845. Hamp-Lyons, Liz. "Applying the Partial Credit Method of Rasch Analysis: Language Testing and Accountability." *LT* 6 (June 1989): 109–118.

Uses examples from a writing assessment to consider the effective and ethical use of latent trait analysis, a nonclassical statistical technique.

1846. Pavitt, Charles. "A Controlled Test of Some 'Complicating Factors' Relevant to the Inferential Model for Evaluations of Communication Competence." *WJSC* 54 (Fall 1990): 575–592.

Concludes that competence evaluation can profitably be explored as a social-cognitive process.

1847. Phillips, Mary Lou Luttrell. "The Language of Naval Performance Evaluation: Officer Promotion as Reader Response and the Ideal Officer Concept." *DAI* 50 (January 1990): 2122A.

Uses Navy evaluations to examine the degree to which readers of a specific cultural subgroup read a written text in a uniform way.

1848. Shaver, James P. "Reliability and Validity of Measures of Attitudes toward Writing and toward Writing with the Computer." *WC* 7 (July 1990): 375–392.

Provides information about the reliability and validity of the Writing Apprehension Scale and the newly developed Attitudes toward Writing with the Computer Scale when used with secondary students. Questions Daly and Miller's unidimensional analysis of writing attitude.

1849. Voogt, Joke. "Courseware Evaluation by Teachers: An Implementation Perspective." *CompEd* 14 (1990): 299–307.

Concludes that computer courseware should motivate students, realize educational objectives better than traditional methods, and reflect teachers' ideas and beliefs.

Subject Index
Name Index

Subject Index

Numbers in the right-hand column refer to sections and subsections (see Contents). For example, entries containing information on achievement tests appear in Section 5, Subsection 5.1 (Evaluation of Students). When the righthand column contains only a section number, information on the subject appears in several subsections. Entries addressing assignments in the classroom, for example, appear in several subsections of Section 4, depending on the kind of course for which the assignments are appropriate.

Name Index

This index lists authors for anthologized essays as well as authors and editors for main entries.

Abbott, Don C., 14
Abbott, Don Paul, 317
Abbuhl, Phyllis Rae, 545
Abdulrazak, Fawzi A., 997
Aber, John, 1289
Aboutorabi, Hamid M. R., 1647
Achinstein, Sharon, 248
Ackerman, John, 41, 116, 1653
Ackley, Alice, 130
Adamczyk, Lawrence Paul, 350
Adams, John L., 1483
Adams, Katherine, 1483
Adjakey, Komi M., 1757
Adler, Mortimer J., 1129
Adult Literacy and Technology Project, 1
Afflerbach, Peter P., 755
Agatucci, Cora, 1595
Agee, Philip, 794
Aghbar, Ali-Asghar, 1427
Agor, Barbara J., 1709
Ahlersmeyer, Thomas Richard, 351
Ainsworth-Vaughn, Nancy, 793
Ajirotutu, Cheryl Seabrook, 546
Akers, Stanley W., 613
Alamprese, Judith A., 475
Albers, Randall K., 1428
Albert, Janice Lee, 1662

Albert, Robert S., 963
Albrecht, Jason E., 782
Alcidamas, 311
Alexander, John, 1758
Alexander, Louis, 1674
Alexander, Thomas Craig, 352
Ali, Basil A., 1775
Ali, Hisham A., 1675
Allaby, Anne Rodier, 1139
Allbritton, David W., 656
Allen, Bryce, 463
Allen, Carolyn, 636
Allen, Jo, 1538
Allen, Mike, 42, 794
Allen, Nancy, 5, 1194
Allen, Philip A., 899
Alston, Kenneth, 507
Altbach, Philip G., 995
Alterman, Richard, 464
Alvarado, Sergio Jose, 465
Amabile, T. M., 963
Amariglio, Jack, 547
Amesley, Cassandra Elinor, 998
Ameter, Brenda, 1195
Anandam, Kamala, 488
Anderson, Charles, 1483
Anderson, Edward, 1399